Talkies, Road Movies and Chick Flicks

Talkies, Road Movies and Chick Flicks
Gender, Genre and Film Sound in American Cinema

Heidi Wilkins

Edinburgh University Press is one of the leading university presses in the UK. We publish academic books and journals in our selected subject areas across the humanities and social sciences, combining cutting-edge scholarship with high editorial and production values to produce academic works of lasting importance. For more information visit our website: www.edinburghuniversitypress.com

© Heidi Wilkins, 2016

Edinburgh University Press Ltd
The Tun – Holyrood Road
12 (2f) Jackson's Entry
Edinburgh EH8 8PJ

Typeset in Monotype Ehrhardt by
Servis Filmsetting Ltd, Stockport, Cheshire

A CIP record for this book is available from the British Library

ISBN 978 1 4744 0689 5 (hardback)
ISBN 978 1 4744 0690 1 (webready PDF)
ISBN 978 1 4744 0691 8 (epub)

The right of Heidi Wilkins to be identified as author of this work has been asserted in accordance with the Copyright, Designs and Patents Act 1988 and the Copyright and Related Rights Regulations 2003 (SI No. 2498).

Contents

Acknowledgements   vi

Introduction   1
1   Talking Back: Voice in Screwball Comedy   9
2   All That Jazz: The Diegetic Soundtrack in Melodrama   44
3   The Alienated Male: Silence and the Soundtrack in New Hollywood   76
4   Brothers in Arms: Masculinity and the Vietnam War Movie   99
5   Subversive Sound: Gender, Technology and the Science Fiction Blockbuster   125
6   Girl Talk: The Postmodern Female Voice in Chick Flicks   149
Conclusion   186

Bibliography   192
Filmography and Other Sources   201
Index   206

Acknowledgements

I am incredibly grateful to Sanja Bahun for her support, guidance and encouragement in the development of this project. During this demanding yet rewarding experience, I am indebted to Sanja who, despite leading such a busy life, has always been there to offer generous comments and excellent espressos! Thanks must also go to the Department of Literature and Film Studies at the University of Essex for funding this undertaking, and for their provision of excellent research facilities. I would like to extend my gratitude to John Haynes, Shohini Chaudhuri, Jeffrey Geiger and Helen Hanson whose enthusiasm for this project has always been appreciated, and whose varied academic perspectives have taught me the merits of looking at things in new ways. I am also indebted to Matthew Carter for his input, guidance and continued friendship.

To my father, Paul Wilkins, thanks for your love, support and for introducing me to *Easy Rider* all those years ago and to my mum, Monica Wilkins, thank you for teaching me to question and argue, and for your never-ending faith in my abilities during moments of uncertainty.

Lastly, I would like to thank my husband and biggest supporter, Peter Cresswell, without whom, none of this would have been possible. Thank you Peter, for your continuous love, support and belief in my abilities, and for sitting through the chick flicks as well as the road movies with me – this book is dedicated to you.

A shorter version of Chapter 3 was previously published as a journal article in *The New Soundtrack* (Edinburgh University Press, 2012)

Introduction

In the 2011 film, *Friends With Benefits*, while watching a romantic movie together, Dylon (Justin Timberlake) loudly speculates: 'why do all these movies have such bad music?' Jamie (Mila Kunis) replies 'It's so that you know how to *feel* every single second'. A conversation ensues about the various musical conventions that have been established by Hollywood to code different emotive or narrative situations, including heartbreak, marriage and sneaking through an office. This self-reflexive summary, within the world of a film which is itself a romantic comedy, while suggesting a historically formulaic approach to the utilisation of sound in American mainstream cinema, also highlights the affective essence generated by music in film. It also demonstrates the extent to which audience expectations of popular film genre conventions are well-established and perhaps, based on Dylon's frustrated questioning, a need or desire for film soundtracks to do something different. Furthermore, this interchange tells us something about gender and sound in film, since Dylon, a twenty-something male is apparently unfamiliar with the film sound conventions of a romantic movie, whereas Jamie, his female counterpart, is well-aware of the intention behind this type of film soundtrack. This snippet of dialogue perhaps establishes an age old paradigm reliant on the perception that female audiences somehow innately enjoy films about romance and thus identify with romantic music, while suggesting that this 'female' film genre is a total mystery, or even a source of frustration, to male audiences.

This book examines a range of so-called 'male' and 'female' film genres in order to uncover the ways in which film sound conveys meanings about gender. The notion of genre has played a key role in the writing of this book, partly because genre and gender are frequently so inextricably linked: action or science fiction films seem to be so often categorised (both inside and outside of academia) as 'male', while romantic comedies or melodramas are deemed 'female'. Rick Altman, in *Film/Genre*,[1] highlights that genre is linked to the recognition of repeated semantic codes or conventions, leading to the categorisation of film texts based on common features. Genre conventions allow filmmakers to work to particular 'formulas' and realise the expectations of film distributors and consumers. This is demonstrated in the example from *Friends With Benefits*, which suggests that Jamie is familiar with the romantic film genre due to repeated viewings. Steve Neale has argued that the pleasure in viewing genre films is derived from 'repetition and difference'[2] emphasising that audiences enjoy seeing how filmmakers can 'play' with or re-interpret genre conventions. Returning to the *Friends With Benefits* example again, we see that Dylon's frustrations seem to be derived from his perception that 'all these movies' (i.e. romantic movies) use 'bad' music, highlighting the importance of re-working genre conventions and perhaps suggesting that while narratives might be re-worked, film sound conventions might be more fixed. This is key to my discussion throughout this book, where I look at the ways in which popular film genres use sound and consider the ways in which film sound conventions are related to representations of gender in popular genres from the 1930s to the 2010s. I furthermore explore how sound is linked to genre transformations, elucidating the ways in which sound genre conventions have evolved over time as perceptions of gender have also changed.

This book covers a wide trajectory of sound in film by firstly focusing on subcategories such as voice and music when discussing early film sound texts. This is due to the more isolated way in which these different aspects of film sound were approached in the early sound period (the late 1920s) to the New Hollywood period of the 1960s where a more holistic approach was then taken by filmmakers in the construction of the soundtrack. Gianluca Sergi has pointed out the validity of critical practice in which the soundtrack is analysed in its entirety, noting that

> by singling out particular elements of a soundtrack, critics have been able to praise individual achievers rather than focus on the much more complex issue of what actually becomes of these 'individual' achievements once they are recorded, mixed and reproduced not as single independent units, but as part of the complex structure that is a soundtrack.[3]

My aim throughout this discussion, rather than focusing on the 'achievements' of individual practitioners is to consider the way that particular aspects of film sound have created meaning about gender in the past. Thus I select elements of sound such as voice, silence or music for close analysis in my early chapters when discussing early sound cinema. From Chapter 4 onwards, I then move to a wider consideration of the whole film soundtrack as a complex structure. I consider technological advancements in film sound, and the ways in which separate elements of sound are layered and arranged in film soundscapes, while always looking at the links between sound and gender. This book begins by looking at the screwball comedies of the 1930s, a key genre of the early sound period. The structure of the book is loosely chronological with each chapter focused on a different genre and linked to key historical moments in US cinema, finishing with Chapter 6 and a detailed analysis of contemporary chick flicks of the 2000s, which explores female voice and the use of bodily sounds in the representation of modern femininity. Due to my interest in the portrayal of gender, a socio-historic approach was taken in the writing of this book; my discussion links film texts to particular moments in American history and their impact on society, culture, politics and perceptions of gender. For example, in Chapter 3, the discussion of New Hollywood films is linked to the emergence of a youth counter-culture in US society and the ways in which this changed societal perceptions of masculinity.

As mentioned above, genre theory was integral to the writing of this book. Each of the six chapters explores a different film genre, which was selected by determining a key genre that was at the height of its popularity in the time period under discussion. This was established through consultation with genre theorists such as Thomas Schatz[4] and Steve Neale[5] who focus their research, as I do in this book, on US cinema. For example, Schatz and Neale both point to the popularity of the family melodrama during the 1950s, and Schatz points to the social and historical link between the family melodrama and its portrayal of the fractures in US society during the post-war Eisenhower era. In this book, I set out to analyse the ways in which film sound creates meaning about gender during these different time periods and chart the changes in genre sound conventions that are linked to changing representations of masculinity and femininity. In each chapter, I set out to contextualise my chosen films by linking them to social, political and cultural events in the chosen time period. I analyse the opening scenes of each film discussed to establish the sound tropes introduced at the start of every film and to follow their development as the narrative unfolds by selecting further key scenes for detailed textual analysis. In each chapter, as I discuss later films of the same genre, I outline the development of sound conventions within particular genres. My aim throughout this book was to cover a wide period of film history and a diverse selection of genres to chart the changing representations of gender through sound.

The first chapter explores voice in screwball comedy from 1934 to 1949. The predominant focus here is on female voice and the ways in which the voices of 'fast-talking dames' (a term appropriated from Maria DiBattista) operated, at the time, as subversive and a challenge to patriarchy. The voice in cinema has been previously discussed by scholars such as Kaja Silverman, Amy Lawrence and Michel Chion; some of this discussion, such as Amy Lawrence's 1991 book, *Echo and Narcissus: Women's Voices in Classical Hollywood Cinema*, focuses on the suppression of the female voice in classical Hollywood. Her feminist approach elucidates the ways in which women are frequently silenced both within the diegetic world and non-diegetically through the filmic apparatus.[6] Whereas in *Overhearing Film Dialogue*, Sarah Kozloff has conversely argued that dialogue is always associated with femininity (and the notion of women speaking 'too much'), she questions the previous lack of scholarly focus on the verbal element of film due to this link with gendered femaleness.[7] This chapter expands on these discussions by exploring female dialogue as well as the volume, tempo and pitch of the voices that pervade this genre. Drawing on scholars such as Aristotle, who has argued that the high-pitched voice is unpleasant, and feminist linguist Sara Mills, who explores masculine and feminine traits in speech, I put forward my belief that far from being supressed, the gendered female voice was a source of power, a challenge to patriarchy, and linked to the changing social status of women during the 1930s. Beginning with *It Happened One Night* (1934), I chart the performances of famous screwball actresses, determining the patterns in speech that were integral to establishing the sound conventions of screwball comedy, which is infamous for its high-speed dialogue. Moving beyond the analysis of dialogue, I explore Barthes' notion of 'the grain of the voice' by looking at the power relations of paralinguistic sounds such as crying and screaming in my discussion of Hildy (Rosalind Russell) in *His Girl Friday*. Furthermore, I explore the utilisation of feminine voicing in Spencer Tracy's performance in *Adam's Rib* (1949) and suggest an early engagement with what Judith Butler has called gender performativity.

The second chapter looks at family melodrama, a popular genre made famous in the 1950s by directors including Douglas Sirk and Nicholas Ray. Their portrayals of the American nuclear family as corrupt and unstable are well-known in films such as *Written on the Wind* (1956) and *Rebel Without a Cause* (1955). This representation is linked to an aspect of the melodrama which is discussed in detail by many film scholars: the genre's perceived subversive comment on Eisenhower's post-war America, which, in recovering from World War Two, was in crisis, both socially and culturally. The latter is summarised by Thomas Schatz who notes that no other genre films projected so complex and paradoxical a view of America: 'at once celebrating and severely questioning the basic values and attitudes of the mass audience'.[8]

My discussion extends these ideas by acknowledging this social shift that was taking place in 1950s society – an era that is so often perceived as sexually and socially repressive, but was in fact undergoing great change. Following the arguments of Barbara Klinger and Laura Mulvey, who have pointed to the obvious presence of sex and sexual liberation in films and other popular cultural products of this era, I look at the ways in which female sexual liberation was clearly present in films of this period, and was subversively signalled via diegetic jazz music. Building on this discussion, I am interested in the power dynamics related to diegetic music whereby a male or female character can potentially control the diegesis and the emotive effects of film sound by singing, performing or playing a record or instrument. I discuss *Mildred Pierce* (1945) as a melodrama that uses diegetic music to signal the lack of power of Mildred (Joan Crawford) in the narrative in comparison to her daughter Veda (Ann Blyth), who often has total control over her mother. The frequent presence of diegetic jazz in family melodramas of this period is also, I argue, linked to the sexual liberation of characters such as Sarah Jane (Susan Kohner) in *Imitation of Life* (1959) or Marylee Hadley in *Written on the Wind* (1956). In this chapter, I conclude by suggesting the idea of this music as an 'acoustic remainder', an aspect of film sound that can stay with audiences, signalling youthful emancipation and freedom from oppressive societal expectations – especially those placed on women.

Chapter 3 explores the link between masculinity, silence and the soundtrack by focusing on a selection of (mostly) silent alienated male characters from renowned New Hollywood films. Based on my observations that in films of this era, there is a distinct lack of dialogue between male characters, the 'type' of silence I often refer to is that described by Paul Théberge as 'a kind of silence that is produced when, for example, music is allowed to dominate the soundtrack while dialogue and sound effects – the primary sonic modes of the diegetic world – are muted'.[9] The films selected for this discussion include *Easy Rider* (1969) where I explore the lack of dialogue between the two male protagonists and build on previous discussions of the film's music soundtrack by Steven Cohen and Ina Rae Clark.[10] I also analyse the silences between the two protagonists in *Bonnie and Clyde* (1968), and the way in which music is used in *The Graduate* (1967) to represent male alienation. I explore the specific use of silence in these texts as well as the ways in which music and diegetic sound frequently express meanings not divulged by the male characters, due to their limited dialogue. I argue that this acoustic construction contributes to a projected sense of alienation of male characters and can also be linked to the blurring of gender boundaries often accounted for by the counter-culture movements taking place in America throughout the 1960s and 1970s.

I continue my discussion of film sound and masculinity in the fourth chapter where I look at two films about the Vietnam War – *Full Metal Jacket* (1987) and *The Deer Hunter* (1978) – and move to an exploration of the soundscape as a whole. In looking at films that depict young men engaging in war, I analyse the ways that music, speech, silence and ambient sounds are used to depict dominant ideological perceptions of what it means to be a man. In *Full Metal Jacket*, the group training sequences in the first part of the film are linked to the notion of 'becoming a man' and in line with Susan Jeffords' research on the 'remasculinization' of America,[11] I look at how non-diegetic music is used to depict this. I develop Jeffords' ideas with my focus on the relationship between

Joker (Matthew Modine) and Private Pyle (Vincent D'Onofrio), which I argue is represented as maternal, and therefore subversive. Analysing sound in scenes of war in both *Full Metal Jacket* and *The Deer Hunter* led me to explore two different depictions of men struggling with the realities of war and the way that silence is used to reinforce a sense of alienation and lack of agency. In the case of *The Deer Hunter*, I look at the acoustic contrast here compared with early scenes of the film in which we frequently hear the comforting sounds of male voices talking, laughing and singing together.

The fifth chapter looks at blockbuster movies of the 1980s, focusing on the science fiction genre, and moves to an exploration of film soundscapes during a period in which sound design came to the fore of filmmaking. Drawing on the research of William Whittington,[12] I discuss *Star Wars* (1977) as a film that pioneered new techniques in Foley and sound design and as a film that uses music to portray unexpected representations of gender, especially in the case of Princess Leia (Carrie Fisher), whom I argue is sounded in a powerful and 'masculine' musical style in the film's opening sequence. I explore the ways in which sound conventions in the science fiction genre have evolved and look at *Aliens* (1986) as an example of a later blockbuster movie, and one that draws on the sound conventions of the horror genre in its depictions of gender. Drawing on Donna Haraway's theories of postmodern women in this technological, post-gender age as being cyborgs,[13] I look at Ripley (Sigourney Weaver) – a highly-discussed female protagonist in film-based scholarship – and the use of music, silence, technology and weapons in representing her as a cyborg. This is set in binary opposition to the male and female space Marines, whose excessive, performative 'male' behaviour is wholly out-dated in the post-gender era of *Aliens*.

The final chapter returns to a discussion of female voice, but this time in contemporaneity: it focuses on postmodern chick flicks and the subversive function of voice and bodily sounds in the female friendship genre, including films such as *Sex and the City* (2008) and *Bridesmaids* (2011). Michel Chion's consideration of the voice deals with the power dynamics of the disembodied (or as he terms it, *acousmatic*) voice. I build on his ideas by looking at the voice-over of *Sex and the City*'s Carrie Bradshaw (Sarah Jessica Parker) and the power and intimacy of her 'unseen' voice. Building on Chion's discussion of female scream in film, which states that the cinema works like a machine to elicit screams from females characters, I discuss what I call 'the engagement scream' – a common response of excitement from women in chick flicks – and unearth other means by which my chosen films express female excitement. In further consideration of non-verbal sounds I look at laughter, drawing on Bahktin's work on the carnival, which suggests that laughter is subversive, a challenge to traditional hierarchies and also is linked to renewal and regeneration. Looking at Bahktin's ideas of the grotesque body, I analyse the ways in which grotesque bodily sounds are used in *Bridesmaids* to construct subversive depictions of unruly female characters. I also look at representations of contemporary women as 'bitchy' in my discussion of voice, music and postmodern narrative techniques in *Bachelorette* (2012). In situating these discussions in the realms of postfeminism, I look at the ways in which such depictions draw out a competitive edge in depictions of modern women, who are often represented as struggling to 'have it all' and strike a balance between a career, a social life and the pressures of marriage and having a family.

Michel Chion has argued that sound in film provides 'added value', enriching the images we see on the cinema screen so that 'we never see the same thing when we also hear; we don't hear the same thing when we see as well'.[14] According to Chion, this audiovisual 'contract' accounts for why we are often unaware of the sounds emitted by cinema, which often seem to be 'naturally' emitted from, or by, the world of the film. If this is the case, sounds that are linked to the representation of gender could also be considered 'natural' or somehow 'obvious' in their representations of men and women onscreen. Returning to the *Friends With Benefits* example from above, whatever meaning can be derived from the music Dylon refers to as 'bad', the very fact that Dylon and Jamie engage in a discussion about the use of sound in romantic movies is significant. This moment perhaps identifies a shift in the way that we can think about gender and sound in film and suggests that there is a need to question why established, seemingly 'natural' sound conventions continue to be utilised in popular genres, or indeed if this is actually the case. As such, it has been my goal in this book to look at six film genres and seventeen film texts over nearly eighty years of film history to explore the use of music, dialogue, sound effects and silence to establish how film sound is used to represent gender. Throughout my discussion I put forward alternative interpretations of seemingly 'natural' or 'obvious' sounds and often discover unusual, sometimes 'un-natural' or subversive sounds that are present throughout the soundscapes of mainstream American cinema. I draw these disparate discussions together to offer an overarching vision of the complex interrelation between socio-political realities, the operation of gender in society, and its cinematic representation on the level of sound.

NOTES

1. Rick Altman, *Film/Genre* (London: British Film Institute, 1999).
2. Steve Neale, *Genre* (London: British Film Institute, 1980), 48.
3. Gianluca Sergi, *The Dolby Era: Film Sound in Contemporary Hollywood* (Manchester: Manchester University Press, 2004), 6.
4. Thomas Schatz, *Hollywood Genres: Formulas, Filmmaking, and the Studio System* (Boston, MA: McGraw-Hill, 1981).

5. Steve Neale, *Genre and Hollywood* (London: Routledge, 2005).
6. Amy Lawrence, *Echo and Narcissus: Women's Voices in Classical Hollywood Cinema* (Berkeley: University of California Press, 1991).
7. Sarah Kozloff, *Overhearing Film Dialogue* (Berkeley and Los Angeles: University of California Press, 2000).
8. Schatz, 223.
9. Paul Théberge, 'The interplay of sound and silence in contemporary cinema and television', in Jay Beck and Tony Grajeda (eds), *Lowering the Boom: Critical Studies in Film Sound* (Chicago: University of Illinois Press, 2008), 51.
10. Steven Cohen and Ina Rae Clark, *The Road Movie Book* (London: Routledge, 1997).
11. Susan Jeffords, *The Remasculinization of America: Gender and the Vietnam War* (Bloomington: Indiana University Press, 1989).
12. William Whittington, *Sound Design and Science Fiction* (Austin: University of Texas Press, 2009).
13. Donna Haraway, 'A cyborg manifesto: Science, technology, and socialist-feminism in the late twentieth century', in Amelia Jones (ed.), *The Feminism and Visual Culture Reader* (London: Routledge, 2010).
14. Michel Chion, *Audio-Vision* (New York: Columbia University Press, 1994), xxvi.

CHAPTER 1

Talking Back:
Voice in Screwball Comedy

During a rickety, uncomfortable bus journey that takes place in *It Happened One Night* (1934) the character of Oscar Shapely (Roscoe Karns) loudly exclaims, 'there's nothing I like better than a high-class mama who can snap em back at ya!' The 'high class mama' to whom he refers is runaway heiress Ellen Andrews (Claudette Colbert) and her ability to 'snap em back' refers to the speed at which she verbally retorts his wanton advances, throwing words back at him as quickly as he dishes them out – much to his delight. This instinct to verbally 'snap back' is a common trait of the screwball comedy heroine of the 1930s and 1940s and the ability to provoke these verbal retorts is a key function of the male characters. The skilfulness of actresses such as Claudette Colbert, Katharine Hepburn and Rosalind Russell to talk at speed was a key acoustic feature of these early 'talkies'. Antagonistic relationships with their male counterparts, including actors such as Cary Grant and Clarke Gable, became a key narrative feature of the genre and the entertaining verbal battles that entailed were fundamental to the success of screwball comedy.

Emerging in the 1930s, screwball comedy became one of the first genres to achieve widespread success in the early sound period. The arrival of synchronised sound in Hollywood between 1926 and 1929[1] inevitably had a significant impact on cinema. Film had always been accompanied by sound in one form or another,[2] but the 'talkies' introduced the prospect of a wider variety of film genres within mainstream narrative cinema that had not been possible during the silent era: genres that were reliant on language and verbalisation rather than mime and gesture. This development marked a change in film performance and acting style. As noted by Robert B. Ray: 'Sound and the new indigenous acting style encouraged the flourishing of genres that silence and grandiloquent acting had previously hindered: the musical, the gangster film, the detective story, screwball comedy and humour that depended on language rather than slapstick.'[3] Although silent slapstick comedy remained in Hollywood, championed by the Marx Brothers, among others, the 'talkies' created great demand for a new generation of actors, those who could speak; it also generated a near-panic when these proved to be not that easily obtainable.[4] Writers and directors of screwball comedy seized this opportunity, recognising that the comedy genre needed to incorporate the possibilities offered by synchronised sound.

Such foregrounding of the voice in mainstream cinema at this time was a liberating experience for women in film. These developments arguably emancipated actresses from being an overwhelmingly visual screen entity and gave women a distinct aural presence, which contrasted the markedly visualised – silent and silenced – appearance of actresses of the 1920s.[5] John Belton notes the passive narrative status of glamorous leading ladies of this period, who tended to be relegated to the submissive position of romantic objects – visual icons – to be won or lost by the hero, rarely indulging in slapstick humour, which was considered unladylike.[6] Thus, the verbal premise of screwball comedy presented a vast opportunity for female actresses to showcase their vocal capabilities. The genre required strong leading ladies who could talk and think on their feet and male counterparts who could keep up with them. Maria DiBattista refers to this type of woman as 'the classical American comic heroine – the dame who attained her majority with the birth of sound – [who] became a fast talker not just to keep up with the times, but to run ahead of them'.[7]

The verbal talents of screwball stars became integral to the emergence of screwball comedy at a time of increased film censorship. In 1934, the Production Code (first introduced in 1930) was revised and enforced in response to increased public concerns over the perceived immorality in Hollywood movies throughout the 1920s and 1930s. Much of the Production Code dealt with the plot, or the moral attitudes espoused by the characters, and what viewers may infer from the moving image. But some portions of it dealt specifically with language, often stipulating offensive words that could not be used to describe male and female characters, for example, 'broad' or 'alley cat' to describe a woman or 'SOB' or 'tom cat' to describe a man. In her discussion of dialogue in Hollywood narrative cinema, Sarah Kozloff calls attention to the particular aspects of language that fell under the Code's censorship decree, such as those that stipulated that the inclusion of vulgar expressions should be kept to a minimum, that oaths should not be used for comedy purposes and that the name of 'Jesus Christ' should only be used in reverence.[8] Despite these new vocal restrictions, Kozloff cites them as one of the reasons for the success of the screwball comedy genre, since it relied on clever manipulation of language. Double entendre and innuendo were part of the viewing pleasure of screwball since they relied on a secret knowing in the audience: 'In every screwball, a disparity exists between the literal meaning of the sentences and the inferences – ironic, extratextual, sexual – that the sophisticated viewer is supposed to perceive. This disparity works to flatter the viewer's sense of sophistication.'[9] This sense of sophistication associated with language highlights an unprecedented focus on clever verbalisation and voice in screwball, and a move away from an emphasis on the visual glamour associated with earlier cinema. These changes brought in a new type of Hollywood actress, proving catastrophic for sexually defined 'goddesses' of the pre-Code Hollywood. While the code was repressive, it was simultaneously liberating for a new kind of on-screen presence, more congenial to the current taste: 'a driving, hyperactive woman, a heroine . . . the "working woman" [who] was more at ease pursuing a career . . . than languishing in a love nest.'[10]

This discussion of screwball comedy predominantly focuses on the voices of such female characters. While the sound of the male voice is important, not least because it frequently complements or matches the sounds of the female voice (and as such will be treated to a certain extent in this chapter), my discussion here focuses on female voice. This is in part due to the social changes taking place in society at the time, including marked female emancipation and changes in attitudes to marriage and work. It is furthermore due to observations by myself and other scholars, including David Shumway and Diane Carson,[11] that numerous screwball leading ladies seem to 'lose' their verbal proficiency towards the end of the film. This often coincides with the screwball heroine falling in love with the film's male protagonist. Shumway argues that in order for a feisty, attractive screwball heroine to find true love, her submission is 'required' for the romance to be consummated and for marriage to take place.[12] Such narrative–aural dénouement could suggest the overpowering of the screwball heroine, as the wayward female voice appears to be ultimately controlled and re-inscribed by patriarchy. But screwball comedy also operates in more complex ways, which I elucidate in this chapter.

Through close analysis of the voice performances in four key screwball films, I probe Shumway's theory of apparent 'submission' to ascertain firstly, how this is reflected through changes in sound performance and secondly, if these changes should be considered a sign of weakness and of patriarchal control. I propose that this transformation actually demonstrates remarkable female versatility and the ability to take on a new role in a new situation, emphasising that the fast-talking dame is just one of many roles our heroines choose to perform. By drawing on Judith Butler's notion of gender performativity, I furthermore point to the playful and self-reflexive approach to voice exhibited in key films as the genre developed. My discussion begins with the voice of the obstinate heiress Ellie Andrews in *It Happened One Night* (1934), for it is Claudette Colbert's varied vocal expressive registers that inaugurated the sound performance of the fast-talking dame. Moving on to the character of Hildy Johnston in *His Girl Friday* (1940), I analyse the sounds of a strong, confident woman of the male-dominated workplace embarking on a verbal and emotional battle with her male counterpart, at a time when the conventions of the screwball genre had become more fixed. The discussion continues with Katharine Hepburn as Susan Vance in *Bringing Up Baby* (1938) whose distinctive upper-class Boston accent and effortlessly super-fast speech maintains its lively attributes throughout the movie and which, I argue, is part of the reason that David (Cary Grant) falls in love with her. Lastly, I consider *Adam's Rib* (1949), also featuring Katharine Hepburn, where I examine her voice performance, and also that of her male counterpart, Spencer Tracy, who uses female vocal performance to orchestrate the 'remarriage' narrative. In each film discussed, I begin my analysis by focusing on the opening scenes of each film. This seems an appropriate moment to begin an analysis that charts the changes in the aural dimensions of the female voice, since the opening scenes tend to establish the sounding of the female characters when they are at their strongest and feistiest. I then select other appropriate moments in each film to demonstrate where changes in voice performance take place, and establish the meaning produced by the variations in voice.

Before it was ever recorded for film, the female voice had already carried a set of ideological assumptions.[13] Gina Bloom argues that in early modern England, the female voice, through its link with the female body, was perceived as unmanageable and porous since it secreted blood and milk: 'the disorderly flow of voice from women's bodies served as an analogous symptom of the female body's extraordinary porous boundaries'.[14] Accordingly, men during this period were expected to control the potentially wayward voices of their wives, daughters and female servants, demonstrating the anxiety that has historically been associated with uninhibited female vocal expression. The later recorded female voice seems to exacerbate some of these anxieties. The phonograph technology, which became commercially available between 1893 and 1914, gave owners the unique opportunity to record their own voices in their home, or play pre-recorded records featuring comedy, monologues and other forms of drama. This device was responsible for the first recordings and wide dissemination of the recorded female voice. But it is telling that, as Anne McKay highlights, the female voice on the radio caused controversy from the outset. In 1925, she notes, 'the public refused to buy recordings of women talking' for, according to a reader response in *Radio Broadcast* magazine, 'the voice of a woman when she cannot be seen "is very undesirable, and to many, both men and women, displeasing"'.[15] McKay speculates that this uneasiness about the recorded, or relayed, female voice could be related to the intimacy of radio. Thus the recorded female voice, particularly when heard within the home, was apparently objectionable to both men and women, especially when women were featured as announcers. But, as my following discussion will highlight, this anxiety, and its various later manifestations, was also linked to the preconceived ideological assumptions about some physical properties of the female voice, some of which date as far back as Aristotle. These include, among others, the assumptions made about the comparatively higher-pitched voices of women, the woman's presumed loquaciousness, and the seeming 'unruliness' of their speech.

Some of these anxieties around the female recorded voice were perhaps amplified by the changing social status of women at this time. The working woman emerged in American society throughout the 1920s and is often featured in screwball comedies of the 1930s and 1940s. Marjorie Rosen asserts that at this time, since World War One, women in the workforce had been 'carving out their small but tenacious niches. Their number had escalated in manufacturing and mechanical industries, in professional services, and it had more than doubled in clerical occupations since 1910.'[16] The women who starred in screwball comedies were often featured as professional workers, such as newspaper reporter Hildy Johnston (Rosalind Russell) in *His Girl Friday* or lawyer Amanda Bonner (Katharine Hepburn) in *Adam's Rib*, both of whom are discussed in this chapter.

With the social changes taking place in attitudes towards women and work, also came a change in attitude towards marriage and relationships. The 1930 Production Code insisted on respect for the sanctity of marriage, an institution that had fallen under threat throughout the 1920s due to changes in the divorce law. Stanley Cavell asserts that screwball comedy narratives serve to enlighten audiences about marriage, through the concept of the term he has famously coined 'remarriage'.[17] David Shumway conversely believes that screwball comedies in fact mystify the concept of marriage, by portraying it as the goal of romance, but not the end of it. Shumway quotes Elaine Tyler May in his discussion of America's marriage crisis in the 1920s:

> During the late nineteenth and early twentieth centuries, American marriages began to collapse at an unprecedented rate. Between 1867 and 1929, the population of the United States grew 300 percent, the number of marriages increased 400 percent, and the divorce rate rose 2000 percent. By the end of the 1920s, more than one in six marriages terminated in court.[18]

It was believed by some that women's emancipation and the new liberal divorce laws were partly to blame for this decline in marriage, yet Elaine Tyler May convincingly argues that rising expectations of personal satisfaction and happiness had put an increased burden on marriage that it was unable to bear.[19] Furthermore, she suggests that Hollywood itself was in part responsible for these rising expectations, through its portrayal of love and romance. Likewise, Tina Olsin Lent discusses Hollywood's perpetual portrayals of 'ideal love' as well as the wider manifestation of this concept in the popular culture of the 1920s and 1930s. She believes that the screwball comedy specifically addresses love and marriage by building on three key sources: 'a redefined image of woman, a redefined view of marriage and a redefined idea of cinematic comedy'.[20]

This 'redefined view of marriage' to which Lent refers meant that women of this period devoted less consideration to the social and economic status of a potential husband, and put more focus on the prospect of romantic satisfaction, sexual gratification and friendship.[21] Lent argues that language, words and verbal exchange are key to the representation of this companionship, particularly between the lead male and female characters in the screwball comedy. As mentioned above, despite dialogue being restricted by the 1934 Production Code, the language of screwball comedy was frequently cleverly manipulated to suggest the potential romantic connection between a fast-talking dame and her male counterpart. The heroine of screwball comedy, with her distinctive voice, often begins the movie talking fast and loud, frequently appearing as brash and outspoken. In line with this proposed connection between words and attraction, this aural pattern is often instigated by male characters, who frequently provoke fast-paced banter. Shumway argues: 'Verbal exchanges function mainly to create a sense of attraction, an "electricity" that stems first from the claim made by the man on the woman and her resistance to it.'[22] Indeed, by the end of the screwball comedy movie, the man who provokes the fast-talking dame wins her love.

Thomas Schatz identifies Frank Capra's *It Happened One Night* as the first screwball comedy, highlighting that its themes and narrative introduced a dimension that would effectively reconstitute Hollywood's romantic comedy tradition.[23] This is true of the film's narrative features and also of its use of sound. Released in 1934, seven years after the first feature film to use synchronised sound (*The Jazz Singer* in 1927), it is part of a body of early 'talkies' that took advantage of the great developments in sound technology at this time. The narrative focus is Ellie Andrews (Claudette Colbert) who is introduced as the headstrong, independent and outspoken heiress of Mr Andrews (Walter Connolly), who despite his best attempts, seems unable to control her. The movie begins aboard the Andrews' yacht, where Ellie is on hunger strike in protest of her father's disapproval of her recent marriage to King Westley (Jameson Thomas); her father intends to annul the marriage. In one last desperate attempt to be with her new husband, she dives from the yacht, escaping her father and his staff for most of the movie. She boards a bus to New York where she plans to meet King and on the way meets newspaper reporter Peter Warne (Clarke Gable). Like many familiar romantic comedy storylines, the couple clash initially and are then gradually drawn towards one another and build a strong rapport as they journey together. Eventually, after they separately admit to Ellie's father that they love one another, Ellie leaves King and the movie ends with the couple married and on their honeymoon.

In her discussion of Colbert's performance in one of her later films, *The Palm Beach Story* (1942), Sarah Kozloff observes Colbert's alternation between two expressive registers. One she refers to as '"woman of the world" is lower pitched and a little throaty . . . the other voice is high-pitched, more girlish, the "damsel in distress" voice'.[24] These expressive registers are also undeniably present in *It Happened One Night* where, throughout the movie, Ellie's voice frequently fluctuates from one of power and determination, to one of childish dismay and also to one of woe and heartbreak when Peter initially rejects her romantic advances – denoting the change in persona explored in this chapter. It is clear that in this, the earliest screwball comedy film, there are more noticeable fluctuations in Colbert's vocal registers, which then became more honed by other actresses as the genre conventions evolved. The tempo of Ellie's speech is as important as her vocal register. She frequently speaks at high speed, particularly when arguing, and delivers quick responses to often inflammatory comments made to her by male characters throughout the movie. This particular aspect of voice was then utilised by many other screwball actresses and partially defined the conventions of the genre. But Peter's voice is also of great importance for the figuration of meanings in this film since his vocal expressions are often matched with Ellie's, giving the audience early clues that the couple are well-matched and seem destined to be together, despite initially belonging to two very different social worlds.

It Happened One Night begins on the Andrews' yacht. The non-diegetic waltzing musical score from the title sequence fades and the sounds of gently lapping water and cawing seabirds creates a peaceful ambience to the movie's beginning. Yet the first loudly spoken words from Ellie's father, 'hunger strike eh?' in reference to Ellie, immediately disrupts this sense of calm, instead introducing a notion of conflict. This sense is highlighted when Mr Andrews' staff inform him that his daughter has not eaten in two days despite their frequent attempts to give her food. Mr Andrews suggests the crew 'jam it [food] down her throat' implying both the potential physical overpowering of Ellie, and also a means of controlling her vocal protest against her father, preventing her from voicing her views.

Sound is used as an initial introduction to Ellie in the following scene as we see the bewildered male crew eavesdropping on her argument with her father. From the beginning of this sequence, the prominent sound of Ellie's voice is at the forefront of the acoustic milieu. It is distinct because she is the only female, but also due to the high pitch, careful precision and fast speed of her speech. Her voice loudly fills the diegesis, raising its significance and allowing an initial judgement of her character based on what is heard, rather than seen. Her first words are directed angrily at her father: 'I'm not going to eat a *thing* until you let me off this boat!' Her words, spoken in a clear, upper-class accent ascend to a loud, high-pitched screaming crescendo during their altercation, demonstrating Ellie's anger and frustration at her father's attempts to dominate her. In comparison, her father's voice is lower, and spoken in a slow and calm manner as he confidently replies, 'Aw come on now Ellie, you know I'll have my way', to which she continues in her high-pitched shout 'Not *this* time you won't, I'm already married to him!' Aristotle distinguished female voice from male voice due to its higher pitch, noting that 'the female in all animals that are vocal has a thinner and sharper voice than the male'.[25] His use of negative adjectives here seems to construct the sound of the female voice as a piercing, sharp weapon. Indeed, one need not probe too far into ancient mythology to come across females capable of death with their voices – sirens and gorgons being two notable examples. As such, we can say that the higher-pitched female voice has historically been perceived as sounding alluring, but also as a threat to masculine power, emphasised by some versions of these myths where the females must die in order to restore masculine control. More contemporary discussions of female voice by feminist linguistic theorists, such as Sara Mills, have likewise highlighted that female voice has frequently been characterised as 'deviant in relation to a male norm'.[26] Yet further examination of this so-called 'norm', reveals that male speech tends to be characterised as 'direct, confident and straight-talking'.[27] This initial introduction to Ellie confirms that she, according to this feminist linguistic theory, exhibits masculine traits in her vocal performance. Mills, rather than classing this type of vocal performance as 'deviant', prefers the term 'discursively competent'. Yet within the world of this film, Ellie's verbal competence might lead us to question if her display of so-called 'masculine speech' is in fact more of a threat to masculine control than her 'feminine' high-pitched voice, as exemplified in her defiant shouting at her father.

This preliminary view of Ellie also constructs an aspect of her personality frequently referred to as 'brat' by Peter later on in the film. This is his shorthand for his perception of her as a spoilt rich girl rebelling against her father; screaming and shouting when not having things her own way. However, as the opening scene continues, the changes in Ellie's behaviour and vocal register begin to build more complex aspects to her character. For example, when Andrews tells her he is having Ellie and King's marriage annulled, she simply looks at him in a jaded and somewhat amused manner, rolls her eyes whilst confidently puffing on her cigarette and repeating the word 'annulled!' before loudly asserting 'I'll have something to say about that! And so will King!' The length, complexity and speed of Ellie's sentences here allow her to dominate the conversation so that, as observed by Elizabeth Kendall, 'we scarcely have time to follow the argument between father and daughter.'[28] At times, she does not allow him to get a word in: 'Can't you get it through your head that King

Westley and I are married! Definitely, legally, actually married. It's over, it's finished, there's not a thing you can do about it, I'm over twenty-one and so is he!' At this point, her voice is deeper, slower and more controlled, revealing a mature and capable side to Ellie, not merely a 'daddy's girl' having a tantrum. This 'woman of the world' voice, as referred to by Kozloff, is the aspect of Ellie's character that frequently surprises Peter throughout the film. This voice is often linked with a display of determination and strength of character that one would hardly expect from a 'brat'.

A further facet of Ellie's vocal abilities is revealed in this scene with her father when he says she has always been 'a stubborn idiot', she instantly replies, 'I come from a *long line* of stubborn idiots!' showing her ability to quickly retort remarks and insults thrown at her. Her emphasis is placed on the words 'long line', which are spoken louder and which she draws out for maximum impact. In this way, she is cleverly turning the argument around and effectively blaming her father and his ancestors for her stubbornness. This line also demonstrates Colbert's skills with the snappy comical delivery of lines that are meant to poke fun at male characters throughout the film.

This scrutiny of voice in the opening scene suggests that the scene has foremost function in the soundscape of the film: it introduces the variety of ways in which Ellie vocally expresses herself, and these will be built upon as the film progresses and as her relationship with Peter evolves. Her range of vocal registers constructs her as a multi-faceted character who is self-assured, confident, and determined that her father will not dominate her. We have also witnessed her ability to quickly retort amusing insults with perfect comic timing, which will be key to the development of her relationship with Peter, and part of our viewing pleasure. Yet there is also a childish element to some of her vocal expressions; indeed, at the end of this scene, she screams and shouts at her father, before knocking over his dinner tray and then making her escape by diving from the boat. At the culmination of this opening sequence, Mr Andrews shouts at his bewildered staff in frustration, 'Of course she got away; she's too smart for you!' He goes on to instruct one of the crew to inform his detective agency 'daughter escaped again', telling us this is not the first time that this young woman has succeeded in outsmarting all the men on the Andrews' boat.

Ellie's vocal tones at the start of the film are matched by the introduction of her male counterpart Peter Warne having a drunken and heated argument with his boss, a New York newspaper editor, over the telephone at the bus station. His vocabulary and the sound of his voice denote that he is of a lower social class than Ellie, yet he is unquestionably linked to her through the way he talks. Like her, his voice is high-pitched and when involved in this confrontation, he speaks quickly and also uses amusing insults such as 'monkey face' and 'gas house palooka!' introducing him as funny, witty and charming and with this use of slang confirming he is a working-class character. His voice has a scratchy, grainy quality to it, constructing him as a man who talks a lot and as having a rugged or down-to-earth quality. He also comes across as a stereotypical newspaperman of the 1930s era, which audiences of 1934 would have recognised from Hollywood's 1932–3 newspaper comedies which typically featured 'the rogue newsman who was as rascally, soused and undependable as he was talented'.[29] Significantly, he is referred to as 'king' by his fellow newspapermen when finishing his telephone conversation: 'make way for the king!' This draws an instant parallel between him and Ellie's new husband, perhaps an early verbal indication that Ellie could find herself with this 'king' by the end of the movie. This also highlights that he is greatly admired by his fellow workers for standing up for the downtrodden working man. However, as the audience, we also possess the privileged knowledge that this admiration is partly based on an untruth since we saw that the most impressive and insulting words to come out of Peter's mouth were actually spoken after his editor had already hung up the phone – this draws a further interesting parallel between him and King Westley as we can see that Peter could be referred to as a 'phoney' king, and King Westley is constantly described as a fake and a 'phoney' throughout the film.

When entering into a new confrontation, this time with the bus driver, we see Peter, like Ellie, also possesses the ability to retort snappy insults; when told by the bus driver that he needs 'a good sock on the nose' he retorts with a lengthy and comical remark that he is fond of his nose, even if others are not. Kozloff discusses screwball comedies' use of accents and dialogue to distinguish the fast-talking and quick-witted protagonists from everyone else: 'just as Westerns use dialogue to separate the laconic Westerners from the tenderfoots, screwballs use language to separate the quick-witted stars from the duller clods around them'.[30] If we compare Peter's funny, quick retorts with the bus driver's slow southern drawl, we see that the bus driver is completely ineloquent, repeatedly responding with a mere 'Oh yeah?' while Peter verbally runs circles around him.[31] Here Peter is immediately identifiable as Ellie's verbal equal whilst also aurally distinguishable from other, lesser characters.

The sounds of interaction between Ellie and Peter fluctuate throughout the movie. Their initial interchange begins with confrontation when Ellie sits on the bus seat that Peter has just argued for. Throughout these disputes, Ellie's vocal performance features distinct changes whereas Peter's tends to maintain the same tones heard in his argument with the bus driver. For example, when he approaches Ellie after her bag is stolen, she adopts her deep, confident voice: 'I don't know what you're raving about young man, and furthermore, I'm not interested.' She speaks quickly and her tone is calm and condescending until she realises her bag has been stolen whereby she reverts to her high-pitched childlike voice: 'Oh my heavens! It's gone! . . . all I have here's four dollars . . .' only to return to a deeper, hostile voice register once Peter suggests they report the missing case: 'Will you please keep out of my affairs! I want to be left alone!' Again, she talks to him in a hostile manner when she realises he has deliberately missed the bus in Jacksonville in order to travel with her. Then, once again, she sheepishly reverts to a childlike persona when she realises he does this for her sake when he gives her the lost bus ticket that she had unknowingly misplaced. Throughout these interactions though, we see a chemistry developing between the characters as they both talk at speed and both frequently include witty phrases or comebacks. Their voices are similarly high-pitched and furthermore they seem to enjoy engaging in these fast-paced battles of wits.

The long bus journey provides further opportunities for Ellie to display her verbal wit. In the scene briefly mentioned in the opening of this chapter, Ellie (having fallen out with Peter) chooses to sit next to a passenger named Oscar Shapely who attempts to charm Ellie by creating a sexist pun from his own name: 'Shapely's the name and that's the way I like 'em!' He guffaws loudly and with delight when Ellie quickly comments with distain on his continual talking, also noting her upper-class accent and applauding her snappy comeback. Shapely also calls attention to game-playing linked to words when Ellie 'snaps back' for a second time and he says she is 'two up' on him. Indeed, Ellie's ability to cut this man down to size with her sharp words is impressive and funny, further demonstrating her strong and capable characteristics and diminishing her 'brat' persona. The importance of play in screwball comedy has been highlighted by Manuela Ruiz Pardos.[32] It seems that voice and words form a key role in this concept; as Shapely points out, Ellie is 'two up' on him, unfortunately, she is not interested in 'playing' with him. However, the scene where Ellie and Peter pretend to be a working-class couple to evade her father's detectives marks a change in their previously antagonistic relationship as Peter becomes aware of Ellie's capacity for 'play'. The sequence provides key evidence of the fast-talking dames' ability to abruptly switch roles and also demonstrates Ellie's awareness of the differences in social classes – perhaps gained in the previous scene where she met several working-class women in the shower queue. When the detectives enter the cabin, Peter and Ellie quickly assume the roles of a lower-class couple, primarily by changing their voices. Peter's becomes low, aggressive and excessively loud, whereas Ellie's becomes high-pitched and she assumes a country accent complete with southern drawl. The scene seems to revolve around the concept of a lower-class marriage involving the husband shouting and the wife wailing as Peter charades as a jealous, protective husband at the suggestion that his 'wife' has looked at another man. Stanley Cavell asserts that their attempt to demonstrate that they are 'a seasoned couple . . . is to bicker and scream at each other'. He then questions

> what does a happy marriage sound like? Since the sound of argument, of wrangling, of verbal battle, is the characteristic sound of these comedies . . . an essential criterion for membership in that small set of actors who are featured in these films is the ability to bear up under this assault of words, to give as good as you get, where what is good must always, however strong, maintain its good spirits, a test of intellectual as well as of spiritual stamina, of what you might call 'ear'.[33]

What Cavell does not mention, however, is the narrative function of the vocal figuration in this scene. While this particular aural representation of a working-class marriage is somewhat disconcerting – especially for a contemporary audience – it is deliberately played out in such a way that it creates unease for the detectives, encouraging them to leave out of embarrassment. Peter repeatedly yelling 'quit bawling!' over Ellie's screeching successfully perturbs the detectives who hastily leave the cabin lest the sound becomes more unbearable. So whilst the bawling and shouting makes for uncomfortable viewing – or listening – it serves the purpose of making the intruders leave. This demonstration of 'play acting' is a key moment in the film where, as observed by Kozloff, 'through combining forces to mislead the opposition, and through finding out how well they can pick up on each other's cues, the two leads discover their bond'.[34] Ellie's quickness on the uptake impresses Peter – 'You've got a brain haven't you?' – while she is equally impressed with his performance. The sound of their gleeful laughter denotes the bond that is forming between the pair, which has been strengthened through their participation in play and willingness to perform. But the impact of this sounding is not exhausted in this narrative rescue. More profoundly, through the characters' incredible aural competency and 'self-knowledge', the film highlights to the viewer the power of the voice and its potential impact on others. Cavell is right to assert that this scene is an assault on the ear. It is meant to be so.

Ellie's true feelings for Peter are revealed later on in the film when she declares her love for him, displaying a further expressive register and what Shumway would refer to as our heroine's 'submission'. From the other side of the blanket or 'Walls of Jericho' that divides their bedroom, Peter paints a beautiful and romantic picture with words of his ideal love, a woman who would join him on his island in the Pacific: 'she'd have to be the sort of girl that'd jump in the surf with me and love it as much as I did'. Given the developments we have seen in their relationship, it is obvious that Ellie is the girl that Peter describes, and when seeing Ellie's response to his words, it is equally clear that Ellie is drawn to the vision he is painting. Cavell refers to Peter's words as penetrating Ellie: 'her body expands with the imagination of what he is envisioning . . . she is drawn towards Peter's vision, hence to Peter'.[35] Next we see Ellie, a shadow of the outspoken, confident young woman seen earlier in the film, crying and sobbing on Peter's lap, begging her to take her to his island: 'please Peter, I can't let you out of my life now, I can't live without you!' This moment in the film could be taken as evidence of Ellie's submission. Conversely, I argue that her admission of her feelings for Peter here actually represent a new level of freedom and choice available to women during this period, whereby, as mentioned above, decisions about marriage were being formed based on friendship, rather than economic or societal concerns. Ellie Andrews is an example of an honest, open and candid fast-talking dame who embraces new opportunities available to modern thinking women. Kozloff similarly makes this claim about screwball women who 'dare to speak so frankly . . . [in] moments when you'd think that the heroine would be polite, evasive, coy, or blathering, she speaks with complete candour. Such breaking of constraints of expected decorum is a form of independence – of rebellion'.[36] What makes this particular moment of openness and honesty appear negative in its portrayal of Colbert's character is Peter's sharp and immediate insistence that she return to her bed, which – in line with Production Code stipulations – he invariably does because she is married and because he is a character who plays by the rules, unlike rebellious Ellie who throws caution to the wind, hence the reason she embarks on this trip in the first place.

This is the last time the couple are seen on screen together since their 'happily ever after' moment at the end of the movie is achieved metaphorically through the dropping of the blanket, or 'the Walls of Jericho', which is also marked by emphatic sounding. Cavell refers to the blanket as 'the most famous blanket in the history of drama', drawing attention to its 'metaphysical isolation' in dividing the two characters within the space of the room. He also draws attention to the significance of Ellie being on the 'Israelites' side of the blanket, who have the relevant trumpets, 'whether the walls come down will depend on whether the right sounds issue from her side of the wall'.[37] Indeed, in the final moments of the film, it is the sound of a toy trumpet being played and a shot of the blanket dropping to the floor that represents the union of the happy couple and the physical consummation of their marriage. This closing flourish represents Ellie's vocal tenacity throughout the film since it is her who first confesses her love for Peter, and her who ultimately decides to leave King and marry Peter – albeit with encouragement from her father.

Claudette Colbert's portrayal of Ellie Andrews inaugurated the first screwball comedy heroine performance, introducing the Great Depression audiences to women who were active, expressive and who had more freedom to choose the life they wanted for themselves. Maria DiBattista refers to the ending of *It Happened One Night* as the 'elating comic climax'[38] in which Ellie follows her heart. She points out that marriage to the 'wrong' man 'is the original sin of the comic world, because it is through marriage that comedy signals its commitment to a social future populated by happy, compatible, and, it is hoped, fruitful human beings'.[39] This relationship bond is manifested in the voices of the two protagonists.

In Howard Hawks' *His Girl Friday*, the fast-talking dame is likewise reunited with a 'wrong' but natural and most obvious partner. The film begins with the female protagonist, Hildy Johnson, announcing to her ex-husband and ex-boss, newspaper editor of *The Morning Post*, Walter Burns (Cary Grant), that she is engaged and very soon to be married to Bruce Baldwin (Ralph Bellamy), a dull insurance salesman. Furthermore, she intends to leave her profession as a journalist in order to start a family and a new life in Albany. The film follows Walter's numerous deceitful efforts to tempt Hildy back into the newspaper business, including getting her fiancé put into jail twice and bribing Hildy to write a heartfelt article about a prisoner who is due to be executed the following day. Eventually, Hildy regains her spark and enthusiasm for being a 'newspaperman' and the film ends with Hildy being reunited with Walter, who was clearly her true counterpart throughout the movie, despite – in his own admittance – not being the best husband.

Unlike the serene sounds heard at the start of *It Happened One Night*, *His Girl Friday* opens to the diegetic sounds of a busy newspaper office, immediately setting the scene in a frantic, fast-paced environment. The ambient sounds consist of typewriters tapping at high speed and the constant buzz of male voices as several newspapermen go about their daily routines. The camera tracks quickly along the length of the office, capturing the staff busy at work, finally stopping on two women working on the telephone switchboard at incredibly high speed; their voices are the first distinctive speech heard in the movie. Their repetitive lines '*The Morning Post*, just a moment please . . .' intermingle as they talk constantly and at speed over one another, conveying the energetic nature of the newsroom and also setting the tempo for the fast-paced speech which is to pervade what Maria DiBattista has referred to as 'the fastest of the talky comedies'.[40] Like Ellie's voice at the start of *It Happened One Night*, their high-pitched and fast-paced voices are distinctive and they stand out amongst the lower-pitched male voices that prevail in this environment.

When Hildy Johnston enters the office, everything about her distinguishes her from the men, and also from the other women at *The Morning Post*. She is dressed in a dark, tailored, pin-striped, masculine suit, she wears a tall hat, putting her physically on par with the men in terms of her height, and she speaks quickly and curtly. Her overall demeanour denotes confidence and capability and also an exceptional verbal performance skill: the moment she steps into the office her mouth is moving quickly in mime as she talks to Bruce. Her first distinguishable words are 'oh hiya skinny' to a young male worker as she whisks through the newspaper office, denoting familiarity with her co-workers and showing that playful banter is something that comes easily to her within this male-dominated environment. A short, amusing conversation then takes place between the two switchboard women and Hildy, belittling Walter Burns before we actually see him (Hildy asks if 'the lord of the Universe' is in, they reply saying that he is in a bad mood that morning, suggesting 'someone must have stolen the crown jewels'). This short episode foregrounds a female dynamic/female chatter within the film, establishing an environment where women poke fun at men, sometimes privately, amongst themselves, but also face to face. It is at this moment that Hildy refers meta-cinematically to the force of her own voice: when one of the women asks if she would like to be announced to Walter, she replies, 'oh no no, I'll blow my own horn!' We can perhaps draw a link here between Hildy's metaphorical horn and Ellie's trumpet from *It Happened One Night*, demonstrating to the audience that Hildy intends to continue the screwball tradition of forceful female voices in this genre. Indeed, Hildy's voice is one that creates an impact the moment she enters a room.

The conversations that take place between Hildy and Walter throughout the film have become legendary in screwball comedy. The speed at which both characters talk is incredibly fast and often difficult to follow and their dialogue is frequently based on witty insults, wordplay and innuendo. Kozloff notes the performative nature of their quarrels, where they apparently perform to each other, verbally challenging one another; she argues that Hildy and Walter are the kind of characters who impersonate themselves,[41] gesturing at the self-reflexive, playful aspect of voice performance that I expand on below. When Hildy first enters Walter's office, this sense of performative play is emphasised in their banter, denoting, in turn, familiarity between the two characters, particularly in moments such as Hildy predicting what Walter is going to say ('anytime, any place, anywhere!'). Their rapid dialogue is fraught with contradictions and non sequiturs, which serve to embody their madcap marriage: lines such as, 'I tell you what, come back to work on the paper. If we find we can't get along in a friendly fashion, we'll get married again!' To begin with, all this auditory and semantic onslaught is novel and entertaining but as the film goes on and the tension between the characters raises, the pressure increases within the audience as well; we are gradually made to realise that raised voices talking over one another can actually be quite distressing to listen to. Schatz attributes much of this tension to the existing narrative relations between the lead couple, which he describes as 'a difficult marital union that simply will not disentangle'. He notes that the central characters in the remarriage narratives are frequently more anarchic and outrageous than those screwball couples in the courtship stage.[42] This sense of anarchy is exemplified at several points during the film, with frequent sounding of Walter, Hildy, Bruce and other newspapermen talking over one another.

Throughout the film, all the men onscreen converse with Hildy as if she is one of them, demonstrated clearly by Walter at the start of the movie when he does not bother with the usual expected courtesies, such as offering her a seat or a cigarette when she enters his office. Hildy similarly does not observe usual courtesies towards him, such as knocking and waiting to be invited into the office. This makes it difficult to judge their relationship as a heteronormative courtship since the familiar boundaries of their relationship are already established (and in some cases distorted) from the start of the movie. It is the first conversation between them that sets up this unusual dynamic. From the way that Walter flirts with Hildy, it is evident that there is still intense attraction and affection between the two characters but also that Walter's male pride has been damaged by Hildy's decision to divorce him and marry Bruce. There is also an amount of overt playfulness between them, which provides an explanation as to why their marriage ended.

> HILDY: Would you mind if I sat down?
> WALTER: There's been a lamp burning in the window for you honey, right here (pats his knee).
> HILDY: Urgh, I jumped out that window a long time ago Walter.

The interplay of words between Hildy and Walter is like a game of ping pong. The couple bat words and phrases back and forth, each consistently interrupting the other and attempting to take verbal control, or outwit the other. In the scene where Walter takes Hildy and Bruce to lunch, the first two dominate the conversation and their quick thinking and fast speech dictate the narrative action. Kozloff notes the patterns and rhythms in their speech that point to their chemistry:

> The two apparent antagonists speak in an identical rhythm, in identical cadences, singing perfect verbal duets – which reveal that the two are spiritually and truly one. Their minds click away at the same pace and in the same rhythm (as opposed to the slow Bruce), just as their words do.[43]

Indeed, it is Bruce who points out this speech-pace compatibility: 'everybody else I've ever known, well, you could always tell ahead of time what they were going to say or do, but Hildy's not like that, you can't tell that about her . . . it's nice'. In contrast, when we hear Bruce embark on his laboured, long-winded speeches, it is immediately obvious that he is not the right man for Hildy. He is portrayed as slow, unadventurous and dim-witted; this is reinforced through Walter's continual mockery of him, which Bruce is too slow to pick up on. Cavell notes that the existing intimacy between the couple means that they communicate 'in a lingo and tempo, and about events present and past, that Bruce can have no part in'.[44] Thus, from the film's outset, we realise that Hildy is far better suited to an unconventional and volatile relationship with Walter than a predictable, 'ordinary' marriage with Bruce.

The fast-talking world of the newspaperman is further aurally reinforced in the episode in the press room at the court house. The audio-space is shaped by continual speech or noises of telephones ringing, denoting a constantly busy atmosphere, even if the main activity taking place is a card game. The voices of the different men intertwine, leaving no breathing space or silent pauses. As Hildy enters the room, she immediately slots into this environment with her fast speech and quick thinking as she engages in, and dominates, amusing banter with the newspapermen about her impending marriage, her hat and her mother-in-law to be. This scene confirms that Walter Burns is not the only man she is able to play verbal ping pong with, and denotes her flair and confidence at conversing with alternative verbal sparring partners.

Sara Mills views this type of powerful female speech as being socially determined, linked to an individual's status within a given social system, such as a place of work.[45] Thus we could attribute Hildy's vocal strength to her position in the newspaper office hierarchy – that is, almost on a par with Walter. This could furthermore explain their verbal wrangling and why she is the only character able to engage with Walter and his vocal performance. The physical presence of Hildy's voice (her 'horn') can be felt throughout the film, especially in her fast interchanges with Walter. At times, the fraught conversations that take place between them actually move beyond the realms of language and become, on Hildy's part, cries of anguish and frustration. Here it is important to consider the ways in which the voice's physical manifestations (speaking, singing, etc., but also paralinguistic sounds like crying, laughing, and others) are also invested with social meanings; an act of 'voicing' is not solely determined by linguistic content. Roland Barthes addressed this issue with his notion of 'the grain of the voice', whereby the voice could be interpreted solely through sound, separating it from language and embracing the non-verbal meanings that can be produced by it.[46] But even the grain of the voice is inescapably gendered, as argued by Leslie C. Dunn and Nancy A. Jones who highlight that voice is a product of a complex interplay between anatomical differences and socialisation into socially prescribed gender roles.[47] Such gendering is seen in, for example, nineteenth-century opera, where the range of female voice is foregrounded but its bearers, female leads, are repeatedly silenced or killed.[48] Dunn and Jones assert that this treatment of female vocality occurs throughout Western literary and musical traditions, which are testament 'to the persistent desire of male artists to control through representation the anxieties aroused by the female voice, even while they licence the display, and the enjoyment, of its powers'.[49]

Certainly, within the world of *His Girl Friday*, the male characters, especially Walter, enjoy Hildy's display of female powers through voice, which often take the non-verbal form of laughing or yelling; his enthusiastic interaction with her is testament to this. But, in such a markedly performative and gender-performance aware film as *His Girl Friday*, things are not so simple. In the scene at the start of the film, where Hildy tells Walter she is engaged, their energetic, fast-paced banter rises to a crescendo in which Walter's words increase to an unintelligible speed, which is then mocked by exasperated Hildy who deliberately interrupts him, making sounds that can only be described as high-pitched, nonsensical gibberish that one might hear from an auctioneer, finally loudly exclaiming, 'sold American!' The function of this performative outburst is to demonstrate the character's awareness that their fast-paced banter often flows out of control, becoming mere sounds battling against one another. These sounds emitted by Hildy, however, also suggest the perpetual frustration she experiences in her interchanges with Walter. Paradoxically, what she is really trying to tell Walter with this intentional use of paralinguistic crescendo is that she is not interested in playing frustrating verbal games with him anymore, and is instead settling for a slow-paced life with Bruce. Yet as the whirlwind narrative continues, we see Hildy becoming irresistibly drawn to a world that she believed she could no longer relish.

Perhaps this frequent, energetic interaction with Walter explains why, more than any other screwball heroine, Hildy's later change in persona is so surprising. At the end of the film she is reduced to tears because she thinks that Walter doesn't love her anymore – a far cry from the independent and capable Hildy we see at the start of the movie. However, it is necessary to consider Hildy's alternation of expressive registers throughout the film; it is this important, if under-discussed, aspect of her aural persona that gives one a 'key' to her character and narrative function. For, there is a softer, gentle side to Hildy's character which actually demonstrates a less brash part of her persona, often left unremembered due to her fast-paced comic performance elsewhere in the film.

In scenes where she converses with Bruce, she always speaks to him in soft, gentle tones, which denote a sense of protectiveness towards his character that presumably was never needed in her previous pairing with Walter, who can easily take (verbal) care of himself. Vulnerable Bruce, however, is spoken to in quiet, delicate tones as she gently tells him to give her all their money, or to put a cheque in the lining of his hat. During these moments, we see Hildy changing her vocal performance to a slow, gentle pace to match with Bruce's own verbal capabilities. This again emphasises him as a character in opposition to quick-thinking Walter and demonstrates Hildy's ability to flexibly switch between different vocal performances, a feat not displayed by any of the male characters throughout the film. Likewise, in the scene where she interviews Earl Williams, in a soft, low tone of voice she quietly convinces him that his shooting of the gun had been influenced by the 'production for use' soapbox politics to which he had been unwittingly exposed. In scenes such as these, we hear an alternative expressive register from Hildy, which reveals her softer side, yet simultaneously demonstrates her clever ability to act pragmatically – to manipulate tonalities to influence susceptible male characters such as Bruce and Earl.

The moment when Hildy breaks down in tears at the end of the film is represented as the turning point at which Walter's creative antics throughout the narrative have finally worn her down. Interestingly, it is when he stops 'playing' with her and is seemingly ready to let her go to Bruce that she breaks down in tears. Walter's surprised response, 'You never cried before!' reiterates that he has always played games with her; and when she finally discovers that he is, in fact, still trying to manipulate her away from Bruce, she is relieved. This is certainly a surprising change in Hildy's character, but her lively interactions with Walter throughout the movie affirm that her ultimate, unconventional choice in partner is the right one for her. As with Ellie in *It Happened One Night*, this reversal can also be construed as a moment of strength and honesty in which the fast-talking dame dares to reveal her feelings and choose a mate with whom she has chemistry, rather than one who can provide a stable and conventional lifestyle. Like Ellie, however, Hildy also displays versatility and the ability to adopt varied personas through her aural performance, as represented in her contrasting quiet moments with Earl Williams and Bruce. The concluding emotional display from Hildy, although surprising, is, one realises, just one of many varied expressive registers that we have witnessed her skilfully using throughout the film. Whatever the values we may ascribe to these tonal, linguistic and paralinguistic performances, such closure ties in well with changing attitudes towards marriage during this period in American society. Importantly, the film ends with the two fast-talking, madcap protagonists reunited, emphasising heterosexual union based on friendship, 'chemistry' and compatibility rather than any rational arrangement.

Bringing Up Baby also features Cary Grant playing the mild-mannered palaeontologist, David Huxley, as he attempts to secure one million dollars' worth of funding for his museum from corporate lawyer Alexander Peabody (George Irving). His efforts are comically thwarted by Susan Vance (Katharine Hepburn), who falls in love with David and manages to sufficiently distract him from his work and his fiancé, Miss Swallow (Virginia Walker), with the help of a leopard named Baby. After driving to Connecticut, losing his clothes, having a confusing dinner with Susan's aunt, the leopard escaping, David and Susan being put in jail, and the loss of his much-cherished dinosaur bone, the exasperated David returns to his museum having lost both his fiancé and the million-dollar funding. In the final scene, Susan has recovered the bone and returns it to David, also informing him that she/her aunt intends to donate a million dollars to the museum. She confesses her love for David and he admits that he loves her too ('I love you . . . I think'). The film ends with Susan accidentally destroying the enormous brontosaurus skeleton to which David has dedicated years of research, but with David embracing her and presumably her funny, madcap ways.

The opening sequence again provides a useful ground for analysis. The music over the title sequence is jaunty and jolly, depicting the light-hearted and slapstick events that are to take place in this movie. Unlike in other screwball comedies discussed in this chapter, we do not meet the female protagonist until we are quite a few minutes into the film. Rather, *Bringing Up Baby* begins with a quiet and peaceful environment in which David Huxley sits atop a high platform in the Natural History Museum, deep in thought, looking at a single bone from a skeleton of a brontosaurus. But the first words of the film do make reference to noise – in particular speech – as some kind of irritant or distraction for Dr Huxley, as Miss Swallow immediately 'shushes' the professor who enters the room speaking loudly, by asserting that David needs absolute quiet while he thinks. This semi-parody of quiet, academic contemplation foregrounds the introduction of Susan, who creates nothing but noise in David's life – either through her own voice, the voices of other people who seem to aggregate around her, car engines, dogs barking, telephones ringing or through David's own voice when he shouts at her in exasperation. These noisy moments – such as David's repeated shouting of 'I'll be with you in a minute Mr Peabody!' which usually accompanies a chaotic episode, caused by Susan – comprise much of the comedy in the film.

Bringing Up Baby features the repeated use of wordplay and double entendre leading to the misinterpretation of words by the various characters in the film. The ability of verbal dialogue to carry multiple meanings is made apparent in David's very first words in the movie; he says, 'Alice, I think this one must belong in the tail'. However, through Grant putting emphasis on the '-long' part of the word 'belong', what he states clearly sounds like 'I think this one must be *long* in the tail'. By modulating vocal expression, we are led to conclude, the same word can come across as 'belong' or 'be long', and it can indicate, on the one hand, where to place the bone in the dinosaur skeleton and, on the other hand, could describe the dinosaur as having a long tail. We can grasp the intended meaning of his words only when Alice replies 'nonsense, you tried it in the tail yesterday and it didn't fit'. And, even so, the true meaning of the uttered phrase is still not entirely apparent since this reply could still refer to either the length of the tail or where on the dinosaur the bone actually belongs. This short interchange foregrounds two very important aspects of voice in this film – firstly that the verbal misinterpretations that take place throughout the movie are entirely plausible since the viewers have just partaken in a potential confusion of words themselves, whilst secondly, that vocal performance of double-meaning words and phrases is the domain where much of the comedy is found in the movie, especially when it involves gender issues. Later in the narrative, David becomes 'Mr Bone', a name bestowed on him by Susan, demonstrating gendered sexual innuendo through names and wordplay as well.

As in the screwball comedies discussed above, there is the sense that the couple, as they are introduced at the start of the movie, are not a good fit for each other, which is reflected in their speech and interaction. Everything that Susan embodies in audio-performative sense is the exact opposite of what the character of David wishes. That much is adumbrated in the opening scene: Miss Swallow briefly exhibits a display of excitement when reading the telegram about the discovery of the intercostal clavicle dinosaur bone, yet David's overly amorous display of affection towards her in reaction to this news seems to bring her quickly back down to Earth, especially when discussing their impending marriage. She henceforth reverts to the conservative behaviour and speech demonstrated at the very start of the movie: she tells David that she sees their marriage as merely a symbol of dedication to his work, which should not 'entail any domestic entanglements of any kind' including children, emphasising that – much to David's disappointment – this is to be a loveless, sexless partnership representing an old-fashioned view of marriage based on convenience or status. In this part of the discussion, and the remainder of the film, her voice is linked to her name, as she seemingly 'swallows' her brief display of livelier performative speech and reverts to a reserved verbal performance that maintains its monotone and lacks intonation. Her voice is then in stark contrast with David's, which is surprisingly expressive and lively and includes slang phrases such as 'gee whizz' and 'I'll knock him for a loop!' For this – and its inappropriateness considering his social status – he is reprimanded by Miss Swallow: 'remember *who* and *what* you are!'

This short introduction to Miss Swallow sets the viewer in the mood to expect an opposite character to be the female protagonist of the movie. Maria DiBattista discusses this opposition as a rivalry between two kinds of women, 'the rationalist miss, all work and no play . . . and a fast-talking dame with a natural talent for game – and role – playing'.[50] Kozloff similarly refers to the film as presenting a contrast between the serious world of the Natural History Museum and the playful world of the enchanted forest, noting that what makes *Bringing Up Baby* so resonant is that the movie itself embodies a wedding between discipline and zaniness.[51] Indeed, when we meet Susan in the following scene, she could easily be described as a 'zany' free-spirit, compared to Miss Swallow. On the wide, open green of the golf course, wearing a white, flowing dress with curly flyaway hair, she is visually the opposite of Alice who wears a dark, smart suit, a neat hairstyle and resides in the dusty confines of the museum. Ironically, the cold diegetic silence that Miss Swallow occupies in the museum is replaced by the sounds of carefree bird song in the first shot of Susan, positioning the former as a caged bird, restricted by the confines of her profession. This sense of opposition is fully reinforced only when we hear Susan speak. Her first words are 'here's hoping!' as she prepares to take a swing at David's golf ball, suggesting that she is not reliant on her skills as a golfer, but merely on luck to make a good shot. In the middle of David's protests about her hitting his ball, she lightly cuts him off: 'you shouldn't do that you know ... talk while someone's shooting ... well anyway I forgive you because I got a good shot'. She talks at speed and there is a curtness to her voice that cuts through David's attempts to get his words across, yet she also has what could be described as a 'smiley' tone – her voice is upbeat and jovial, making her a character who is instantly likeable. She is also impeccably polite and her upper-class, characteristically Bostonian pronunciations[52] suggest someone who is at home on the golf course and in the scene that follows in the Ritz, yet also someone who is comfortable talking to those from all walks of life, as shown in her playful interactions with the bartender. Susan's fast talk matches her movements in this short section as she breezes across the golf course and quickly sinks David's ball. Her fast pace and self-confidence means that she dictates the action of this scene, as she does in subsequent scenes, instructing the men present to take the pin out of the hole and in David's case to 'be quiet please', again with impeccable manners and a light, airy vocal tone.

Through her speech in the film, Susan comes across as a contradictory character, which is another part of her appeal since the audience – and David – can never accurately predict what she might say from one moment to another. At one point in the golf scene, she says, 'if I sink this putt I'm gonna beat my record', suggesting that she is a keen player with a competitive spirit. Yet once she has sunk the putt she makes a joke about the shape of the golf ball and quickly says, 'well what does it matter? It's only a game anyway', implying a light-hearted and somewhat childish approach to game-playing that does not quite make sense when compared with her previous competitiveness with herself. Much of the dialogue is self-reflexive – reflecting the key elements and 'game-like' or random plotlines of the screwball comedy genre. Her speech is also full of clever plays on words and snappy replies to David's continued attempts to make her understand her apparent mistakes in playing his ball and driving his car: 'your car, your golf ball, is there anything in the world that doesn't belong to you?' David replies, 'yes thankfully, you!' showcasing his own capability to deliver snappy, witty replies. Such voice performance is an early indication of the compatibility of the screwball couple, and is also just one of many amusing repartees that comprise much of the entertainment of the film.

When compared with those of the other actresses discussed in this chapter, Hepburn's performance is the most comical and part of her humorous resonance resides in the sound and delivery of her voice. Its exceedingly high pitch and delicate fast tempo appears effortlessly performed, and this performance maintains it light-hearted essence throughout the film, despite the bizarre events that might be taking place around Susan. Ann Carson, in her discussion of Aristotle and Aristophanes, explains that the high-pitched voice, according to the Ancient Greek philosophers, carried negative connotations linked to loose morality. 'High vocal pitch,' she relates, was seen as going 'together with talkativeness to characterise a person who is deviant from or deficient in the masculine ideal of self-control'.[53] Talkativeness was something that Democritus similarly perceived as a negative, or inappropriate, trait in women since it was linked with argumentation, which was a tool for what was then seen as the exclusively male activity: philosophising.[54] In the character of Susan Vance, we see an extremely talkative, sometimes argumentative female character, with an exceedingly high-pitched voice who does present a threat to the traditionally male domain of science and philosophy, as vigorously confirmed at the film's conclusion: there we see her conclusively destroying the brontosaurus skeleton David has been researching. Yet her high-pitched, fast-paced speech also reveals an alternative way of looking at the world and thus a unique new philosophy; as David says, 'Susan, you look at everything upside down, I've never known anyone quite like you!' The discursive reframing provided by Susan and the unconventional situations in which he finds himself in turn lead David to alter, or reposition, his own discourse and philosophy, so that the latter appears as 'skewed' as Susan's; for 'when a man is wrestling a leopard in the middle of a pond, he is in no position to run'.

Much of the initial comedy that comes from the interplay between Susan and David is physical – such as him riding out of the golf club on the running board of a car, or slipping on an olive that Susan drops on the floor. Yet as their relationship develops, we see their voices complement one another, as David appears to be the only character who can keep up with and engage with Susan's energetic dialogue. Gerald Mast, in his discussion of the making of the film, recalls the frequent use of dialogue improvisation by the key actors in the film, or frequent last-minute changes made to the script by director Howard Hawks himself. He notes the effect that this had on the aural impact of the film's voicing: 'this stream of breathlessly rapid chatter not only gives the film's dialogue a spontaneous energy; it also converts articulate patterns of human speech into the pure physicality of sound, a kind of verbal music'.[55] As such, we could say that Grant and Hepburn's voices are presented as being in harmony. This is frequently reflected in the balanced spatial compositions of shots throughout the film, where the two characters tend to occupy equal amounts of space on screen, their visual presence signalled as harmonised. This harmony is aurally represented through the song 'I Can't Give You Anything But Love (Baby)' (1928),[56] which the couple sing to the leopard when they arrive in Connecticut, inserting their own *ad lib* words as they shepherd the large cat into a pen. Their later repeat performance of this song, complete with growling and howling from George the dog and Baby the leopard, shows the couple singing in harmony in an aural representation of their increasingly harmonious, although highly unusual relationship.

At this later point in the film, more voices have been incorporated into the diegesis, exacerbating David's preference for contemplative peace and quiet. This aural accretion begins with the inclusion of Aunt Elizabeth (May Robson) and her dog, George. The dog barks incessantly at various moments in the narrative, including when Susan and her aunt talk quickly together at the same time, often arguing about David, who cannot get a word in. Later on when all the characters are in jail they all talk at once, over one another, so that Constable Slocum (Walter Catlett) cannot make sense of anything they are saying. Here we see simultaneous performative dialogue building to a loud crescendo, which increasingly irritates David, whilst also presenting an aural – yet comical – assault on the ears of the film viewer.

Unlike in the vocal performances of the other actresses discussed so far, whose voices (at least) seem to change as a result of falling in love with the male protagonist, the viewer is left in no doubt that Susan's voice alters only to manipulate those around her. She has a brief tearful moment in the woods when David tells her to go away, yet there is an overriding sense that these are exaggerated and fake tears, intended to provoke sympathy rather than representing genuine upset as in the case of Ellie Andrews or, to some extent, Hildy Johnson, discussed above. This strong performativity is made audible in particular in the scene in jail, when Susan adopts the persona of 'Swingin' Door Susie', complete with New York accent and swaggering gestures. This performance supports my argument that fast-talking dames easily adopt alternative roles in order to suit the situation in which they find themselves. She tells the constable in a confident New York drawl, 'I'll talk. I'll talk so much it'll make your hair curl!' Susan proceeds to excite the police officers with her tales of the imaginary Leopard Gang to which she claims they all belong, encapsulating them with her words in her convincing portrayal of a stereotypical gangster moll. It is her fast-paced speech during this episode that facilitates her escape since Elmer (John Kelly) is unable to type at the same speed at which she talks. As the confused men gather round the typewriter to confirm Susan's story, she jumps out of the window.

Throughout *Bringing Up Baby*, it is Susan's quick, energetic voice that frequently pushes the hectic narrative forward. Her voice seems infectious and manages to whisk everyone along with it as the other characters are seemingly carried away by the bizarre turn of events that take place in the film, all caused by Susan. Despite David's frequent objections to Susan's carefree attitude to life, at the end of the movie he admits that he had the time of his life with Susan. Thus, in a significant reversal of screwball comedy choice pattern,

David, much like Hildy in *His Girl Friday*, opts for the quirky, but definitely more fun and fulfilling relationship with his natural screwball counterpart. This reversal in narrative pattern, one premised on a male's (rather than a female's) choice of the partner who has pursued him, demonstrates just one of the ways in which later screwball comedies began to play with and subvert traditional gender roles. Grant's lively aural performance throughout and his infamous use of the word 'gay' whilst dressed in women's clothes can lead the viewer to question the representation of particular behaviours associated with masculinity and femininity, as well as the heteronormative narrative crux of screwball comedy itself. This point takes the discussion forward to a consideration of Spencer Tracy's portrayal of the character of Adam Bonner in *Adam's Rib* who, I argue, orally embodies female behaviour in order to reconcile his relationship with his wife. Not unlike the three screwball heroines discussed so far, who change their voices and performances to facilitate a partnership based on rapport and friendship, in *Adam's Rib* we likewise see a male performer changing his voice and delivery to initiate the remarriage narrative. In this instance, we see the male character adopting a female gendered vocal performance in order to manipulate his wife. This turn merits further attention, as it sheds light on another aspect of sound performance in screwball comedy, which is inchoate in the films previously discussed but foregrounded in this 1949 film.

The film opens with Doris Attinger (Judy Holliday), gun in hand, shooting at her husband and his lover in order to scare them. Amanda Bonner (Katharine Hepburn) is a lawyer who makes it her mission to defend Doris in court. She is happily married to Adam Bonner, the assistant District Attorney, who is given the task of prosecuting Doris in court. The film frequently features Amanda making lengthy speeches about women's rights and specifically about how women should be entitled to fair and equal treatment under the eyes of the law. Her convincing argument wins her the case in court, but results in the loss of her husband as Adam leaves Amanda due to her lack of respect for him and for the law. During a subsequent meeting at their accountant's office, it seems that the couple are prepared to permanently separate, until Adam suddenly breaks down in tears, evoking Amanda's sympathy and resulting in their reunion. Adam later tells Amanda in the film's culmination that his tears were fake and that he is able to produce them at any given moment, revealing his apparently emotional disclosure to be a mere performance.

In discussing *Adam's Rib*, a 1949 comedy film, when contemplating the character of Adam, we could firstly reflect on his tearful performance in line with post-war shifts in gender relations. We can furthermore consider his character in line with Judith Butler's notions about gender performance, as explored in her seminal 1990 book, *Gender Trouble: Feminism and the Subversion of Identity*. In this book, she argues against biologically, culturally or socially established notions of gender that situate men and women as universal binary opposites, instead positing the notion of gender as an always moving, changeable, reiterated social performance. This performance, according to Butler, can be affected by the situations in which an individual finds themselves, and is thus not reflecting any prior gender 'identity'. This approach disparages the idea of an intrinsic essence or identity linked to gender that causes a particular behaviour and instead views gender performances as a varied and ever changing series of performative acts that constitute (rather than express) a 'gender'. In concluding this chapter, I consider the ways in which this concept can be applied to the vocal performances in *Adam's Rib* and the ways in which the character of Adam, in particular, uses traditionally female performed behaviours to facilitate the remarriage screwball narrative.

When we first meet the couple, they are in bed eating breakfast and their friendly chatter denotes a happy marriage founded on warm affection and mutual respect for one another. Adam's voice is soft, calm and deep; at this point some of his words are nonsensical. Narratively, this is justified since he has just woken up; but this lack of eloquence also establishes a verbal pattern to feature throughout the film, where Adam often struggles to articulate his words. Amanda's voice, in contrast, is of a higher pitch, and is bright and sharp; she speaks quickly in comparison with his slow, sometimes slurred speech. This initial interchange establishes some key narrative dynamics of the film, such as the couple's mutual interest in news and current affairs, Amanda being a Yale law graduate,[57] and the couple's use of affectionate nicknames for one another, most notably Adam being called 'Pinkie'. The latter seems to connote a childlike innocence about their relationship, but the operation of the nickname is more complex. The nicknaming of the male protagonist with a colour traditionally associated with femininity establishes at the outset a dynamic of the subversion of or playfulness with gender roles, I argue. Not incidentally, this nickname also humiliates Adam when he accidentally uses it in court later in the film, just before he loses his case. In this opening scene, however, their initial conversation about the noises Adam emits when sleeping is fairly mundane and their discussion is slow-paced and relaxed. Yet, on reading the stirring news of Doris Attinger's attack on her husband, their interaction speeds up as they begin a lively debate that is to continue throughout the movie. Hepburn's strong voice and confident presence gives her speech compelling resonance as they continue their discussion in the car. In this film, unlike in *Bringing Up Baby*, her voice is deep and authoritative, but still carries the clipped, sharp tone that is key to many of her other vocal performances in the films of the 1930s and 1940s. She still speaks at speed and frequently talks over Tracy, whose character is then often placed in situations in which he has to request if he can speak or say something to avoid her verbal domination.

From the outset, Amanda is constructed as the one in charge of their relationship. This is but one way in which Amanda is masculinised throughout the film, while Adam is feminised. Orit Kamir correctly notes that Amanda 'is the articulate Yale graduate who runs an aggressive private practice, while he is a gentle, easygoing, stuttering public servant. She drives them both to work, while he cooks, wearing an apron.'[58] Such gender role reversal suggests a progressive agenda behind the film's representation of a powerful female lawyer and a subservient male character, and speaks of the films post-war context. However, through this type of characterisation, the film actually reinforces socio-cultural expectations, emphasising a particular patriarchal agenda about expected gender-based behaviours, whereby it is seen as 'natural' that the female (or the effeminate) should cook, while the man drives. Thus Adam's crying later in the film might, to some viewers of the time, be justified by his partaking in other apparently female activities such as cooking. Yet, I argue that in the realm of screwball comedy, which is known for its playful resolve, these are examples of the characters playing with actions that might traditionally have been considered male or female with a great deal of self-reflexivity. Such reading is supported by the early court scenes, when both protagonists loudly and convincingly argue their cases to the surrounding characters in the courtroom, but then in secret, quietly whisper and blow kisses to one another under the table, switching between these contrasted performances with ease. Therefore, I argue, in line with Judith Butler's theory of gender performance expounded in *Gender Trouble* that, rather than being 'masculinised' or 'feminised', the characters play both roles, using so-called male or female behaviour to their advantage.

As the film continues, their relationship becomes increasingly fraught as Amanda's uncompromising conduct in defending Doris causes a divide between them. Adam objects to Amanda being, as he puts it, a 'new woman', saying he wants a wife, not a competitor. He is not comfortable with his wife's gender performance, which skilfully fluctuates between 'masculine', forceful, uncompromising verbal tirades in amplified and resonant voice, gentle and intimate utterances in half-whisper and lively banter with other women in court. These moments in the film appear to support Anita La Cruz's argument that Adam's 'old-fashioned' preference for two different sexes and their expected behaviours underlines the fact that men of the post-war era were 'informed by a patriarchal ideology [and] were aware more than ever of the precarious nature of man's supremacy'.[59] Thus the gender behaviour anxiety that is present from the film's outset signals, from La Cruz's perspective, a female threat to masculine supremacy; as such, the film, in La Cruz's reading, presents an attempt to revert to, or maintain, the status quo of male supremacy. However, as mentioned above, the sense of gender play that is prevalent throughout the film does not entirely support this argument when we later see both characters begin to further embody alternative gender performances in order to achieve their respective goals within the narrative. I argue that this is not as much a case of a desire to maintain male (or even female) supremacy, but more that of a desire for a kind of ludic equality between the sexes, a mantra frequently championed by Amanda. Adam discovers that to find himself on an equal plane with his wife requires him to break out of expected masculine behaviours and freely embody female gender performance – or to playfully layer gender performances.

After Adam has left Amanda, the viewer witnesses the ways in which this new narrative situation affects the verbal performance of the characters. During the court summation, Amanda's voice has become loud, aggressive and angry – i.e. 'masculine' – as she beats her fist on the bench in front of the jury. She clearly and carefully concludes her arguments, stressing the importance of equal rights for women, engaging the jury to imagine what their judgements might be if Doris Attinger were a man. She then uses strong emotive words to encourage empathy from the court, finishing her argument with a soft, gentle ('feminine') tone that paints Doris Attinger as a victim, rather than an attempted murderer. Adam disparages her case, referring to Amanda's arguments as 'sound, mere sound' which has no bearing on the case, suggesting that Amanda's speech was a meagre performance with no legal substance. But it is Amanda's 'sounding' that wins the day. During his summation, Adam's own words are frequently muddled, featuring spoonerisms and other verbal errors. This disrupts his usual low-pitched, steady confident tone, especially when, during a flustered moment, he inadvertently uses the couple's nickname, loudly instructing Amanda: 'sit down Pinkie!', which further disrupts his performance and causes giggling within the courtroom. At this point, Stanley Cavell argues that 'she knows, he knows, we know ... that she has won, that he is not able to fight her as an equal in public'.[60] Thus it seems that Amanda's clever play with both male and female 'sounding' has won her the case and, in this narrative, Adam, who at this point does not fully embrace varied gender performances, is not Amanda's equal.

At two separate points in the film Adam makes reference to 'female' tears as a powerful means by which to gain sympathy. When Doris Attinger breaks down crying during the court's questioning of her, she loudly bawls into her handkerchief, gaining the sympathy of all in the courtroom except Adam, who attempts to use this emotional breakdown to suggest that she is an unstable woman and an incapable wife and mother. In the following scene, he is equally unsympathetic when Amanda cries after they argue about the court case. Adam clearly feels that tears are habitually used by females as a tactic to manipulate men. He calls them a 'guaranteed heart-melter! A few female tears! Stronger than any acid' contending 'but this time they won't work!' Yet in these comments, he is acknowledging the potential power attached to tears, especially since they usually elicit an empathetic emotional response from others. This reference to 'female' tears, twice in the film, foregrounds Adam's later decision to use a powerful female gender performance not only to save his relationship but also to put himself back on equal standing with his wife.

In the scene when he cries, Adam's tears are silent, but as they appear in his eyes and are seen by Amanda. The look of complete shock on her face confirms that this 'female' behaviour is not something she has seen from him before, suggesting a 'new' gender performance. The scene takes place in the office of their accountant, Jules Frikke (Emerson Treacy), where Adam appears to struggle with the notion of separation from Amanda. Conversely, she remains cool and distant throughout the discussion and continually reiterates their division, sharply exclaiming 'I can't help that' when Adam says he wants to pay for the repair of a coat he bought her, and correcting his 'we like a lot of plants' into the past tense with a sharp 'liked!' This abrupt vocal reprimanding causes Adam's subsequent voice performance to become slower and drop in pitch, denoting his increasing sadness at the demise of their marriage and friendship. At one point he erupts into amused high-pitched laughter when the accountant queries a cheque for a lost bet, jovially asking Amanda, 'oh yeah, remember that?', whilst chuckling. On seeing Amanda's stony expression, however, he immediately reverts back to his reserved, sad demeanour. It is the cheque for the final mortgage payment on their house in the country that causes Adam to break down; his usually deep, velvety voice quivers with emotion as he says they are 'free and clear' of mortgage payments. Amanda's linguistic reversion here to present tense – 'we, erm, own it now' – and her now quiet, softened tone of voice reflects her own melancholy at the demise of their relationship. This reveals her previous unyielding behaviour to have been a facade, or a performance, and now cues Adam's tears. There is complete silence in the film's soundscape and an extreme close up on Adam's face as tears begin to well in his eyes and run down his face. Such formal strategy ensures full attention is placed on the act of the male protagonist crying. Together with his continual glances upwards at Amanda, ensuring that she sees his tears, such aural isolation highlights this moment as performative: as his shrewd attempt to use 'female' tears – 'stronger than any acid' – to win her over. As he turns his face away from her and Jules, Amanda, won over by his crying, suggests they drive up to their farm in Connecticut. Throughout this sequence, the high-pitched, nasally voice of the accountant, with his harsh New York accent, serves as an aural contrast to Adam's silent crying. His voice does not detract attention from the act or gentle sounds of Adam's sobbing; his high tempo, scratchy voice – divulging complex and uninteresting facts about tax law – fades into the background, yet serves as an aural substitute for the silences and quiet words exchanged between Adam and Amanda. Adam adds emotion to his performance by saying in a shaky, high-pitched voice, 'you don't really want to go' as his sobbing augments. He then begins to sniff and emit louder, high-pitched sobs as Amanda gently shuffles his stooping, weeping form out of the office; his female performance has successfully saved their relationship.

Of course, Amanda has no clue that this was a mere performance. Once settled at their home in the farm, she jokes with Adam about being his political rival when he announces a potential change in career to 'County Court Judge Pinkie' (here the repeated use of their nickname signals a complete reconciliation in their relationship). Adam's response to this is a threat that he will cry again. He reveals to a surprised Amanda how he is able to 'turn on' his tears whenever he needs to, promptly giving her a repeat silent performance, including an explanation of where and why he adds in the loud sobs. This performance of 'female' tears – as they are called throughout the film – and acknowledgement of their threat and power demonstrates the ways in which male and female characters can play with gender, choosing which behaviours they want to exhibit. Such gender performativity here facilitates the remarriage narrative in *Adam's Rib* whilst also seemingly upholding the patriarchal agendas and, as discussed by La Cruz, apparently containing the strong-willed female character 'within' the narrative conclusion.

Yet through Adam's playful, self-reflexive gender performance, the very notion of some universal condition of patriarchy is actually put into question. For, if Adam's performance of gender – whether masculine or feminine – can always be perceived as only a performance, then he cannot be interpreted as a representative of any patriarchal identity, because the notion of patriarchy itself is constructed through his acts. If, as Butler suggests, 'there is no gender identity behind the expressions of gender'[61] and gender identity is 'performatively produced by the very "expressions" that are said to be its results', perhaps this final attempt to control the wayward female actually 'constructs' (in a Butlerian sense) rather than 'expresses' (in a traditional sense) patriarchal masculinity. The narrative closure suitably fulfils genre conventions whilst alleviating potential anxiety related to the subversion of gender roles witnessed throughout the film. Nevertheless, the sheer amount of parodic performativity (including that associated with David Wayne, discussed below) also leaves some 'cracks' in the narrative and the viewer's experience (cf. Commoli and Narboni).[62] It is these cracks, and the comic performativity which ultimately does not refer to anything seriously, that destabilise our picture of 'universal' genders.

Adam's Rib is replete with other characters who play with gender performance. For example, the women whom Amanda gathers to speak in court include a quiet, stern-voiced female doctor with an impressive list of degrees and other qualifications, a loudly spoken female foreman and a curvy, country-accented female performer and weightlifter, who humiliates Adam by lifting him above her head during the court hearing, displaying a physical form of gender subversion, while Adam cries out in anger and annoyance. When considering the film contemporaneously, these female characters, alongside the female protagonist, would have been perceived as engaging in traditional masculine endeavours and behaviours. Thus, as well as Adam's self-reflexive gender performances, we see women embracing behaviour traditionally associated with men, but in such exaggerated fashion that these staged behaviours move from the realm of usual performance (which, in Butler's reading, refers to some stable identity) to that of pure performativity (which, according to Butler, does not refer to anything but itself, highlighting the constructed nature of gender as such).

In *Gender Trouble*, Butler discusses drag performance as an example of exaggerated display of gender performance.[63] This sense of embellished performance can also be found in *Adam's Rib* in the Bonner's piano-playing neighbour Kip Lurie (David Wayne), described by Stanley Cavell as having 'a mild show-biz homosexual tinge'.[64] His effeminate mannerisms are represented as an irritant to Adam and as an unsubtle suggestion to the audience that his character might be homosexual. His smooth, deep voice has a performative essence to it, as he playfully flirts with Amanda, takes frequent jibes at Adam, and often expresses his thoughts loudly in song. The narrative, significantly, remains absurdly inconclusive: Kip's obvious desire for Amanda, embodied in the song he writes for her, and his later attempts to seduce her, suggest he is a heterosexual male, with marked feminine characteristics, or, more accurately, as a male playing (with) female gender performance. In reference to the court case, though, Kip fully supports Amanda's cause, saying 'you've got me so convinced, I might even become a woman', to which Adam replies, 'and he wouldn't have far to go either!' This exchange further reinforces the sense that Kip's play with gender performance, as extreme as it is, may also be dangerous in heteronormative society; Adam's comment, however, also adumbrates and contextualises his own later performance. These and other examples of varied gender performance and their comedic quintessence suggest not just the humorous aspects of gender performance, but also its emancipatory element. Butler notes the sense of liberation that accompanies exaggerated gender performance, such as drag, which, she writes, has the effect of perpetually displacing the notion of an individual's 'original' gender, instead constituting 'a fluidity of identities that suggests an openness to resignification and recontextualisation'. She furthermore notes that such parodic performance deprives hegemonic culture and its critics of the claim to naturalised or essentialist gender identities.[65] Through this lens, we can perceive the resignification and recontextualisation of the aural personas of the characters discussed here as a means of emancipation from previously rigidly and narrowly defined voicing and performance associated with 'male' and 'female'.

Indeed, the varied examples we see of characters playing with ideas related to masculinity and femininity shows a light-hearted, self-reflexive attitude towards gender and its aural dimensions throughout *Adam's Rib*. As alluded to above, in the earlier screwball comedies discussed here, such as *It Happened One Night*, the divisions between male and female gender performances are clearly delineated, especially in the performances of Clark Gable and Claudette Colbert. Gable's gruff sounding masculinity and Colbert's varied, but always distinctly feminine vocal registers denote a film with a traditional take on gender that, as Adam Bonner puts it, likes 'two sexes'. Yet we must not forget the performative aspect of this film, which undoubtedly had great influence on the sense of subversion and play to hereafter pervade the screwball comedy genre. This is apparent in such scenes as Ellie and Peter impersonating a working-class couple. Whilst this does not necessarily demonstrate the ways in which gender can be played with through voice, and/or be questioned as a 'substantive appearance',[66] Ellie and Peter still adopt the vocal tones of a certain 'type' of male and female, establishing a sense of light-hearted performativity that would frequently feature in later incarnations of the screwball comedy narrative.

Beyond the question of the construction (or not) of gender identity, it is certain that early screwball comedies capitalised on the audibility of what is normatively seen as 'subversive elements' of female voice. In the case of Ellie Andrews, her formidable voice carried the ability to destabilise the patriarchal power of her father, and in the case of Hildy Johnston, she was able to cleverly manipulate male characters such as Bruce and Earl with her varied vocal performances as well as perform lightning-speed dialogue with Walter, who at times struggles to keep up with her. Such adept vocal skill can be seen as having a huge influence on the pacey performances of Hepburn in *Adam's Rib* and Tracy, who sometimes equally struggles to maintain high-tempo dialogue – or even get a word in – with his screwball counterpart. In the case of Claudette Colbert, we must also remember that she was one of the earliest actresses to appear on screen with an audible, synchronised voice. Therefore, she was one of the first women to introduce cinema audiences to active, expressive onscreen women. In films such as *It Happened One Night* and *His Girl Friday*, where women frequently used their quick, witty, vocal capabilities to outsmart or poke fun at men, this sense of performativity provided a basis for later films such as *Adam's Rib* to aspire to, or as I have argued, to 'play' with.

All of the female protagonists featured in this chapter have a moment where they break down in tears. As discussed above, this narrative situation mostly occurs when they realise their love for the male character, with whom they have formed a powerful bond of friendship. Thus the act and sound of crying appears to be as much a part of the screwball comedy genre conventions as fast-talking and living 'happily ever after'. As such, Adam's crying is markedly genre self-reflexive, as is the whole world of *Adam's Rib*. Indeed, his own detailed explanation of his crying performance suggests a meta-cinematic awareness of the trope of female crying in screwball comedy, or even film in general, and the politics of its use.

In considering gender performance in the 1938 film *Bringing Up Baby*, which comes chronologically before *His Girl Friday* in 1940, again we see glimpses of play with gender roles, such as when David appears wearing a negligee and tells Susan's aunt that he 'just went *gay* all of a sudden', leaping into the air on the word 'gay'. This fleeting and surprising example of gender play (and a moment often cited as the first time in a Hollywood film the word 'gay' was used to describe homosexuality)[67] is an early example of screwball comedy characters playing with ideas of gender performance. Like all films discussed here, the sense of performativity is prevalent throughout *Bringing Up Baby*, particularly where Susan is concerned. Her impersonation of a gangster moll demonstrates playfulness with characterisation and a self-reflexive portrayal of movie-type gangsters; furthermore, her naming of David as 'Jerry the nipper' (a name he is called by Irene Dunne in *The Awful Truth*; McCarey, 1937) in the jail scene, adds a further intertextual element to her performance, moving it, potentially, beyond the realm of performance into that of meta-cinematic performativity. It is by referencing back to this history of performativity in previous screwball comedies that *Adam's Rib*, then, can question the notion of gender identity itself.

NOTES

1. John Belton, *American Cinema, American Culture* (New York: McGraw-Hill, 2005), 148.
2. See Rick Altman, *Silent Film Sound* (New York: Columbia University Press, 2004).
3. Robert B. Ray, *A Certain Tendency of the Hollywood Cinema 1930–1980* (Princeton: Princeton University Press, 1985), 30.
4. Maria DiBattista, *Fast Talking Dames* (New Haven: Yale University Press, 2001), 13.
5. For more extensive discussion of this issue, see Molly Haskell, *From Reverence to Rape: The Treatment of Women in the Movies* (New York: Holt, Rinehart and Winston, 1975), 6–8.
6. Belton, 186.
7. DiBattista, 11.
8. Sarah Kozloff, *Overhearing Film Dialogue* (Berkeley and Los Angeles: University of California Press, 2000), 22.
9. Kozloff, 179.
10. Haskell, 92.
11. David R. Shumway, 'Screwball comedies: Constructing romance, mystifying marriage', *Cinema Journal*, v. 30, no. 4 (Summer, 1991); Diane Carson, 'To be seen but not heard: *The Awful Truth*', in Diane Carson, Linda Dittmar and Janice Welsch (eds), *Multiple Voices in Feminist Film Criticism* (Minneapolis: University of Minnesota Press, 1994).
12. Shumway, 15.

13. Amy Lawrence, *Echo and Narcissus: Women's Voices in Classical Hollywood Cinema* (Berkeley: University of California Press, 1991), 9.
14. Gina Bloom, *Voice in Motion: Staging Gender, Shaping Sound in Early Modern England* (Philadelphia: University of Pennsylvania Press, 2007), 11.
15. Anne McKay, 'Speaking up: Voice amplification and women's struggle for public expression', in Caroline Mitchell (ed.), *Women and Radio: Airing Differences* (London: Routledge, 2000), 23.
16. Marjorie Rosen, *Popcorn Venus: Women, Movies and the American Dream* (New York: Coward, McCann and Geoghegan, 1973), 73.
17. Stanley Cavell, *Pursuits of Happiness: The Hollywood Comedy of Remarriage* (Cambridge, MA: Harvard University Press, 1981).
18. Cited in Shumway, 8.
19. Shumway, 8.
20. Tina Olsin Lent, 'Romantic love and friendship: The redefinition of gender relations in screwball comedy', in Kristine Brunovska Karnick and Henry Jenkins (eds), *Classical Hollywood Comedy* (London and New York: Routledge, 1995), 316.
21. Lent, 320.
22. Shumway, 13.
23. Thomas Schatz, *Hollywood Genres: Formulas, Filmmaking, and the Studio System* (Boston, MA: McGraw-Hill, 1981), 150.
24. Kozloff, 194.
25. Aristotle, *History of Animals* (Whitefish, MT: Kessinger Publishing, 2004), 114.
26. Sara Mills, *Gender Matters: Feminist Linguistic Analysis* (Bristol: Equinox Publishing Ltd, 2012), 230.
27. Mills, 230.
28. Elizabeth Kendall, *The Runaway Bride: Hollywood Romantic Comedies of the 1930s* (New York: Cooper Square Press, 2002), 40.
29. Kendall, 41.
30. Kozloff, 172.
31. Kozloff, 172.
32. Manuela Ruiz Pardos, 'Addicted to fun: Courtship, play and romance in the screwball comedy', *Revista Alicantina de Estudios Ingleses*, 13 (2000).
33. Cavell, 86.
34. Kozloff, 180.
35. Cavell, 98.
36. Kozloff, 185.
37. Cavell, 81.
38. DiBattista, 20.
39. DiBattista, 21.
40. DiBattista, 14.
41. Kozloff, 181.
42. Schatz, 163.
43. Kozloff, 174.
44. Cavell, 167.
45. Mills, 233.
46. Roland Barthes, *Image-Music-Text* (London: Fantana, 1977), 179–89.
47. Leslie C. Dunn and Nancy A. Jones (eds), *Embodied Voices: Representing Female Vocality in Western Culture* (Cambridge: Cambridge University Press, 1996), 2.
48. See Catherine Clement, *Opera, or, The Undoing of Women* (London: I. B. Tauris, 1997)

49. Dunn and Jones, 3.
50. DiBattista, 179.
51. Kozloff, 187.
52. Bruce Babington and Peter William Evans, *Affairs to Remember: The Hollywood Comedy of the Sexes* (Manchester: Manchester University Press, 1989), 17.
53. Ann Carson, 'The gender of sound', in Ann Carson, *Glass, Irony and God* (New York: New Directions Publishing Corporation, 1995), 119.
54. Prudence Allen, *The Concept of Woman: the Aristotelian Revolution, 750 BC–AD 1250* (Grand Rapids: W. B. Eerdmans Publishing, 1997), 36.
55. Gerald Mast, *Bringing Up Baby*, (New Brunswick, NJ: Rutgers University Press, 1988), 9.
56. Written by Dorothy Fields and Jimmy McHugh, performed as a cappella by Hepburn and Grant.
57. The Yale School of Law began to enrol women in 1918, but in 1949, the time setting of *Adam's Rib*, women graduating from law schools were still very much a minority. Throughout the US, female law graduates found themselves discriminated against and struggled to find work as lawyers. In 1940, women made up 2.4% of those working in the profession of Law; in 1950, this had increased to 3.5%. For more information, see Cythia Fuchs Epstein, *Women in Law* (Champaign: University of Illinois Press, 1993) and Virginia G. Drachman, *Sisters in Law: Women Lawyers in Modern American History* (Boston, MA: Harvard University Press, 2001).
58. Orit Kamir, *Framed: Women in Law and Film* (Durham, NC: Duke University Press, 2006), 142.
59. Anita La Cruz, 'Is "Who wears the pants" an empty question? Comedy and marriage in *Adam's Rib*', *Bells: Barcelona English Language & Literature Studies*, v. 9, no. 2 (1998): 139.
60. Cavell, 199.
61. Judith Butler, *Gender Trouble: Feminism and the Subversion of Identity* (New York and London: Routledge, 1990), 25.
62. Jean-Louis Comolli and Jean Narboni, 'Cinema/ideology/criticism', *Screen*, v. 12, no.1 (Spring 1971): 27–36.
63. Butler, 134–41.
64. Cavell, 214.
65. Butler, 138.
66. Butler, 25.
67. Ed Sikov, 'Laughing hysterically: Sex, repression, and American film comedy', in Martin B. Duberman (ed.), *Queer Representations: Reading Lives, Reading Cultures* (New York: New York University Press, 1997), 94.

CHAPTER 2

All That Jazz: The Diegetic Soundtrack in Melodrama

As modern film audiences, we are well aware of the capacity of music soundtracks to perform a multitude of functions in film. Music, whether diegetic (a part of the world of the film) or non-diegetic (outside of the world of the film), has the capacity to create emotion or humour; to be narrative or symbolic; to create atmosphere or provide information about a setting; and in its various forms, music is integral in creating meaning about film characters. This chapter looks at the use of music in melodramas of the 1940s and the 1950s. Melodrama is a film genre that notoriously makes use of music for its emotional capacity and for its ability to generate meaning about female protagonists in film texts that have been historically labelled as 'women's films' or 'female weepies'. Thomas Elsaesser defines melodrama as 'a dramatic narrative in which musical accompaniment marks the emotional effects'[1] and notably, the word melodrama itself is derived from the Greek word '*melos*' meaning music, and the French word '*drame*' meaning drama or performance. Kathryn Kalinak characterises the function of film music by 'its power to define meaning and to express emotion'.[2] Schatz notes that 'Hollywood's use of background music to provide a formal aural dimension and an emotional punctuation to its dramas extends back even into the "silent" era'.[3] In his historical study of film music, Mervyn Cooke observes that much musical film scoring was influenced by melodramatic theatrical traditions, which throughout the nineteenth century had developed a set of musical codes and conventions for symbolising emotion. He quotes Shapiro's 1984 study that highlights 'the well-established symbiosis between music and drama that had in the nineteenth century shaped the development of major theatrical genres such as opera, ballet and (above all) melodrama'.[4] Subsequently, when melodrama was integrated into film, this occurred with a series of musical conventions already in place and which were understood by audiences, particularly where non-diegetic music was concerned.

Yet, in this discussion, I am interested in the use of diegetic music in melodrama, the function of which appears more difficult to outline. This might be because it forms a part of the world of the film and therefore is audible to the characters, as well as the film viewer. Like non-diegetic music, music within the diegesis can also be used to signify emotion or atmosphere, as argued by Claudia Gorbman: 'the mood of any music on the soundtrack, be it diegetic or non-diegetic, will be felt in association with the diegetic events'.[5] However, Buhler *et al.* assert that for diegetic music to have a meaningful impact, it must be foregrounded on the soundtrack, otherwise it 'tend[s] to recede to something nearer the commentative role of underscoring'.[6] Diegetic music is also crucial in providing semantic information about characters and in establishing time and place; Buhler *et al.* cite examples such as 'a marching band, a gamelan, a jazz combo, [or] a symphony orchestra' as music that is effective in quickly establishing an acoustic milieu.[7] Yet what links can be drawn between diegetic music and the representation of gender in melodrama?

Heather Laing, in her discussion of 1940s melodrama, explores the link between diegetic music, female characters and dynamics of power. She argues that where diegetic music forms part of the sound design, it has great implications on the film's female protagonist and the viewer's ability to empathise with her. Firstly, she argues that diegetic music often denies the viewer access to the protagonist's emotions since it often 'fills' a space where the non-diegetic track would be fulfilling a narrative and/or emotional role. Secondly, she draws attention to the fact that the playing of diegetic music, be it a record, a piano or a full singing and dancing performance, leaves the protagonist somewhat powerless if they cannot control the sounds, since 'the actions and reactions – and therefore the emotions – of the listener are contextualised by music that remains under the complete control of another character ... thus rendering them passive in terms of both narrative and emotional agency'.[8] She develops her argument to focus specifically on the role of the male performer and the female listener, demonstrating her ideas through a detailed analysis of *Letter from an Unknown Woman* (1948). She argues that Stefan's piano playing and frequent performances deny the viewer 'access' to Lisa's emotions at crucial moments in the narrative, leaving her powerless.

Laing's argument provides an interesting starting point for a discussion of diegetic music and power relations, yet her focus on the male performer and the female listener does not account for the potential power of the female performer or for female characters who are in control of diegetic music in melodrama.[9]

I am interested in the power dynamics related to the 'control' of music in a film's diegesis as well as the role this music plays in establishing meaning about female characters. In this chapter I discuss three successful melodramas of the classical Hollywood period: *Mildred Pierce* (1945), *Written on the Wind*

(1956) and *Imitation of Life* (1959). Following Laing, I look at two aspects of the diegetic music in these films. Firstly, I look at the ways that it can demonstrate dynamics of power (or lack thereof) between female characters and their counterparts. This is often signified through 'stronger' characters appropriating the sound diegesis by playing records or instruments, or through singing in musical performance. Secondly, I consider the proliferation of jazz music within the films' diegeses, which is repeatedly linked to the female characters in these films, frequently resulting in a construction of these characters as immoral and rebellious, due to the social and cultural meanings attached to jazz music, which I discuss below.

Melodramas of this period frequently portray female characters torn between desirable, yet usually immoral choices. These texts explore the tension between social expectations placed on women during the 1940s and 1950s and the subversive desire to break free from such ideological restraint. Schatz characterises the films as 'popular romances that depicted a virtuous individual (usually a woman) or couple (usually lovers) victimised by repression and inequitable social circumstances, particularly those involving marriage, occupation and the nuclear family'.[10] The nuclear family was an institution that was perceived as being under threat in the US in the 1940s and the 1950s, when the social fabric of America had begun to transform.[11] The nuclear family had previously symbolised America's middle classes and patriarchal social order, yet the Second World War and the US involvement in the Korean conflict had led to a fragmentation in the family when men in service were sent overseas and women were made to leave the home and join the workforce. Jackie Byers argues that these developments incited a change in gender perceptions of men and women and a questioning of previously rigidly defined gender roles.[12] This social anxiety about the nuclear family and in particular the role of the mother was a focal point of the family melodrama subgenre narrative, which I discuss here. Schatz highlights that, in family melodramas, the family unit is no longer subject to external conflict such as crime or war, but instead becomes a site of conflict itself. Janet Walker has highlighted that between the end of the Second World War and the early 1960s an 'optimistic' image of America was fostered by Hollywood, as well as by other forms of media: 'Commentators defined domesticity, respectability, security, TV, advertising, affluence, suburbia and superhighways as the order of the day.'[13] Yet beneath this glossy facade, lay a society that had been shattered by the horrors of war and which Christine Gledhill describes as a 'bourgeoisie "decaying from within" in Eisenhower's America'.[14]

This sense of 'regression' in moral values is explored in Barbara Klinger's discussion of the ways in which Douglas Sirk's *Written on the Wind* was publicised in the 1950s. She notes that although this period is often retrospectively perceived as a socially and sexually repressive era, this depiction of the 1950s ignores the high visibility and complexity of discourses on sexuality that characterise this age: 'Along with its sedate images of the nuclear family,' Klinger argues, 'the 1950s saw an explosion of discussions and representations of explicit sexuality that made sex an aggressively integral part of public life.'[15] Klinger suggests that far from sexual repression, a form of sexual emancipation was taking place, as evident in adult film genres at the time, such as melodrama. Her exploration of the promotion of such 'adult' films and other forms of popular culture in the 1950s highlights that the promise of narratives featuring sexual themes such as 'homosexuality, sexual initiation, prostitution, rape, abortion, adultery, sexual frustration and temptation, alcoholism and murder'[16] was exciting and attractive to adult audiences. Furthermore, Klinger notes a heightened awareness of 'alternative' sexual choices in this period through the existence of organised gay subcultures and the beatnik movement that advocated 'free love' and resisted monogamy. The 1940s had seen the emergence of Betty Grable as wartime 'pin-up' girl, the 1950s saw the arrival of the nude pin-up into the public sphere with the first issue of *Playboy* published in 1953 featuring Marilyn Monroe. Publications such as *Playboy* were 'devoted to an anti-family philosophy of male freedom'.[17] Such prevalence of sex and sexuality in the 1950s led to reformist groups becoming more intent on challenging what they perceived as a decline in morality. This subsequently led to an era that was 'driven by contradictory and sometimes combative representations of sex, manifested in a wide range of popular forms from Monroe and *Playboy* to *Father Knows Best* and Walt Disney films'.[18] Klinger's observations of the prevalence of sex in 1950s society supports Laura Mulvey's prior assertions that melodrama, far from hiding gender and family-related oppositions beneath the surface, places them at the forefront: 'ideological contradiction is the overt mainspring and specific content of melodrama, not a hidden, unconscious thread to be picked up only by special critical processes'.[19] Like Klinger, Mulvey believes that audiences were fully aware of the subversive elements of melodrama, stating that melodrama works by 'touching on sensitive areas of sexual repression and frustration; its excitement comes from conflict not between enemies, but between people tied by blood or love'.[20]

I examine this 'contradiction' or conflict between morality and sexuality in relation to the diegetic jazz music that is frequently linked to the female characters in these films. This music, I believe, represents female characters embracing youthful and sexual emancipation from the societal rigidity of the 1950s and embracing the subversive undercurrent that was emerging in US society. John Belton notes that during this post-war period, American female sexuality, which Hollywood had previously confined to the domestic sphere of the family, 'suddenly rebelled, revealing its dangerous potential' in genres such as film noir and melodrama. Whilst this rebellion tended to be controlled by the film's male protagonist or dealt with in the narrative via the downfall of the female character, Belton believes it revealed 'that sexuality nevertheless emerged as revolutionary, empowering (albeit briefly) the women who possessed it'.[21] This empowerment is particularly evident in the female characters discussed in this chapter, and whilst its emergence is generally contained by the film's narrative, I argue that the act of empowerment and emancipation – because it is represented acoustically – remains in the mind of the film viewer due to the marked presence of diegetic jazz music.

Jazz music began to be used more frequently as part of the Hollywood film score in the 1950s after the demise of the studio system, which, due to financial constraints and the rise in the sale and availability of pop records, saw a decline in the use of classical orchestral music. Although 1950s melodramas still utilised the classical Hollywood score, jazz music became subversively prevalent in genres such as melodrama and film noir, and frequently related to the female protagonist. In the films discussed here, jazz is often linked to the female adolescent characters. Kathryn Kalinak states, when it is incorporated effectively, 'jazz is narratively motivated and is exploited in much the same way that the classical score used atmospheric or mood music'.[22] The following discussion will demonstrate that in the melodramas of the 1950s, jazz in fact rarely performs a narrative function yet is frequently used to create an atmosphere of sex, seduction or danger. The use of such music, I argue, can also be linked to the emancipation of female adolescents from familial bonds as well as sexual liberation, which although often linked to a 'decline' in morals, can also be perceived as a positive opportunity for women to break out of their previously rigidly defined social roles.

David Butler has written extensively about the use of jazz music in film, drawing on various other critical discussions of its primitive rhythm, associated sexual dance movements and even its alleged link to sex through the phallic qualities of the jazz trumpet. In his discussion of jazz music in film noir of the 1940s he notes 'jazz became a useful means of suggesting a number of sordid and immoral themes that the censorship laws prevented from being explicitly depicted'.[23] Buhler *et al.* similarly assert that jazz was often used to signify 'seedy urban settings' or 'the dangerous world of crime'.[24] Kalinak explains that jazz became related to the sexual depiction of women due to the musical conventions that had been developed in classical Hollywood scoring of the 1930s to represent prostitutes:

> The classical Hollywood film score collaborated in the dominant ideology which punished women for their sexuality. Visual displays of female sexuality were accompanied by a nucleus of musical practices which carried implications of indecency and promiscuity through their association with so-called decadent forms such as jazz, the blues, [and] ragtime.[25]

The decadent forms to which Kalinak refers include the use of woodwind or brass instruments and characteristics such as 'blue notes',[26] instrumentalisation, swinging syncopated rhythms,[27] and improvisory-like textures'.[28]

Butler calls attention to jazz as an 'inferior' type of music that could sit among the classical orchestral score without threatening it. He argues that 'the use of jazz did not contradict the values of the classical Hollywood score ... because jazz was a black music, and by implication an inferior music'[29] Kalinak similarly asserts the link between jazz and otherness:

> The classical score frequently encoded otherness through the common denominator of jazz. For white audiences of the era, jazz represented the urban, the sexual, and the decadent in a musical idiom perceived in the culture at large as an indigenous black form. Playing upon these culturally empowered stereotypes, the classical score used jazz as a musical trope for otherness, whether sexual or racial.[30]

Yet at the same time, jazz has also been associated with the notion of emancipation and rebellion of the young against the old from the very beginning of sound film (cf. *The Jazz Singer*, 1927). Therefore, whilst on one level jazz signifies sex and immorality, to an adolescent in the 1950s it potentially represented an expression of freedom from restraint.

Tracing music gender coding as far back as Gregorian chanting and Old Roman singing, Leo Treitler has demonstrated that historically and ideologically, particular musical patterns or features have been coded as male or female. He argues that traditionally, music featuring traits such as 'softness, roundedness, elegance, charm, grace'[31] and music that is able to transgress limits can be semiotically coded as feminine. In Heather Laing's discussion, she also links these ideas with more unfixed musical forms such as improvisation and melodic elaboration. This is in opposition to masculine coding which Treitler defines as featuring 'clarity, system, understandability, strength, vigour, power and reason'. Although I do not intend to deny that jazz is a powerful and vigorous musical genre, features of jazz such as its softness, roundness and its infamous use of improvisation instead of rigid musical structures could also be coded as distinctly feminine and, at the very least, aimed at disrupting the patriarchal order. Therefore, when juxtaposed with a rigid, highly structured classical, non-diegetic score, jazz arguably becomes not just a representation of femininity but also a metaphor for female rebellion against patriarchy.

Historical and cultural links between jazz and femininity also stem from the constitutive role played by women in jazz. For example, the highly influential and infamous jazz singer Billie Holiday's distinct vocals and improvised performances link to the aforementioned notions of feminine musical coding. Furthermore, Kristin A. McGee notes that the great success of theatrical and cabaret performers such as Bessie Smith and Sophie Tucker, combined with the 'highly desired chorus-girl acts and solo jazz dancers . . . created an image of jazz as feminine during the Jazz Age'.[32] In the context of melodrama, I assess the potential liberation that underlies female musical performance. I suggest that performance, whilst partly symbolising female sexuality and therefore posing a threat to male patriarchy, also symbolises female emancipation by showing women as active performers rather than passive listeners. The frequent use of jazz music within the melodramatic diegesis constructs female, adolescent characters as rebellious and wayward as well as sexually promiscuous through jazz music's social and cultural connotations with sex and otherness.

In the films discussed here, jazz music is repeatedly used diegetically to create a link to female characters to suggest immoral traits and socially unsanctioned behaviour. In *Mildred Pierce*, jazz music codes not just Mildred (Joan Crawford) but also her daughter Veda (Ann Blyth) as improper and immoral through their frequent link to diegetic jazz, and often to the men who incorporate this type of music within the film's diegesis; the latter can also be considered to behave in a socially aberrant manner. In Douglas Sirk's *Written on the Wind*, the character of Marylee Hadley (Dorothy Malone) is accompanied by suggestive jazz melodies virtually every time she appears on screen, including the moment in which her father tumbles to his death. In Sirk's *Imitation of Life*, we again see a mother and a surrogate daughter coded with jazz music and women as performers, demonstrating a more empowering and rebellious use of jazz music.

Mildred Pierce begins with the murder of Monte Beragon (Zachery Scott), Mildred's second husband, and with the police questioning Mildred about his murder. The remainder of the narrative is presented as a flashback narrated by Mildred to the police, leading up to the point where Monte is murdered. The flashback shows Mildred as a struggling lone mother with two children, her husband Burt (Bruce Bennett) having left her for another woman. Her eldest daughter, Veda, frequently complains about their lack of money, which motivates Mildred to open her own restaurant. With the financial assistance of rich, handsome Monte Beragon and her ex-husband's friend, Wally Fay (Jack Carson), she becomes wealthy and successful. Mildred falls in love with Monte and has an affair with him, thus introducing Veda to a lavish, luxury way of life through her relationship with him. Meanwhile, Veda marries wealthy Ted Forrester (John Compton) and pretends to be pregnant in order to extort money from his family, at which point, Mildred cuts all ties with Veda and throws her out of the house. After some time away, Mildred returns to find Veda performing in a cheap club; she refuses to return home unless Mildred can provide her with a life of riches and luxury. Mildred asks Monte to marry her in exchange for a third of her business, which he does and Mildred is reunited with her estranged daughter. However, on the evening that Mildred discovers Monte is selling his share of the business, rendering her bankrupt, she also discovers Monte and Veda are having an affair. It is suggested at the beginning of the film that Mildred is responsible for Monte's murder, yet we now discover that it is Veda who shoots him when he tells her he does not love her. Despite everything, Mildred is still willing to protect her daughter by pretending to be responsible for Monte's murder.

In terms of its classification within a genre, *Mildred Pierce* has been discussed as both a film noir and a melodrama since it features aesthetic devices associated with noir, such as the use of chiaroscuro lighting and the accentuation of distorted shadows, as well as narrative specificities such as flashback and voice-over. Furthermore, the character of Veda has often been discussed as the film's destructive femme fatale. Yet predominantly, the narrative framework focuses on a female breaking free from the domestic realm, and her struggle for success within a rigid, patriarchal society. Therefore, in my own discussion, I treat it as a melodrama with noir features. The use of jazz music linked to the femme fatale, however, is one such noteworthy feature of the late 1940s and 1950s film noir. I would like to suggest that this diegetic acoustic coding in *Mildred Pierce* could perhaps be responsible for the continued use of jazz in the melodramas of the 1950s. Here we see melodrama adopting an element of film noir acoustic coding and making it active within its own genre, therefore taking over the associated subversive meanings of jazz, and the spectrum of social meanings it conveys.

Mildred Pierce presents us with a female protagonist who, in many ways, presents herself as a powerful, independent and headstrong individual. Joyce Nelson asserts that Mildred's eventual demise is her attempt to be financially independent: 'if Veda's crime was murder, Mildred's was independence – especially in economic terms'.[33] Mildred's determination is driven purely by a desire to provide her materialistic daughter Veda with an expensive and lavish life of luxury. Yet this is her ultimate downfall; many critics cite this as justification for her demise as a mother in the context of narrative economy of Hollywood melodrama. Furthermore, her sexual representation seems to further justify her demise; through her relationships with Monte and Wally, 'Mildred was doomed not to "have it all" because, consistent with the noir universe, the passionate need for Monte Beragon corrupted her and dulled her decent impulses'.[34]

Much critical discussion of *Mildred Pierce* focuses on the various visual similarities between Mildred and Veda. Kathleen Anne McHugh observes that they 'appear to be mirror images of each other . . . the film dresses and coifs the two actresses very similarly'.[35] Therefore, it seems quite apt that both women, whose behaviour is signalled as overtly sexual and therefore immoral by social standards of the 1950s, are frequently coded with diegetic jazz music.

The main difference between the two female protagonists is that Mildred herself does not ever appropriate this music. By contrast, such appropriation is frequently undertaken by Veda, Monte and Wally, who control Mildred throughout the narrative. This manipulation is, then, symbolised acoustically through the use of diegetic music.

The film's opening shot is of a dark, gloomy beach house at night. The diegetic sound of the splashing waves is merged with the non-diegetic classical music, which is soft and harmonious, creating an almost idyllic atmosphere as the camera draws closer to the house. This melodious situation is immediately disrupted with the sound of five loud, staccato gunshots, demonstrating early on how sound in the diegesis can quickly break audience involvement with the emotive aspects of a scene. The scene quickly cuts to inside the beach house and shows a medium shot of a man, Monte, clutching his stomach and falling dramatically to the floor, at which point he manages to utter the word, 'Mildred'. The absence of a reverse-shot revealing the character wielding the gun leads us to draw the conclusion that the film's namesake, Mildred Pierce, is the perpetrator of the crime, therefore instantly coding her as a corrupt character.

This is reinforced in the next scene in which Mildred is seen walking along a dark pier, staring into the murky water. Andrea Walsh notes that 'darkness and ambivalence surround our introduction to the female protagonist'[36] conveying an initial sense of ambiguity about her character. Indeed, as Mildred walks along the pier, the non-diegetic music features ominous-sounding low-pitched brass but also what appears to be a high-pitched harp playing up and down the musical scale at a fast tempo. This slightly mismatched scoring denotes Mildred's emotions as fluctuating and disordered and as we now see a medium shot of her face, the music builds to incorporate emotive strings and dramatic brass typical of melodrama. As Mildred stares into the shadowy water, tears run down her pale cheeks. The music now builds to a crescendo as she grabs the railings, intending to throw herself into the water, yet she is stopped – audibly by the sound of a policeman rapping his baton loudly on the railing. This signals a moment where the non-diegetic music stops and is replaced with the policeman's loud scolding, accentuating the sound of his reproachful voice. This interruption obstructs our access to Mildred's emotions. The significance of this emotive moment being interrupted by a police officer cannot be overlooked. At this point we literally see Mildred's emotions being 'policed' by a symbol of the patriarchal order. As he scolds her and sends her on her way, our access to her emotions is obstructed by the law; this is the first of many instances where the non-diegetic music that signals Mildred's emotive state is interrupted by another character or sound in the diegesis.

It is from this point onwards that we frequently find Mildred underscored with jazz music. As she walks slowly along the dark pier, low volume, brassy jazz drifts over her from Wally's club. Since we are placed outside with Mildred, the music is initially quiet and not overly imposing on the soundtrack. Yet once we too are seeing Mildred from Wally's point of view, through the window inside the club, the jazz soundtrack[37] immediately increases in volume as Mildred turns on her heels and looks towards Wally, and the viewer. The jazz music gets instantly louder at the moment she turns, giving us our first full-length view of Mildred, properly lit, as if she is announcing herself to us. This moment is even slightly reminiscent of a performance, accompanied by a lingering and suggestive jazz tune coding her as 'improper' and yet also active, in one of the opening and semantically establishing scenes of the film. As Mildred enters the club, the jazz music gets louder again as she and Wally sit down and the camera makes a notable pan to focus on the female performer onstage, singing and dancing to the jazz tunes – a clear foreshadowing of Veda's similar performance that is to come later in the narrative and which symbolises her 'demise' from classical music to popular music. In this opening scene, we are given further clues about Mildred's sexual behaviour where she says to Wally 'you always made love so nicely' and he questions the whereabouts of her husband. This almost 'justifies' the use of jazz music to underscore part of her introduction in the film, whilst also presenting her as a character who could be defined as sexually liberated and rebelling against the rigidities of 1950s patriarchal society.

The continual link between jazz music and Mildred's socially unsanctioned behaviour is later accentuated as the film plays out in flashback. In the scene where Mildred and Monte meet at his beach house, jazz signals their experience as a purely sexual, rather than romantic encounter. Such meaning is confirmed by the constant references to female bathing suits belonging to Monte's 'sisters': the proliferation of bathing suits suggests that Mildred is just one in a long line of women who have been seduced at Monte's beach house. While Mildred dries her hair in front of the fire, a low-pitched oboe plays from the jazz record[38] which we see Monte playing at the start of the sequence: the act of Monte putting the record on demonstrates his control of the diegesis, and therefore denies Mildred's emotional expression outside of the diegesis. The ambient music signals a strong sexual attraction between them; in spite of that, the lack of emphasis on romance and overemphasis on sex is made clear aurally at the climactic moment in which they kiss. Traditional classic Hollywood romantic sounding would likely underscore such a moment with lavish, orchestral, light-hearted, harmonic music. Yet the moment in which Mildred and Monte kiss is instead aurally underscored with the harsh, repetitive, scratching noises of the record player's needle as the record reaches its end. Such diegetic sounding emphasises this as a sexual moment, not one of romance. Elaine Roth asserts that Mildred's role as a mother and her desire for sex represent a problem: 'while romantic longing is a familiar theme in many Hollywood films, and melodramas in particular, the possibility of a sexual mother poses a crisis in representation'.[39] Due to the aural coding of this sequence, there is a sense that this is a crisis moment, instead of a climactic moment and signals that Mildred is behaving immorally as a mother. Indeed, this seems to be reinforced by the narrative, since in the scene that follows, Mildred's younger daughter, Kay, dies in what can easily be construed as punishment for her own sexual behaviour.

There are further, 'non-sexual' moments in the film where Mildred is associated with jazz music and therefore with rebellion against accepted societal codes. For example, Mildred as a lone parent running her own restaurant (albeit with partial financial backing from two men) is an example of one way in which she is a threat to 1950s patriarchal society. As Joyce Nelson observes, 'running a restaurant chain is not all that far removed from running an efficient home kitchen, except for the important difference of earning an income'.[40] Therefore, Mildred simultaneously maintains her place within the women's realm of domesticity, yet transgresses into the traditional male domain of business and entrepreneurship. In the scenes where Mildred is opening her restaurant, lively instrumental jazz music plays in the background from a jukebox. On the one hand, this loud music provides contextual information: it is the type of music popular at the time, particularly in urban settings such as diners. On the other hand, jazz signals the subversion of the patriarchal order: the music symbolises Mildred's 'improper' behaviour and deviation from the strict social codes of the 1950s. Such codes would not have condoned a woman running her own business instead of fulfilling her perceived role as wife and mother in the suburban home.

The ways in which Veda is coded by the film's diegetic music charts an interesting transformation in her character as we see her develop from a young girl playing classical piano music into a rebellious adolescent performing jazz on a stage. Throughout *Mildred Pierce*, she is frequently underscored by diegetic music and is the only main character to perform on a number of occasions. The fact that Veda is learning the art of music, having singing and piano lessons, is referred to several times throughout the film. It appears that Mildred is determined that Veda should be equipped with what would perhaps be considered 'proper' female accomplishments, suggesting that Mildred is keen on her daughter exploring her creative desires and encouraging her as a performer, rather than learning skills appropriate for simply being a housewife. Her first 'performance' in the film is the 'Brilliant Waltz' (1834)[41] which she initially plays at Mildred's request; it is a low-key, simple, ordered melody signalling 'proper' virtues and innocence when compared with the jazz numbers that come later in the film. When Veda performs this song for Mildred on the piano, it is the only time in the film's diegetic soundtrack that Mildred requests to hear her play. Such construction of narrative power relations indicates that, at the start of the film, Mildred has 'power' over Veda.

Later in the film we see Veda playing popular tunes on the piano whilst Kay sings and dances.[42] This episode shows Veda's growing awareness of other popular forms of music, and signals Veda as a controlling character, since she has dressed up Kay in a costume and make-up and makes her sing and dance. This control is especially augmented in the same episode in which Mildred angrily confronts Veda when she discovers her work uniform in her closet. Arguably the power relations between them have changed once Veda discovers Mildred's uniform; there is a sense of embarrassment in Mildred's anger, since Veda has discovered a humiliating secret about her undertaking (what Veda would consider to be) menial paid employment. Throughout their altercation, Veda continues to control the diegesis by gently playing the piano while Mildred shouts at her. By doing this, and maintaining her calm, smug attitude, we see the control that Veda has gained over Mildred and also the control she has over the viewer's access to Mildred's emotions. For in this scene, Veda is manipulating the diegesis and whilst we can attempt to empathise with Mildred's anger and frustration, we are never truly witness to it due to Veda's control.

As the film continues, we see Veda's frequent alignment with popular jazz music and a move towards Veda becoming a female performer. For example, on the night of Mildred's restaurant opening, she dances with Monte to a jazz tune on the jukebox as Wally sings along and Mildred and Ida (Eve Arden) watch and admire. Much later on, Mildred returns from an extended trip to find Veda performing a jazz tune onstage in Wally's club.[43] Mildred is horrified to see Veda dancing suggestively with her midriff bare, her performance accompanied by wolf whistles from the sailors in the audience. This moment symbolises Veda's social 'demise' but also her (albeit temporary) emancipation from her already fragmented family. When Mildred attempts to take her home, she speaks of her employment as a performer as a form of liberation: 'I'm free now, no one tells me what to do and what not to do'. Indeed, whilst Veda is clearly an immoral character throughout this film, she also represents female emancipation through jazz performance and I would argue that this moment in the film reveals Veda at her most honest. She apologises to Mildred for the way she has behaved and acknowledges that she is essentially a spoiled brat. It seems that freedom from Mildred has allowed Veda to experience the 'real world' and taught Veda much about herself. Arguably, it is her return to Mildred that ultimately corrupts her.

In her discussion of duplicity in *Mildred Pierce*, Pam Cook argues that Mildred's rejection of Bert as husband and Wally as replacement husband and her attempts to assume the male role of family provider represents a threat to the patriarchal symbolic order. As such, she effectively denies her own castration and is 'masculinised' throughout the film. This visual 'masculinisation' is discussed by numerous scholars who highlight that over the course of the film, her clothing changes from patterned housecoats to broad, masculine suits, leading to an increasingly masculine appearance. Mildred's behaviour, which revolves around business and providing the financial means to fund Veda and Monte's expensive tastes, is also traditionally seen as male. Cook argues that this masculine appropriation results in 'the collapse of all social and moral order in her world',[44] accounting for Mildred's apparent failure as a wife, mother and entrepreneur at the end of the film. She states that, for order to be restored, Mildred must undergo castration, symbolised through the removal of Veda, and be reunited with her first husband. Furthermore, Cook asserts that the final image of the two women on their knees cleaning is 'an image of sacrifice which closes the film with a reminder of what women must give up for the sake of the patriarchal order'.[45]

In the context of the association of jazz music and female emancipation in *Mildred Pierce*, my perspective on the resolution of this film differs. I argue that an altogether contrary message lingers at the film's closure, one that inheres in the subversive coding provided by the use of jazz music, but also in the narrative line itself. Whilst the narrative is seemingly resolved in line with the traditional codes and conventions of male patriarchy, there are many questions that still remain, such as, is it really conceivable that Mildred would happily return to a relationship with Bert? And as for the two women cleaning the steps, whilst partly representing women undertaking menial paid work, at the very least this is still a representation of women as part of the workforce – the very thing that women were being dissuaded from throughout the late 1940s and the 1950s. It does appear as a compromise, but the continual focus on women in the workplace that we witness throughout the film is an important aspect that is represented in an obvious way at the end. This accentuation of women's capacity to work and financially provide for themselves and their families is not unrelated to the choice of diegetic music in this film. It is the frequent use of jazz in this melodrama that allows a lingering message of female and youthful emancipation to remain. For the points in the narrative where jazz is incorporated within the diegesis represent key moments in the unfolding of this story of emancipation (for example, the issue of female performance): they present us with women who are active, rather than passive characters. Veda's words about her feelings of freedom accentuate this. Other key moments that are coded with diegetic jazz are Mildred's business endeavours as well as her sexual relationships with Monte and Wally. Again, whilst this behaviour represents immorality in the context of 1940s societal codes, at a subversive level it is a signal of female liberation.

The signification imparted by the diegetic use of jazz music is key to the ideas that can be taken away from *Mildred Pierce*. Unlike the classical musical scores of earlier melodramas, the use of jazz within this sound design incorporates a musical genre that encourages and frequently requires (both female and male) audience participation, rather than merely listening. It is a musical movement which represents rebellion, subversion and the breaking of boundaries and which, as mentioned above, has been linked with an increasing awareness of the younger generation's potential to overthrow the old. Therefore, it is highly significant that this type of music has been used throughout the film to signal female and youthful emancipation. It leaves an acoustic remainder lingering in the audience, one that could potentially be reignited once viewers stepped into a diner and heard jazz on the jukebox. I would argue that the use of jazz in *Mildred Pierce*, which is often classed as film noir, had a great influence on its continued use to represent these subversive aspects of society in melodramas of the 1950s.

One of the most eminent directors of melodramas in the 1950s was German-born director Douglas Sirk. He made his most celebrated melodramas in Hollywood between 1954 and 1959 and the subversive aspects of his work have been widely discussed by film critics since the 1970s. Leerom Modovoi summarises his films as 'brilliantly wrought works of irony whose uses of generic excess and cliché reveal a subtly achieved critical perspective on postwar America'.[46] This generic excess is often achieved through highly stylised, lavish interiors and is also an applicable description of the use of sound in his films, which is often overt and affective in its portrayal of female characters in particular. Both *Imitation of Life* and *Written on the Wind* make use of jazz music to an excessive extent which, like in Curtiz's *Mildred Pierce*, is often linked to subversive female behaviour.

Part of this subversion is represented through the character of the single mother as the 'breadwinner' of the household in *Imitation of Life*. Like the issues raised in *Mildred Pierce*, the film questions the implications of a woman's resistance to the role of housewife. *Imitation of Life* also explores the implications of racial inequality through the teenage character of Sarah Jane who, like Lora, is resistant to the roles available to her as a young, black woman, instead choosing to 'pass as white' and become a vaudeville performer. The audible coding of each of these two characters is linked to jazz, more so in the case of Sarah Jane, who is represented as the most rebellious figure in the movie.

The first part of *Imitation of Life* introduces Lora Meredith (Lana Turner) meeting Annie Johnson (Juanita Moore), a black, homeless widow and her pale-skinned daughter Sarah Jane (Karin Dicker). She invites them to temporarily stay with her and her young daughter Susie (Terry Burnham). Annie quickly becomes Lora's maid and supports her in becoming a successful Broadway actress. The second half of the film is set in the suburbs of Connecticut where both young girls are now teenagers. Lora's daughter, Susie (Sandra Dee), is the 'good girl' who benefits from her mother's success with first-rate schooling and a luxurious lifestyle. Yet Lora's success causes her to be a frequently absent mother resulting in the demise of their relationship. They grow apart and Susie falls in love with Steve Archer (John Gavin), Lora's eventual fiancé, while Lora is working abroad. Sarah Jane (Susan Kohner) meanwhile repeatedly attempts to deny her black heritage and pass as white, eventually leaving home to become a vaudeville performer. She severs all contact with her family causing Annie great mental anguish, eventually leading to her death. The film ends with the coming together of Lora and Steve with Susie and Sarah Jane, suggesting the reestablishment of some kind of nuclear family, whilst never really confirming it, leaving the film's ending at a typically Sirkian, ambiguous conclusion.

Sirk's 1959 version of the film is the second treatment of the original novel written by Fanny Hurst and published in 1933. The first treatment, directed by John Stahl in 1934, features key narrative differences – most notable of these is that the white woman, Bea Pullman (Claudette Colbert), and black servant, Delilah Johnson (Louise Beavers), enter into co-ownership of a profitable pancake business together. Sirk explains that narrative changes were necessary for a 1950s treatment of the story since during this period a successful black woman could conceivably buy a house instead of having to remain dependent on a white woman. Sirk explains: 'I had to change the axis of the film and make the Negro woman just the typical Negro, a servant, without much she could call her own but the friendship, love, and charity of a white mistress'.[47] Therefore, Sirk's decision to not have the black woman as jointly successful with the white character forces her into a subservient role. This narrative decision underscores a sense of inequality between Lora and Annie, and foregrounds the issue of race in the film.

The film's musical score is central to the representation of the effects of this inequality. Written by noted Hollywood composer Frank Skinner, the music is orchestral and lavish in places, signifying moments of extreme emotion between Annie and Sarah Jane. In other places the music is contemporary and jazzy, signifying female and youthful emancipation, principally represented through Sarah Jane. Such musical strategy provides a discernible contrast between the classical Hollywood emotive scoring and the use of lively jazz tunes. Unlike the use of jazz in *Mildred Pierce*, however, the jazz in *Imitation of Life* frequently verges on excessive and is often overly dramatic. Yet this acoustic coding is consistent with Sirk's general aesthetic of excess and 'distanciation'.[48]

In juxtaposing my discussion of women and jazz in *Mildred Pierce* with *Imitation of Life*, an obvious link appears between Lora Meredith and Mildred Pierce – namely their determination to work hard for personal and professional success and provide for their daughters with material wealth. Marina Heung also links these films, observing that in both films 'worldly success for women usually necessitates failure as wives and mothers'.[49] In the case of Lora, her obsession with her career consistently prevents her from fulfilling her maternal responsibilities and stops her from becoming a wife at all. Jackie Byers notes, 'Lora's passionate commitment to her acting career functions as an attempt to dislodge "mother", expressing an emerging ideology.'[50] This is represented in her refusal to embrace the role of wife and mother in the early part of the movie by declining Steve's marriage proposal. This emerging ideology of the working mother is, however, arguably presented as the 'wrong' choice since Lora eventually finds her career altogether unfulfilling. Therefore, by the end of the film she accepts that she must ultimately, as Steve puts it, 'grow up' and get married.

Unlike Mildred Pierce, however, there is less sense of Lora being a morally corrupt character. Despite her continual narcissism and often selfish treatment of her daughter and Annie, she is never portrayed in comparable sexual liaisons, for example, as Mildred is and does not tend to be surrounded with the corrupt characters that seem to facilitate Mildred's downfall. Medovoi has observed that 'her status as a mother notwithstanding, it is clear that, from the beginning, the aspiring quality of Lora Meredith's character gets associated with a girlish idealism over and against a womanly maturity that would be more appropriate to her age'.[51] As such, there is a distinct difference in the aural configuration of Lora when compared with Mildred whose frequent transgressions are signalled acoustically through jazz. By contrast, the aural characterisation of Lora is frequently marked by classical, orchestral sounding which often sounds lively and even cartoonlike in places, confirming this connotation of her character as somewhat childlike. There is one exception to this aural coding where Lora is underscored with jazz. Significantly, this is also the moment where we witness her overriding idealism and happens during a meeting with her theatrical agent, Mr Loomis (Robert Alda).

This meeting, which takes place after office hours in his darkened, shadowy, empty office, shows Lora as a potential sexual being. She enters the office wearing a sophisticated black evening dress as the non-diegetic soundtrack introduces a slow, jazzy and bluesy tune. The low-key drawn-out notes suggest a potential sexual liaison and the contrastive, shadowy noir lighting with the music creates a sense of ambivalence and seductiveness about their meeting. Like Mildred, in this liaison Lora is given borrowed clothes by her male counterpart – this time, a mink coat that Loomis apparently lends only to his 'very special clients'. This loan is seemingly part of his seduction routine since it leads to him putting his arms around Lora and kissing her neck as he drapes it over her shoulders. Unlike Mildred, however, Lora's reaction to his advances is one of disgust; she delivers a dramatic speech about how she will never demean herself in order to be successful: 'You're trying to cheapen me but you won't. Oh I'll make it, Mr Loomis, but it'll be my way!' With this, she dramatically throws the mink back at him and leaves the office. The use of non-diegetic jazz throughout this scene imbues Lora with a sense of sexuality and suggests the power and sway it might afford her. However, her refusal to 'comply' with what is apparently the norm for Loomis' mink-clad clients removes the idea of Lora as a sexual being and therein lies the distinction between her and Mildred. Whereas at first sight the jazz coding seems to be attached precisely to what Lora rejects – namely, the treatment of women as sexual objects – a closer inspection reveals that it also serves the opposite purpose: to accentuate a moment of female emancipation. In this case, the use of jazz highlights Lora as a character who forcefully rejects the aid of patriarchy and in doing so becomes successful in her own right.

As mentioned above, the real 'rebel' in this movie is Annie's daughter, Sarah Jane. Heung identifies Sarah Jane as 'the centre of disturbance in this film'[52] and indeed, the breakdown of the relationship between Lora and her daughter pales in comparison to the unrest caused by Sarah Jane's actions in the film. Much like Veda Pierce, Sarah Jane is presented as rebelling against the rigid confines of her family – her mother's love is frequently presented as stiflingly oppressive – but also rebelling against her own race by pretending to be white. She does so in the same way as Veda Pierce, by performing jazz songs on stage. Laura Mulvey states that Sarah Jane 'attempts to find escape and a solution to the problem of appearance through performance'[53] and much critical discussion related to Sarah Jane focuses on her apparent attempts to imitate Lora, who through her own success in performance represents the potential opportunities available to talented and determined white women. However, I argue that Sarah Jane's rebellion is not just racially motivated but also linked to teenage rebellion against the older generation. This rebellion is embodied in Sarah Jane's jazz performances that highlight the power of her physical presence when underscored by powerful, performative jazz melodies. Elena del Rio asserts that while we may regard Lora's successful white, wealthy body as the more powerful force in the film, its effects pale in comparison with 'the force and intensity that accompany the onscreen presence of Sarah Jane's body'.[54]

The power of Sarah Jane's body is emphasised from the moment we encounter her as a teenager. This is reinforced through the diegetic music that underscores her first rebellious act – when she feigns illness to avoid a family picnic and instead secretly meets her boyfriend. When she confides this secret to Susie in her bedroom, she turns the radio on and a low-volume, low-key tune plays as the girls whisper. The music features the same brassy instruments familiar in jazz music but is much slower in pace and moreover conveys a sense of tragedy as Sarah Jane explains her need to hide her race in order to have a white boyfriend. Whilst this form of jazz is in contrast with the fast-paced, performative jazz that comes later in the movie, it creates an aural link between Sarah Jane's misdemeanours and popular jazz music while also emphasising the instant access the girls have to popular (potentially rebellious) music via their bedroom radios. This strategic introduction of diegetic radio music serves to underscore Sarah Jane's likely awareness of popular styles of music. Furthermore, Sarah Jane's active incorporation of music into the sound diegesis at this 'secretive' moment demonstrates the ability of music to help Sarah Jane hide her transgressions since it audibly covers the girls' whispering. This use of diegetic jazz music as a form of concealment is confirmed and augmented later in the film where musical performance allows Sarah Jane to pass as white and hide the secret of her black heritage. Therefore, I argue that the introduction of music via the radio shows Sarah Jane utilising popular music to signal her rebellious behaviour and hide her transgressions.

Arguably, this acoustic moment also informs Susie's own sexual awakening about boys. Modovoi states that Susie, the 'good girl' is shocked by Sarah Jane's rebellion since she 'has barely begun thinking about boys'.[55] Yet her previous questioning of Annie at the picnic about boys and kissing would suggest otherwise. Arguably, this musical moment and awareness of Sarah Jane's experiences fuels Susie's own transgressions as she now falls deeper in love with Steve. This is a misdemeanour in itself since Steve is part of the older generation and also a surrogate father figure. For Sarah Jane, this exciting adolescent moment is quickly spoiled by Susie asking 'is he coloured?' about her boyfriend. This reinforces the preconception that even Susie expects that Sarah Jane will only date black boys. Hence the meanings conveyed by this piece of diegetic music are markedly important: the music signals Sarah Jane's noncompliance with societal expectations, yet the cultural and racial associations of music from her black heritage remind us of her own ethnicity.

This moment is in contrast with the next time we see Sarah Jane in her room when her rebellious awakening is in full flow. Whilst she briefly observes Susie and Steve partaking in the wholesome activity of horse riding, she looks on in distaste and listens to loud, showy jazz records, which are strewn about her room demonstrating that she has actively purchased the music that signals youthful emancipation. The music has now changed to upbeat, performative jazz and as she listens, she dances around her room, seductively, practicing for her stage performances that come later in the film. As she dances, she ends her choreography by kicking a symbolic cuddly toy lamb across her room with the final beat of the music – signalling her rejection of innocence and embracing the world of youthful emancipation and adulthood.

The most disturbing use of jazz in association with Sarah Jane is the moment when she is beaten by her boyfriend after he has discovered she is black. This episode marks a turning point in the film where she completely rejects her black roots in order to pass as white and become a performer. Sarah Jane waits for Frankie (Troy Donahue) on a dark street corner, whilst a non-diegetic quiet jazz tune plays. The minor-key music features a high-pitched woodwind instrument, low-pitched quivering piano notes that slowly waver up and down in tone and a light percussive cymbal, which taps quickly, apparently representing Sarah Jane's anxious heartbeat. Medovoi states that this sound 'thematises the urban bohemia where he [Frankie] and Sarah Jane have shared their romance'.[56] Indeed, this non-diegetic music underscores the first moments we are privy to an exterior, urban environment (excepting our very brief glimpses of Lora's experiences in New York). Yet arguably, and more importantly, I assert that this music allows us access to Sarah Jane's interior emotions as the use of jazz brings a certain edginess to this scene, creating an air of moody ambivalence about their meeting. When Frankie arrives the music keeps its steady pace and as they talk it gradually builds, incorporating a simple melody and further percussion. Frankie and Sarah Jane's quiet vocal tones match the gentle jazz as she happily suggests they elope together. Frankie's voice, which we soon realise he has been struggling to keep under control, suddenly and unexpectedly rises, bringing a feeling of ensuing violence as he abruptly bellows at her, 'Is it true? Is your mother a nigger?' At this juncture, a strong, quick drumbeat is heard and the music instantly changes to fast-paced, energetic jazz. Frankie continues to yell at Sarah Jane before violently attacking her. The sounds of high-pitched brass, woodwind, piano, high tempo cymbals and drums combine to create a thriving, vigorous piece that would be suited to a staged jazz performance. Yet simultaneously, this music is combined with the loud, exaggerated staccato sounds of Frankie's hard slaps on Sarah Jane's body and her piercing screams, thus creating an air of contradiction and disjointedness about the scene and its musical underscoring, perhaps leading the viewer to question why such upbeat music is used to accompany such a tragic, violent moment. However, the notion of contradiction is rather pertinent in relation to their coupling since Sarah Jane's response to his question about her mother's race is 'what difference does it make? You love me!' We have previously heard Sarah Jane tell Susie that Frankie wants to marry her someday; therefore such musical accompaniment could serve to represent Frankie's own internal contradictions. The fast-paced, exciting jazz embodies a sense of exhilaration and freedom which could represent their teenage love, yet the loud slaps and screams represent Frankie's conflicting feelings of anger. He has said he loves Sarah Jane, yet the disjointed soundtrack accompanying this moment of extreme violence demonstrates he is evidently not prepared to transgress accepted social boundaries regarding interracial relationships. Perhaps it furthermore indicates that for Frankie, this is a performance – maybe he is in love with Sarah Jane and this performance demonstrates his own frustrations about the impossibilities of them being together, or serves as a performative statement of his hatred of black people.

Significantly for Sarah Jane, this non-diegetic, performative music leads to her pursuit of a career on the stage, often performing to precisely the type of jazz music we hear in the background at this juncture. Therein lies a third contradictory aspect since this moment of violence is a result of Sarah Jane's black cultural roots. However, this experience precisely leads to her embracing a music that has its origin in black culture. Yet another turn has it that, in order to become a successful performer, she ultimately must pass as white and conceal her black heritage. This paradox seems to echo the fact that throughout the film, Lora successfully 'performs' while Annie is reduced to the body, never capable of transcending her black, female form. Thus, when examining the multi-layered contradictions that are manifest in this aspect of the film, this seemingly mismatched musical accompaniment appears surprisingly apt, and definitely Sirkian.

After this episode we see Sarah Jane's rebellion escalating as she begins working as a dancer at 'Harry's Club'. In the performance we witness she sings a song entitled 'Empty Arms' the lyrics of which, according to Michael Stern, 'invite the lecherous men in the audience to fill up her empty arms'[57] and which some critics interpret as an overt invite for sex. Stern goes on to assert that this 'is a completely demeaning role, ironically so, inasmuch as this represents Sarah Jane's attempt at liberation'.[58] I argue, however, that, whilst this moment in the film does not necessarily represent an idealised version of female liberation, it nevertheless shows Sarah Jane's capacity to break free from the oppression of her mother and her race as well as the confines of a rigid bourgeois home in which she never quite belongs. Here we see Sarah Jane beginning to develop her own identity as a young, white female performer, which is everything she has aspired towards throughout the movie, even as a child. Critics such as Heung discuss this moment as a marginally failed attempt to imitate Lora's own success as a performer,[59] which is made impossible by her 'blackness'. Still, as I mentioned above, Sarah Jane's rebellion is clearly not just racially motivated, but, like many other teens in films of this era, motivated by a desire to rebel against the older generation, which includes Lora and Steve and the middle-class lifestyle they represent. Certainly, Annie is not the only mother figure to whom she objects throughout the movie ('your mother doesn't own me!'). Elena del Rio sees Sarah Jane's performances as 'unique events expressing a constellation of physical, libidinal, and social forces'.[60] Thus, as pointed out by Modovoi, 'the raunch of Sarah Jane's bluesy come-ons seems more attractive and glamorous a style of femininity than the clean-cut white womanhood conveyed by Lana Turner in the flea powder advertisement'.[61] Elena del Rio draws further distinctions between Lora and Sarah Jane's performances throughout the movie (both on and off stage), highlighting that Lora's are frequently immobile: 'a style that favours static posing over mobility, ideality over physicality, and even in the classically centred images the film selects to stand in for her theatrical career'.[62] This representation is contrasted with Sarah Jane's lively performances, which are informed by movement and audience interaction. Her lively routines relate to her overall movement in the film, denoting her as a character representative of motion, change and progression. This is symbolic in relation to the concept of the younger generation as becoming emancipated and changing, whilst the older generation remain 'stuck in their ways'.

This sense of change and refusal of a life like Lora's is embodied in Sarah Jane's jazz performance at Harry's Club. A crucial link can be found here in the words she sings: 'The loneliest word I've heard of is "empty". Anything empty is sad.' The words 'empty' and 'sad' are reminiscent of Lora's earlier comments about her own empty, sad life. She talks about director David Edwards (Dan O'Herlihy) saying that if he ever stopped living his life at a breakneck pace 'he'd be sure to find out how sad he really is . . . and I know that feeling. Funny, isn't it? After all this time, the struggling and the heartache, and you make it, and then you find out it doesn't seem worth it, something's missing.' This is of course Sirk's characteristic critique of the affluent middle classes whose lives are meaningless, and of Lora's 'empty', white identity. Heung believes 'in identifying with Lora, Sarah Jane allies herself with a woman who, in her own way, has risked transgression' and indeed, in some respects she has. Yet, despite the narrative and thematic parallels between the two characters, I disagree that Sarah Jane's performances necessarily come across as any type of alliance with Lora. Rather, they represent her desire for freedom and independence, but also a chance at a life different from Lora's, which is perpetually represented as 'empty' and 'sad'. When Annie visits Sarah Jane after her performance at the Moulin Rouge, she asks if Sarah Jane is happy. She replies that she is (albeit because she is passing as white) and indeed, her experiences in her new life are represented as convincingly happy and fulfilling. Sarah Jane's life is evidently full, busy and exciting in a way that Lora's is not.

Throughout the film, Sarah Jane's moments of liberation are frequently thwarted by her mother: for example, at Harry's Club when Annie's presence results in Sarah Jane losing her job, after which, they quarrel on the street. The musical accompaniment here combines traditional orchestral scoring with jazz as if to incorporate the identities of both characters within the soundtrack. The sequence begins with a jazzy, fast percussive beat as we see Sarah Jane, suitcases packed, leaving Harry's Bar. The fast-paced beat and subsequent quick piano notes playing up and down the scale at high tempo are introduced the instant we see her and (like in the sequence with Frankie) seem to provide direct access to her emotions. The use of low, ominous notes with the light tapping of a cymbal represent Sarah Jane's anger at her mother and create an atmosphere of hostility. As they argue, Sarah Jane walks briskly along the street whilst Annie attempts to keep up with her. The same fast-paced jazz tune is used throughout, increasing in volume and building the tension. This acoustic moment demonstrates Sarah Jane's anger and the fast pace signals her intentions to keep moving quickly in the narrative. Twice during this altercation, Annie physically grabs Sarah Jane by the arm, a tangible demonstration of her role as an oppressive mother, and illustrating exactly what Sarah Jane desires emancipation from. As they argue, and it becomes clear that Sarah Jane has no intention of going home with Annie, high-pitched orchestral strings are heard, now signalling Annie's emotions of grief and distress at Sarah Jane's rebellion and rejection. As Annie finally collapses and sits down weeping on some steps, the orchestral music builds in volume and pitch embodying Annie's sorrow, whilst simultaneously preserving Sarah Jane's musical motif which sustains the upbeat tempo and low-pitched piano notes. The scene ends with Sarah Jane striding off into the city, escaping her mother. She is underscored by the same jazz tune, yet the lavish, orchestral aspect of the soundtrack has now taken over, leaving the audience's overwhelmingly affective response to be one of sympathy for the rejected mother, Annie.

The use of orchestral sounding is continually allied with Annie in the latter part of the film to represent her grief at losing Sarah Jane and later to signal the tragedy of her death, the trope of jazz being reserved for Sarah Jane alone. The film's ending brings in a new genre of music however, that allies Annie and Sarah Jane: the gospel music played at Annie's funeral and performed by Mahalia Jackson. The incorporation of a 'real life' gospel singer, noted for her influence not just in music but also in civil rights, brings a distinct resonance to the ending of the film. Heung highlights that 'the lack of explanation of Jackson's relationship to any of the characters in the film gives her singing at Annie's funeral the semblance of a documentary performance within a fictional film'.[63]

This foregrounds the issue of race as being relevant in the real world and raises its importance above all other issues explored by the film, such as patriarchy or motherhood. Jackson's performance in *Imitation of Life* is given the longest amount of screen time when compared with the performances of Lora and Sarah Jane. Her extra-diegetic existence makes this a 'real' performance as opposed to the acted 'imitations' we see elsewhere in the movie. Richard Dyer observed, 'the fact that Jackson's singing is so "genuinely" emotional that she cannot lip-synchronise herself with any precision draws attention to the artifice of the film medium which is "unable" to "capture" her untrammelled outpouring of emotion'.[64] Again, this imbues the film's ending with a sense of realism that is in contrast with the fantasy elements that pervade elsewhere in the film. Lastly, the foregrounding of gospel music at the culmination of the film, a musical tradition rooted in black culture and religion, precedes the moment in which Sarah Jane enters and flings herself dramatically on Annie's coffin. I argue that this musical moment is presented as 'calling' to Sarah Jane, asking her to return to her roots and re-appraise her cultural heritage – which, arguably she has always embraced through her alliance with jazz music. In this sense, it appears that the use of gospel music in the final moments of *Imitation of Life* bridges the fields of aural signification previously attached to each character – jazz to Sarah Jane and classical orchestral to Annie. The 'calling' of the gospel music leads to Sarah Jane's public declaration of her black roots for the first time in the film ('it's my mother!'). It seems therefore, that Jackson's powerful, affective gospel performance leads to a belated reconciliation between the estranged mother and daughter. It also arguably leads to a resolution between Sarah Jane and her cultural heritage by pointing to the type of music that lies in the roots of jazz.

To summarise, Sarah Jane's rebellion in *Imitation of Life* is largely racially motivated and therefore her continual link with jazz, a traditionally black music, carries racial connotations as well as being linked to the concept of youthful emancipation. However, as previously discussed, links between jazz and female sexuality are commonplace throughout classical Hollywood and in the next film under discussion, *Written on the Wind*, Marylee Hadley's overt sexuality is consistently underscored with excessive, even exaggerated jazz. Such musical associations highlight the subversiveness and danger related to uncontrolled female sexuality. Barbara Klinger identifies *Written on the Wind* as Sirk's 'most overtly subversive text'[65] and Jackie Byers notes that Sirk himself claims the film was conceived as 'a piece of social criticism, of the rich and spoiled and of the American family'.[66] Indeed, the narrative explores the decadent lifestyle of the oil-rich Hadley family, who, despite their lavish possessions and privileged lifestyle (and much like *Imitation of Life*'s Lora Meredith), are desperately unhappy, and morally and socially corrupt.

The film begins with the dramatic death of Kyle Hadley (Robert Stack) on the doorsteps of the Hadley mansion. An extended flashback follows, showing Kyle Hadley as a rich, alcoholic playboy who immediately gives up his hedonistic lifestyle when he meets and marries level-headed Lucy Moore (Lauren Bacall). Kyle's best friend, Mitch Wayne (Rock Hudson), is also in love with Lucy, whilst Kyle's sister Marylee Hadley (Dorothy Malone) is in love with Mitch, and has been since childhood. Throughout the film, Marylee engages in sexual encounters with different men in a desperate bid for Mitch's attention. Yet his love for Lucy and lack of desire for Marylee – whom he claims to see as a sister – is clear throughout the movie. Lucy and Kyle's happy marriage is disrupted on their first wedding anniversary when the family doctor tells Kyle that he might be impotent, causing a return of his alcoholism. The sudden death of Kyle and Marylee's father, Jasper Hadley (Robert Keith), fuels his addiction whilst Marylee's manipulative suggestions make him paranoid that Mitch and Lucy are having an affair. When Lucy announces that she is pregnant, he wrongly assumes that Mitch is the father. He hits Lucy, causing a miscarriage, and attempts to shoot Mitch. Marylee intervenes and the gun goes off, shooting Kyle in the stomach, causing his death as witnessed during the film's opening. Marylee tells the truth at the inquest and the film ends with Marylee sitting at her father's desk crying and clutching a miniature oil derrick while Mitch and Lucy drive away together, united at last.

In her discussion of the female body and sexual display in films of the 1950s, Pam Cook describes Marylee Hadley as the embodiment of 1950s contradictions between female sexual desire and social containment.[67] This sexual desire is frequently represented through Marylee's active pursuit of various men in the film and her outlandish flirting with Mitch – thus expounding the notion of female sexual emancipation. Yet, Cook notes that Marylee is frequently contained or repressed by the *mise en scène* or framing used throughout the film. She notes that, at certain moments, Marylee's antics lead her to break the edges of the cinematic frame 'giving the impression that the cinema screen is too small to accommodate this excessive female body'.[68] Similarly, in *Imitation of Life*, Sarah Jane is often shown through restrictive window frames, doorways or screens. This visual technique seems to highlight an ideological necessity to curb the subversive behaviour of young women who are seen to be breaking societal codes. Such visual techniques are particularly noticeable in moments of excessive sexual behaviour, which are frequently underscored by jazz music.

The concept of Marylee's excess is also discussed by Christopher Orr who argues that Marylee is never contained by the film's narrative. He notes that the inquest scene at the end of the film seems peripheral or like the beginning of another film. It foregrounds Marylee at the end of the narrative since her story seems to exist outside of the film's resolution. He says, 'Marylee has not been contained within the film's circular structure and hence its ideological project.'[69] This is unlike Sarah Jane, who despite her transgressive behaviour throughout *Imitation of Life* is integrated into Lora and Steve's (arguably dysfunctional) nuclear family in the narrative conclusion. Marylee's narrative end is markedly different – the ending of *Written on the Wind* does not just fail to 'contain' Marylee but also casts a shadow over the supposed happy ending – the coming together of Lucy and Mitch, which, like Lora and Steve's coupling, adheres to dominant ideological concepts of suitable parent figures. The memorable image of Marylee clutching the oil derrick as her father's portrait looms over her is far more emphatic than the image of Mitch and Lucy driving away together. Therefore, the prevailing image of *Written on the Wind* is one of subversion represented through the somewhat unusual image of Marylee Hadley as the head of a highly successful oil company. As Byers argues:

> Her happy ending substitutes poorly for the coupling with Mitch she has so actively desired throughout the film. Her 'reward' for flaunting prevailing social definitions of sexual difference places her in a merely figurative couple and at the pinnacle of a thriving oil business. Although this image of woman was rare in the 1950s, it was ideologically more

acceptable than the position in which she was first depicted, in a bar on 'the wrong side of town'.[70]

In my own discussion of Marylee, I do not attach a great deal of significance to the ending of the film, since I believe her actions throughout the narrative are more worthy of extended analysis. I therefore argue that Marylee is barely contained by the film's ideological project at any point in the film. To expand upon the ideas of Cook and Orr, I would suggest that (like Sarah Jane in *Imitation of Life* and Susan in *Bringing Up Baby*) this female excess and lack of containment of sexually driven behaviour is also represented audibly.

Of the four main characters in this film, it is Marylee who is most frequently accompanied by jazz music. Like in *Mildred Pierce*, this is often achieved through diegetic music played by Marylee herself, yet the dire consequences of Marylee's diegetic appropriations far exceed those of Mildred's or Veda's. Elena del Rio discusses the performative aspect of *Written on the Wind*, suggesting that each of the four main characters is paired with a musical theme which enhances the affective dimension of the film. With reference to Marylee, she states that the rounded or circular jazz scores that attend her onscreen performance 'reinforce her oversexualised, curvaceous figure, as well as her circuitous methods of operation'.[71]

In contrast to much discussion of Dorothy Malone's character as sexual and deviant, I would also like to highlight that there are several moments in which Marylee is seen in pastoral surroundings, accompanied by classical non-diegetic music. Such underscoring – true to traditional melodramatic musical coding – exemplifies her feelings of hurt about Mitch's rejection and conveys a sense of Marylee's isolation from her family and the outside world. I argue that such moments construct Marylee in a more sympathetic way and demonstrate the ideological concerns about the consequences of capitalism and the dissolution of the traditional nuclear family. These moments are visually distinctive from Marylee's usual interior surroundings and from her familiar seductive attire: we see her walking barefoot by the river, touching the trees and wearing a checked shirt that could be said to represent a more natural side to her character. The first time we see her in these surroundings is audibly juxtaposed with Mitch saying his love for Lucy is 'strictly one-sided', as is Marylee's love for him. This scene not only represents a more 'natural' side to Marylee but also audibly creates a sense of sadness by playing the childhood voices of her, Mitch and Kyle over this scene, to which she physically reacts with taunted facial expressions, eventually breaking down in tears. We see that at one time, Mitch did return her feelings: 'sure, you're my girl', and we see the physical evidence of their past relationship in their initials scratched into a tree, surrounded by a heart. In this way, we are exposed to a more innocent and pastoral side of Marylee's personality. Yet, this also highlights her isolation from the other characters, since she is still dwelling on bygone days by the river, while the other characters have moved on. In the scene when Marylee and Mitch have a picnic by the river, we see a more relaxed and natural version of Marylee. We witness an aspect of her character that demonstrates her strong desire to fulfil the role of housewife to Mitch as she carefully sets out a picnic. Again, her dress – although bright in colour – is more understated and there appears to be a natural chemistry between the two characters, despite Mitch's clear desire to resist her. The music underscoring them is classical, soft and orchestral, denoting their rural surroundings and the momentary rapport between them. Yet these more classical, pastoral scenes are fleeting and static when compared with episodes featuring Marylee's rebellious behaviour. The latter scenes, featuring drama, excess and jazz are the ones that drive the narrative forward and depict female behaviour that upsets the traditional bounds of patriarchy.

The first time we meet Marylee is crucial in constructing her as a sexual and somewhat deviant character: she is about to have sex with a man she barely knows in the back room of a low-class bar. Prior to this, Marylee has been aurally constructed as a socially undesirable female; her own brother refers to her as a 'devil' and Mitch awkwardly declines Jasper Hadley's wishes for them to be married. Unlike other females discussed in this chapter, she is depicted as wicked and manipulative by her brother, as an undesirable companion by Mitch and as a sexual object by other men in the film – although arguably this is something that she herself orchestrates. Her initial appearance in the film is audibly coded with diegetic jazz music and is linked to sex, alcohol and violence. This scene takes place in a cheap bar, on 'the wrong side of town'. Marylee's physical appearance is coded as decadent and excessive and is first visible in the mirror of the dingy downtown bar – a common Sirkian (Brecht-inspired) technique for framing his characters. Her bright pink, cleavage-revealing dress and blonde hair stand out against the beige colours surrounding her in the cheerless décor of the bar. She appears visually out of place in clothes that depict passion and sensuality. Her behaviour – drunken and destructive (she scratches the table top with a knife) – identifies her as rebellious and she comments that she is bored, again signalling that she is a character who does not seem to 'fit' into the film's diegesis.

It is when their conversation turns to sex that her male companion puts a jazz tune on the jukebox – an acoustic coding that Marylee does not really shake off for the remainder of the film. Like the jazz featured in *Imitation of Life* (again scored here by Frank Skinner), the music is loud, exaggerated and performative, which is directly linked to Marylee's behaviour in this scene. The music features a flamboyant melody played on a jazz trumpet along with other brass, making this a full, vibrant piece with high-pitched, blues notes played at an upbeat tempo. The evocative tune creates an atmosphere of sexual anticipation and is reminiscent of a raunchy vaudeville performance. As the music starts, it seems to announce that sexual behaviour is about to ensue. Marylee's companion puts his arms around her and kisses her neck. However, she does not respond, instead turning away with a sultry smile and pouring herself another drink. The implication here seems to be that her affections for him are merely performative, and also indicate that she has guessed Kyle and Mitch are likely to be on their way to intervene. In this sense, it is as if Marylee is waiting for the 'main performance' to begin and as if on cue, the two men enter the bar, through a beaded curtain and onto the 'stage'. As a fistfight ensues, she laughs with glee whilst punches are thrown as the lively jazz tune underscores the action, further creating a sense of performance. The music continues until Kyle is thrown against the juke box and the music stops abruptly – perhaps indicating the type of physical force required to curb Marylee's sexual endeavours and also signifying a juncture in the narrative which now focuses on male bravado rather than female sexuality. At the end of this sequence, Mitch heroically saves the day and defends Marylee's honour. She exclaims, 'thank you Sir Gallahad, you do care about me don't you', now placing herself in the role of the innocent damsel in distress and highlighting his heroic status in her eyes. This moment demonstrates that Marylee's wayward behaviour is driven by her sexual desire for Mitch and is generally aimed at provoking a reaction from him. It also highlights her capacity for role-playing and performance throughout the narrative, which is not only sexually motivated, but also sexually charged.

When Mitch steps outside the bar and spots Marylee perched provocatively in her bright red convertible, the same jazz tune (heard in the bar) is repeated. She writhes suggestively in her seat, smiling at him and gesturing for him to join her. The jazz tune, which is (unusually) non-diegetic begins at the moment a point-of-view shot captures Marylee, depicting her from Mitch's perspective. Much critical discussion about Mitch in *Written on the Wind* is sceptical about Mitch's apparently platonic view of Marylee; arguably this musical moment supports such notions. The repetition of the erotically charged jazz from the bar at this juncture, conceivably represents Mitch's inner, repressed sexual attraction to this woman whom he knows is socially wrong, epitomising his inner struggle about his feelings towards her. Yet, the introduction of low-pitched, ominous, slower paced piano chords as Mitch climbs into Marylee's car signifies the apparent danger associated with a young woman in charge of her own sexuality. At several moments in the film where Marylee is at her most calculating, she is accompanied by this same tune which seems to become a theme or leitmotif for her character. The low-pitched, deep notes and slow pace imply ambivalence and create a predatory sense to her pursuit of Mitch – which is frequently highlighted as being a physical longing for him, since she says she will 'have' him 'marriage or no marriage'. Such musical coding creates a distinct sense of threat around Marylee and her solicitous behaviour – the power of which is made obvious in the scene of her father's death.

One of the most memorable scenes from *Written on the Wind* is the death of Marylee's father, which takes place whilst she dances to jazz music in her bedroom. Prior to this, the police have escorted her home from a motel, where she was found with a boy she 'picked up' from the petrol station. During this episode (which causes her father great distress), Marylee looks smug and pleased with her actions. Obviously this guise is aimed at Mitch, who appears embarrassed, yet it is her father who is to suffer at the hands of her subversive behaviour. The 'death' scene starts with Marylee putting a record on and proceeding to dance wildly around her bedroom, while clutching Mitch's ornately framed photograph. The jazz record she plays is called 'Temptation' (1933)[72] and she plays it at such high volume that it spreads throughout the mansion, significantly invading her father's office. Here he sits at his huge desk, despairing over his daughter's wild endeavours, while the jazz track seeps over him like a toxic mist: this pervasive, powerful music proves consequential in the next few minutes of diegetic time. Meanwhile, in her bedroom, Marylee undresses and dances in her underwear as the scene cuts back to a shot of her father, looking grieved and worried as the sounds of Marylee's provocative music floods over his office. A cut back to Marylee shows her wearing a long, flowing pink gown as she bursts through her dressing room curtains and the music now becomes more passionate, faster-paced and dramatic. Scenes of her dancing are now repeatedly juxtaposed with images of her father who is now slowly ascending the staircase. Her progressively frenzied performance is linked with her father's slow and vulnerable movements up the staircase. The music and increased editing speed signals impending ferment as it builds to a loud, fast crescendo and then a close up of Jasper's wavering hand on the banisters. Suddenly he tumbles backwards down the staircase, landing in a crumpled heap at the bottom. The exultant music, however, continues, and herein lies the shock. Marylee continues to dance and frolic around her bedroom, laughing and smiling, and even kicking up her heels, oblivious that her wayward behaviour has indirectly caused the death of her father. Christopher Orr suggests that

> the implicit purpose and effect of Sirk's cutting between Marylee's dance and Hadley as he mounts the stairs and collapses – the father's final attempt to contain his daughter's sexuality – is to implicate Marylee in the crime of parricide. The juxtaposition of the shot of Hadley lying dead at the bottom of the stairs with that of his daughter literally kicking up her heels with joy is truly horrifying.[73]

The inclusion of this upbeat, yet rebellious music in this scenario demonstrates how the use of diegetic music can be consequential in terms of plot development. The diegetic impact of this music is established by the ways in which it audibly pervades the Hadley household. Furthermore, its diegetic power seems to physically prevent Jasper from reaching his daughter at the top of the staircase, to attempt to curb her unruly conduct. This specific impact of sound on both the figuration of the story and its symbolic layers is enhanced by its continuation after Marylee's father is dead. It highlights a sense of hedonism about her character whereby she cheerfully carries on dancing, regardless of the grim realities that lay only footsteps away. Yet perhaps a lack of acknowledgement of the consequences of one's actions was integral to the notion of female and youthful emancipation that was mounting in this era.

In concluding this chapter, it is fair to say that the three films I have discussed feature an explicit use of jazz music to denote female sexuality and female emancipation from familial roles and from the 1950s ideology of an older generation. Arguably, as many critics would assert, these subversive females are frequently re-inscribed within a patriarchal ideological system by the narrative conclusions, yet I strongly argue that the continual use of jazz – a music that historically symbolises youthful emancipation – is far more memorable and carries far more impact than the narrative conclusions of these films. Such aural coding leaves an acoustic remainder that stays with the viewer due to its lively features and democratic sense of easy participation. The characters I have discussed in detail – Mildred Pierce, Lora Meredith, Sarah Jane Johnson and Marylee Hadley – are distinctly unforgettable precisely for their sense of rebellion and free-spirit throughout the narratives of their respective films, not for their narrative conclusions.

NOTES

1. Thomas Elsaesser, 'Tales of sound and fury: Observations on the family melodrama', in Christine Gledhill (ed.), *Home is Where the Heart is: Studies in Melodrama and the Woman's Film* (London: BFI, 2002), 50.
2. Kathryn Kalinak, *Film Music: A Very Short Introduction* (Oxford: Oxford University Press, 2010), xiii.
3. Thomas Schatz, *Hollywood Genres: Formulas, Filmmaking, and the Studio System* (Boston, MA: McGraw-Hill, 1981), 221.
4. Anne Dhu Shapiro, 'Action music in American pantomime and melodrama', quoted in Mervyn Cooke, *A History of Film Music* (Cambridge: Cambridge University Press, 2008), 10.
5. Claudia Gorbman, *Unheard Melodies: Narrative Film Music* (London: BFI, 1987), 155.
6. James Buhler, David Neumeyer and Rob Deemer, *Hearing the Movies; Music and Sound in Film History* (Oxford: Oxford University Press, 2010), 186.
7. Buhler *et al.*, 204.

8. Heather Laing, *The Gendered Score: Music in 1940s Melodrama and the Woman's Film* (Aldershot: Ashgate, 2007), 69.
9. Whilst Laing also discusses a reversal of this dichotomy (female performance and male listener) she does so in fairly limited terms and also within the concept of the film noir femme fatale rather than her chosen genre of melodrama.
10. Schatz, 222.
11. Jackie Byers, *All That Hollywood Allows: Re-Reading Gender in 1950s Melodrama* (Chapel Hill: University of North Carolina Press, 1991), 8.
12. Byers, 8.
13. Janet Walker, 'Hollywood, Freud and the representation of women: Regulation and contradiction, 1945–early 1960s', in Christine Gledhill (ed.), *Home is Where the Heart is: Studies in Melodrama and the Woman's Film* (London: BFI, 2002), 198.
14. Christine Gledhill (ed.), *Home is Where the Heart is: Studies in Melodrama and the Woman's Film* (London: BFI, 2002), 18.
15. Barbara Klinger, *Melodrama and Meaning: History, Culture and the films of Douglas Sirk* (Bloomington: Indiana University Press, 1994), 51.
16. Klinger, 40.
17. Klinger, 53.
18. Klinger, 54. (*Father Knows Best* was a 1950s American TV and radio show about a family living in the Midwest.)
19. Laura Mulvey, 'Notes on Sirk and melodrama', in Gledhill (ed.), *Home is Where the Heart is*, 75.
20. Mulvey, 75.
21. John Belton, *American Cinema, American Culture* (New York: McGraw-Hill, 2005), 115.
22. Kathryn Kalinak, *Settling the Score: Music and the Classical Hollywood Film* (Madison: University of Wisconsin Press, 1992), 185.
23. David Butler, *Jazz Noir: Listening to Music from The Phantom Lady to The Last Seduction* (Westport: Greenwood Publishing Group, 2002), 38.
24. Buhler *et al.*, 356.
25. Kalinak, *Settling the Score*, 120.
26. A note that is played at a slightly lower pitch than notes on a major scale – usually a semitone lower – also known as a 'worried' note.
27. The stressing of a beat that is usually unstressed or weak.
28. Buhler *et al.*, 356.
29. Butler, 43.
30. Kalinak, *Settling the Score*, 167.
31. Leo Treitler, 'Gender and other dualities of music history', in Ruth A. Solie (ed.), *Musicology and Difference: Gender and Sexuality in Music Scholarship* (Berkeley and Los Angeles: University of California Press, 1995), 27.
32. Kristin A. McGee, *Some Liked It Hot: Jazz Women in Film and Television, 1928–1959* (Middletown: Wesleyan University Press, 2009), 31.
33. Joyce Nelson, '*Mildred Pierce* reconsidered', in Bill Nichols (ed.), *Movies and Methods: An Anthology, Volume 1* (Berkeley: University of California Press, 1985), 457.
34. Andrew Dichos, *Street with No Name: A History of the Classical American Film Noir* (Lexington: University Press of Kentucky, 2002), 160.
35. Kathleen Anne McHugh, *American Domesticity: From How-To Manual to Hollywood Melodrama* (Oxford: Oxford University Press, 1999), 142.
36. Andrea Walsh, *Women's Film and Female Experience 1940–1950* (New York: Praeger Publishers, 1984), 123.

37. *You Must Have Been a Beautiful Baby*, music by Harry Warren, lyrics by Johnny Mercer (1938).
38. *It Can't be Wrong*, music by Max Steiner (1942).
39. Elaine Roth, '"You Just Hate Men!" Maternal sexuality and the nuclear family in *Gas, Food, Lodging*', in Addison *et al.* (eds), *Motherhood Misconceived: Representing the Maternal in U.S Films* (New York: State University of New York Press, 2009), 112.
40. Nelson, 457.
41. *Waltz in E Flat Major (Grand Valse Brillante)*, music by Frédéric Chopin (1834).
42. *South American Way*, music by Jimmy McHugh, lyrics by Al Dubin (1939), performed by Ann Blyth and Jo Ann Marlow.
43. *The Oceana Roll*, music by Lucien Denni, lyrics by Roger Lewis (1911), performed by Ann Blyth.
44. Pam Cook, 'Duplicity in *Mildred Pierce*', in Ann E. Kaplan (ed.), *Women in Film Noir* (London: BFI, 1978), 75.
45. Cook, 81.
46. Leerom Medovoi, *Rebels: Youth and the Cold War Origins of Identity* (Durham, NC: Duke University Press, 2005), 280.
47. Douglas Sirk, *Sirk on Sirk: Conversations with Jon Halliday* (London: Faber and Faber, 1997), 148.
48. Paul Willemen, 'Distanciation and Douglas Sirk', *Screen*, v. 12, no. 2 (1971): 63–7.
49. Marina Heung, '"What's the Matter with Sarah Jane?": Daughters and mothers in Douglas Sirk's *Imitation of Life*', in Lucy Fischer (ed.), *Imitation of Life, Douglas Sirk, Director* (New Brunswick, NJ: Rutgers University Press, 1991), 303.
50. Byers, 248.
51. Medovoi, 281.
52. Heung, 314.
53. Laura Mulvey, *Fetishism and Curiosity* (London: BFI, 1996), 34.
54. Elena del Rio, *Deleuze and the Cinemas of Performance: Powers of Affection* (Edinburgh: Edinburgh University Press), 41.
55. Medovoi, 285.
56. Modovoi, 288.
57. Michael Stern, 'Imitation of life', in Lucy Fischer (ed.), *Imitation of Life, Douglas Sirk, Director* (New Brunswick, NJ: Rutgers University Press, 1991), 283.
58. Stern, 283.
59. Heung, 316.
60. del Rio, 41.
61. Modovoi, 289.
62. del Rio, 44.
63. Heung, 322.
64. Richard Dyer, 'Four films of Lana Turner', in Lucy Fischer (ed.), *Imitation of Life, Douglas Sirk, Director* (New Brunswick, NJ: Rutgers University Press, 1991), 206.
65. Klinger, 36.
66. Byers, 229.
67. Pam Cook, *Screening the Past: Memory and Nostalgia in the Cinema* (Abingdon: Routledge, 2005), 212.
68. Cook, 212.
69. Christopher Orr, 'Closure and containment: Marylee Hadley in *Written on the Wind*', in Marcia Landy (ed.), *Imitations of Life: A Reader on Film and Television Melodrama* (Detroit: Wayne State University Press, 1991), 381.

70. Byers, 179.
71. del Rio, 51.
72. Written by Nacio Herb Brown, lyrics by Arthur Freed.
73. Orr, 384.

CHAPTER 3

The Alienated Male: Silence and the Soundtrack in New Hollywood

In 1969, a low-budget film about two men travelling across America on motorbikes was an unexpected box office smash. The road movie *Easy Rider* struck a chord with young audiences through its portrayal of rebellion and freedom and arguably through its compelling use of rock music. The first and only audible sound in the opening scene of *Easy Rider* is, appropriately, a revving motorcycle engine. The rumbling sound is loud, harsh and abrasive, immediately confronting the viewer with a dominating tone that serves as an aural motif of resistance and rebellion henceforth. This scope of meaning is supported as the revving gets louder and two motorbikes appear in the bleak, dusty landscape at a shack-like building that is apparently ironically named *La Contenta Bar* ('The Happy Bar'). The motorbikes carry Wyatt, also known as Captain America (Peter Fonda), and Billy (Dennis Hopper) who, with their long tousled hair and dirty, unkempt clothing embody the sense of rebellion suggested by the opening sounds of the movie. Wyatt talks with the men who emerge from the 'happy' bar speaking fast, fluent Spanish. The soundscape is filled with bilingual male banter as the men converse, laugh and embrace, introducing from the outset the notion of, reinforced by the sounds of, male bonding. The Spanish bar and dialogue allows us to deduce that the film's opening takes place in Mexico. As Wyatt and Billy purchase drugs from their Mexican friend, the dialogue continues in Spanish, making the first few minutes of the film partially inaccessible to any viewer not fluent in Spanish. Such aural configuration reinforces a sense of outsidedness, or alienation, augmented by the location of a desolate junkyard behind the bar and also embodied by Mexico itself; but this linguistic estrangement also places viewers in the position of the outsider, alienating them from direct understanding of the narrative events via sound.

Despite the potential language barrier here, non-Spanish-speaking members of the audience are nevertheless able to understand the events taking place, and the use of possibly inaccessible dialogue subsequently allows the physical presence of drugs – another key motif of *Easy Rider* – to be at the forefront of the narrative. In the next scene, during a second drug deal, again, the characters are inaudible; this time due to the location being at the end of a loud, busy airport runway. The deafening roar of jets landing overhead is the only audible noise. The sound engulfs the soundscape, making it impossible for the characters to communicate verbally. Thus, the film's opening emphasises *Easy Rider* as a film that utilises sound to distort and veil meaning. The introduction of the problem of poor understanding or the potential for misinterpretation immediately links Wyatt and Billy to the alienated, misunderstood youth of the 1960s. From the outset, the audience struggle to understand the words of the film's main characters and are not privy to any verbal communication between them in this opening sequence. Thus *Easy Rider* is also presented to us as a film that will feature minimal amounts of male dialogue, proliferating the myth of male silence and augmenting a sense of alienation. This type of alienated male as a representation of masculinity is often explored in New Hollywood cinema. Such representation points to a more general sense of ideological alienation felt by the younger generation in America throughout the 1960s. Michael Ryan and Douglas Kellner point out that many films of this era explored young people's growing sense of alienation from the dominant myths and ideals of US society, and argue that 'film served as both an instrument of social criticism and a vehicle for presenting favourable representations of alternative values and institutions'.[1]

In this chapter, I explore the audible link between masculinity, silence and soundtrack by focusing on a selection of silent, alienated male characters from renowned New Hollywood films. In this discussion, the 'type' of silence I often refer to is that described by Paul Théberge as 'a kind of silence that is produced when, for example, music is allowed to dominate the soundtrack while dialogue and sound effects – the primary sonic modes of the diegetic world – are muted'.[2] The deployment of this technique in New Hollywood perhaps has something to do with Théberge's later observation that in Western culture, silence is a sign of abnormality or of something to be feared.[3] The films selected for this discussion are *Easy Rider*, *Bonnie and Clyde* (1968) and *The Graduate* (1967). I explore the specific use of silence in these texts as well as the ways in which non diegetic music and diegetic sound are used to express meanings not divulged by the male characters, due to their limited dialogue. I argue that this acoustic construction contributes to a projected sense of alienation of male characters and that it can also be linked to the blurring of gender boundaries often accounted for by the counter-culture movements taking place in America throughout the 1960s and 1970s.

The New Hollywood period of the late 1960s and 1970s is renowned for the cultural, economic and political changes that took place in American society.

Lester D. Friedman argues that 'it was an era lacerated by cultural divisions that grew wider and deeper in a jagged trajectory'.[4] The generation of the 'teenager' that had emerged in the 1950s found its feet in the 1960s, resulting in a powerful, rebellious youth counter-culture. Youth was generally defined as anyone under the age of thirty and a key component of the psychological make-up of this youth movement was general opposition to the opinions of the older generation. Young Americans found themselves in what John Belton terms 'an ideological battle with age'.[5] He notes that the two different generations found themselves at odds over all kinds of issues, and the younger generation challenged the repressive codes established by their more conservative elders, who had been brought up in the hard times of the Great Depression.[6] These extreme, polarized opinions of the young and old frequently came into conflict throughout the 1960s and 1970s, decades which were famous for riots and student protests over issues such as civil rights, feminism, nuclear arms and foreign warfare. As Barry Keith Grant highlights, 'all the tensions roiling within American society were inevitably reflected in the cinema of the time even as the industry fought a rear-guard action to attract dwindling audiences'.[7] These tensions are uniquely reflected in the complex, multifaceted sound design of New Hollywood films, as I argue below.

For Hollywood itself, the rise in youth counter-culture was eventually integral to its survival throughout the 1960s and 1970s, which was a period of great economic decline for the industry. The breakup of the studio system in the late 1950s and the increasing popularity of television meant that in the later part of the 1960s and early 1970s, cinema attendance was at an all-time low. As explained by Richard Maltby,

> moviegoing ceased to be a regular habit for most of the American population. By 1953, only half as many people in the US were going to the movies as had done seven years earlier. A 1957 survey found that only 15 percent of the American public attended the cinema as often as once a week, and this group of frequent attenders – three quarters of them under 30 – accounted for nearly two-thirds of total admissions.[8]

Geoff King, furthermore, points to changes in American society such as mass migration to the suburbs where there were few cinemas, as well the increasing popularity of other, more expensive, forms of leisure due to enhanced prosperity among the middle classes;[9] these factors further contributed to the drop in audience attendance. Moreover, as the above data on the age make-up of the cinema audience suggests, Hollywood found itself having to adjust to its new, younger audience. As Peter Biskind puts it, 'the old men who ran the studios were increasingly out of touch with the vast baby boom audience that was coming of age in the '60s, an audience that was rapidly becoming radicalized and disaffected from its elders'.[10] Despite studio attempts to release pictures starring previous favourites such as Rock Hudson and Doris Day, the industry experienced consistent failure. The fact that the customary narrative and artistic formulas, and even stars themselves, ceased to draw audiences suggested a dire need for new creativity and new type of filmmaking. Barry Langford observes that despite European New Wave films causing enormous excitement at festivals and art houses, 'how such radical departures from convention could be imported into the American commercial film industry was unclear'.[11]

However, by the end of the 1960s, with only three of the major eight studios remaining profitable,[12] and with the departure of many of the old studio-era magnates, new young studio executives were prepared to take a chance on an influx of new, university-educated, creative younger directors – frequently referred to as the 'movie brats'. Having studied film and being partly inspired by French New Wave directors, this generation of filmmakers was the first in the history of Hollywood to be critically aware of the Hollywood history, and so inevitably made movies with a new, more self-conscious approach to traditional genres.[13] Changes to censorship laws in the 1960s also had a huge impact on the types of permissible onscreen content. The Hays Production Code had become outdated and irrelevant in contemporary American society and was replaced by the rating system in 1968. America had become a far more permissive society and consequently audiences welcomed overt depictions of sex and violence that had previously been censored in the repressive studio era. Moreover, it was precisely this new and diverse filmic content that attracted viewers back to the cinemas, since such narratives and themes could not be seen on television.

New and diverse approaches to film sound are also evident in many films of this era. This is partly due to many filmmakers abandoning shooting on film sets, instead choosing to shoot on location. The increased portability of cameras allowed young filmmakers to embrace the gritty realism that could be captured by shooting on location.[14] Yet sound recorded on location was sometimes insufficient and required extra post-production manipulation. So, ironically, the transition to realistic location shooting led to less realistic, more artificial sound design within New Hollywood films. Thus sound design seemingly experienced an influx of creativity and experimentation during this period; Paul Monaco observes that after the collapse of the studio system, sound was increasingly used in ways that Hollywood had previously considered 'too jarring'.[15] This shift towards increased complexity and ingenuity in film sound design can again be party attributed to the influence of experimental European filmmakers. William Whittington asserts that the intent of many New Hollywood sound designers was 'to call attention to the constructed nature of sound and its design as an aesthetic element within the film . . .

[this was] derived in part from the influence of the French New Wave.'[16] He argues that directors such as Arthur Penn, Francis Ford Coppola and Martin Scorsese were among the first to encourage their sound personnel to 'blur the lines between audio recording, editing and mixing as a means of transforming image and sound relations'.[17] Indeed, sequences featuring the layering of music, dialogue, Foley sounds and non-linear editing became commonplace; this chapter explores the ways in which these sounds are linked with representations of masculinity.

My transition in this chapter from a discussion predominantly centred on women in previous chapters, to one that is focused on gender relations and the concerns of masculinity is motivated by the proliferation of New Hollywood narratives that focused on men and male relationships. Barry Langford observes this shift in popular films of the 1960s and 1970s, stating that 'a masculine bias was evident in the increasing tendency of hit films to focus not on traditional heterosexual romance but on male friendships and partnerships'.[18] Peter Kramer similarly highlights this transition with reference to *The Graduate*, which accordingly 'encouraged both audiences and filmmakers to shift their attention away from the female protagonists . . . [and] towards male protagonists and the contemporary American scene'.[19] This shift to male-focused narratives in New Hollywood cinema is indicative of a time when much was altering and changing in America, including conceptions of what it meant to be an American man.

Representations of masculinity in New Hollywood films of the late 1960s and 1970s are vastly different to those that prevailed throughout the 1950s and early 1960s. The latter representations embodied the American ideas against which many of the younger generation chose to rebel. The pressures of post-war society are often cited as the reasons for such a shift in perceptions of American masculinity. Brian Baker cites two key anxieties relating to masculinity throughout the post-war period: firstly, the idea of the 'damaged soldier', 'the man so inured to war that he transports violence and aggression back into the peacetime world'[20] and, secondly, the notion that the close contact and forged relationships between men during wartime may not only have disrupted domestic, family life, but heterosexuality itself. Baker argues:

> To counter both the possibility of male violence or homosexuality, and the disruption to the familial and economic structures of capitalist America, masculinity had to be redefined in the postwar period. The ideological work of this redefinition was partly carried out by representations of men in film and popular fictions.[21]

In particular, Benshoff and Griffin highlight the change in the representation of male emotion in film throughout the 1950s, pointing to new antiheroic roles played by older stars such as James Stewart and new, younger introspective, 'method' actors.[22] These young talents included Marlon Brando, James Dean and Al Pacino who were often cast as young men tied in emotional knots and straining under the pressures of being a man. Their roles frequently embodied a sense of yearning for release from the stress of conforming to traditional expectations of masculinity.[23] John Beynon notes that throughout the later New Hollywood period of the 1970s and 1980s, masculinity became far less sure of itself. He cites actors such as Robert Redford and Jack Nicholson who portrayed a succession of 'troubled losers'.[24] Much discussion of men in films of this era refers to a 'crisis' in masculinity and also draws on the spirit of counter-culture revolution that defines this period as an explanation for the breaking down of gender roles.

The 1960s hippie counter-culture became synonymous with feminised images of men with long hair, beaded jewellery and patterned clothing, as encountered in the sequence of *Easy Rider* discussed above. David Savran discusses this feminisation of men throughout this period, linking his argument to hippie counter-culture and its tendency to invert the norms of so-called 'straight' society. He draws on Theodore Roszak's suggestion that male gender roles were disrupted by the counter-culture and that one of its remarkable aspects was its 'cultivation of a feminine softness among its males'.[25] Conversely, the older generation maintained identification with traditional representations of masculinity and remained set in its ways, believing that 'the real man was supposed to be independent, adventurous, competitive, morally upright, and, like [John] Wayne, wholly predictable'.[26] Savran goes on to note that for the majority of counter-cultural youth, this 'aggressive' masculinity was an embarrassment. One does not have to venture far into the New Hollywood canon to discover these polarised representations, which I discuss in more detail below: *Bonnie and Clyde*'s protagonists blur gender boundaries with Bonnie's (Faye Dunaway) assertiveness and gun wielding and Clyde's (Warren Beatty) inability to perform sexually, whilst *The Graduate*'s Ben Braddock (Dustin Hoffman) is physically and audibly surrounded by the predictable, materialistic, 'embarrassing' generation of his parents and their friends. The latter's self-assurance in Ben and his potential future in 'plastics' could not be further from Ben's sombre and often silent aspirations for a life that is wholly 'different'.

The concept of silence is important in a discussion of masculinity and film. Since cinema's inauguration, the representation of the archetypal strong, silent male has prevailed, particularly in genres such as the western, film noir and action films; the latter have typically featured tough, rugged images of masculinity. In his discussion of male myths and the western, Roger Horrocks highlights the phenomena of the 'impassive and silent' male hero. Using Clint Eastwood's infamous western persona as a key example, he goes as far as to argue that his stoic silence is actually 'akin to autism', adding that this representation of male silence suggests that 'the gnomic style of the western hero resists language'.[27] Horrocks questions why such representations of masculinity have been a dominant feature of American cinema for so long:

> Why has this persona – half dead, cut off from feeling, cut off from women – become so dominant in popular cinema? ... This is the demand made by patriarchy to men: deaden yourself, show no feelings, do not speak, carry out your duties and don't complain, and then die ... the hero is obliged to suffer in silence, to show no tears, [and] ask for no compassion.[28]

Brian Baker similarly describes the western male protagonist as a 'lone stranger', emphasising the frequent narrative tendency to reduce the protagonist's dialogue, instead giving way to action or violence.[29] The implication here is that male disputes are not resolvable through discourse and that silent action is preferable to language and passivity. Whilst none of the films discussed in this chapter are (strictly speaking) westerns, the enduring popularity of the genre since the 1930s highlights long-standing audience familiarity with the genre's archetypal constructions of masculinity. Robert Warshow's 1954 article 'Movie chronicle: The Westerner' speaks of the lonesome existence of the western hero as being organic or intrinsic to notions of masculinity, as constructed by the genre. Yet Warshow also argues that the western hero is an archaic figure, considered 'unrealistic' by audiences, since he is encased within the mythical world of the western.[30] Conversely, Steve Neale has argued that audiences narcissistically identify with male western heroes[31] and according to Benshoff and Griffin, western hero John Wayne is 'still considered by some to be the epitome of American masculinity'.[32]

Steven Cohan and Ina Rae Hark discuss identifiable links between the western and New Hollywood films and the road movie in particular. In their analysis of *Easy Rider*, they note the characters of Wyatt and Billy are named after legendary Wild West figures Wyatt Earp and Billy the Kid. They also highlight visual similarities such as the image of the open road and wild landscape. Thematic similarities are also evident, such as the quest for freedom and the absence of civilisation and domesticity.[33] Regarding the acoustic level, Cohan and Hark also discuss the link between silence and masculinity with reference to Clint Eastwood. Here they draw a distinction between the western and road movies such as *Easy Rider* by arguing that Eastwood's silence is formally constructed as something purely *external*, comprising 'a richness of surface, all actions and attitude'[34] rather than an intrinsic essence to the characterisation. They argue that in the road movie, silence comes to represent the unspoken interiority of the protagonist and 'the *literalisation* of the inner journey ... a dual journey, physical and spiritual' [italics in original].[35] As mentioned above, the concept of male interiority was central to many roles played by young actors during this period. In the films discussed here, I believe that this inner journey is reflected (or literalised) through the non-diegetic music and the wide-ranging diegetic sounds which often substitute for male, alienated silence and represent the interior essence of male protagonists.

This interior essence is initially presented in the first few minutes of *Easy Rider* through diegetic 'noise' – motorbike engines, male banter, the snorting of cocaine, shuffling footsteps, the wind on the landscape, and roaring jet engines, making it impossible for the characters to speak, yet connoting rebellion, camaraderie, drug addiction and the open road. However, these harsh diegetic sounds are suddenly interrupted by the non-diegetic intrusion of the song 'The Pusher' by rock band Steppenwolf (1968). This instantly changes the rhythm of the movie to one that is more laid back and less chaotic. The slow, gentle strumming of an electric guitar encapsulates a sense of freedom, and the soulful voice and lyrics create a folk feel to the start of the film as the two men commence their journey. The conversational lyrics, 'you know I smoked a lot of grass ... oh lord, I popped a lot of pills' convey aspects of their characterisation via the score rather than through verbal expression. Thus music is used semantically to evoke meaning about the characters, whilst maintaining a sense of the alienated male through silencing the film's diegesis. They commence their travels to a second Steppenwolf track, 'Born to be Wild' (1968), a now instantly recognisable, iconic road-movie track. Whilst encapsulating the free-spiritedness of the men, the lyrics are arguably inherently masculine, referring to machines ('get the motor running') and to the journey ('head out on the highway, looking for adventure and whatever comes our way'). Throughout *Easy Rider*, details about the characters' lives never emerge – do they have jobs? wives? homes? – none of which seems relevant, since, according to the soundtrack, they were 'born to be wild' and thus, the music here embodies the sense that they are fulfilling what they were 'born' to do. Accordingly, the film focuses on Wyatt and Billy's 'wild' drive across America and the characters they meet along the way. Beginning in Los Angeles, they drive through the Deep South, to New Orleans in time for Mardi Gras. In the final scene of the movie, travelling along an open road, two men in a pick-up truck shoot Billy, leaving him dying on the side of the road. As Wyatt jumps on his bike and speeds off to get help, the men return and Wyatt meets the same fate.

Much discussion about the impact of *Easy Rider* focuses on the effects created by the rock score: Denisoff and Romanowski note that 'songs were carefully placed as a musical commentary throughout the picture'[36] whilst Geoff King argues that *Easy Rider* is 'fuelled' by its music soundtrack, and that its appeal is 'close to that of a musical'.[37] As discussed above, the selected music tracks frequently appear to be a direct representation of the characters' inner thoughts and feelings or serve a narrative function, adding to the overall meaning of the film. Anahid Kassabian, in her discussion about the compiled music soundtrack in film, notes that using recognisable popular music can 'bring the immediate threat of history ... [since] perceivers bring external associations with the songs into their engagements with the film'.[38] Indeed, the fact that young audience members in the 1960s are likely to have known the lyrics to many of the selected tracks, allowed them to associate the words with the characters. Conversely, this apparent 'threat' of external associations could actually allow audiences quickly to identify with the film's protagonists. In his discussion of *Easy Rider* and *The Graduate*, David Shumway argues that the music in these films is 'meant to be not merely recognized but often to take the foreground and displace the image as the principle locus of attention'.[39] For the purposes of this discussion, such musical foregrounding frequently silences the characters and despite the men travelling together, they still appear alienated. Unlike other road movies where the pair may travel by car, the motorcyclist's experience is solitary and does not allow for conversation. Even when Billy and Wyatt stop travelling to camp at night (unable to find motels that will accommodate 'long hairs'), their drug-induced conversation is nonsensical, providing limited insight into their characters and maintaining a sense of isolation through their lack of meaningful interaction.

However, the introduction of the southern lawyer George Hanson (Jack Nicholson) allows male silence to be temporarily broken by his frequent fireside chatter: the longest dialogue sequences are performed by him as he talks to Wyatt and Billy, who barely interact or respond, but seem content to listen. George speaks about high school, his mother, UFO conspiracy theories and his problems with 'the booze'. Such personal details are never heard from our protagonists, who remain consistently aloof and isolated. George momentarily verbalises the opposing generations of 1960s America by explaining the perceived fear attached to individuals such as Wyatt and Billy. His assertion that 'talking about it [freedom] and being it, that's two different things' reinforces Billy and Wyatt as doers, not talkers. It is clear from a scene in a small town café where the three bikers are refused service, that men with long hair suggested animalistic tendencies or homosexuality to those with traditional (or dated) perceptions of what it meant to be a man. George's words now seem to predict the demise of all three characters: moments before he is killed he asserts that those who they offend with their looks and lifestyle are 'gonna get busy killin[g] and maimin[g]'. Throughout the remainder of the film, the two protagonists continue to be underscored by non-diegetic music from counterculture artists such as The Byrds and Smith as they pursue their quest. Much like the earlier part of *Easy Rider*, their story is told through the music and, if anything, their silence is more pronounced in the latter part of the movie after the death of George. *Easy Rider* draws a distinction between such characters through the incorporation of Jack Nicholson's comical portrayal of the Southern lawyer, whose animated chatter seems to emphasise the silence of Wyatt and Billy. Thinking beyond this chapter, one could also draw a distinction between these silent males and the verbose male characters of screwball comedy discussed in Chapter 1. This is augmented in the final scene in which both men are killed and which suggests that the counter-cultural male, who presents a challenge to established gender norms and social convention, appears predestined to be eternally silenced by death.

Arthur Penn's 1968 film *Bonnie and Clyde* similarly features its rebellious protagonists being silenced by death. The film tells the story of the rise and fall of bank robbers Bonnie Parker (Faye Dunaway) and Clyde Barrow (Warren Beatty). When they meet at the start of the film, they are immediately and irresistibly attracted to one another, forming a deep bond of friendship. Early in the film, Clyde reveals that he is impotent which causes a visible and audible rift in their relationship. As they begin robbing banks and stealing cars, they recruit C.W. Moss (Michael J. Pollard) as their driver, and Clyde's brother Buck Barrow (Gene Hackman) and his wife Blanche (Estelle Parsons). They name themselves The Barrow Gang and continue to carry out successful bank robberies until the police track them down and C.W.'s father (Dub Taylor) arranges for the couple to be ambushed by Sherriff Frank Hamer (Denver Pyle). The movie ends with Bonnie and Clyde being mowed down in a hail of police bullets. This graphic, shocking depiction of gun violence had never been seen on screen before. Murray Pomerance asserts that such is the shocking nature of this final scene that the audience itself emerges from the movie 'spattered with metaphorical blood and riddled with wounds'.[40] This sensation is augmented by the deafening sounds of diegetic gunfire, which assault our aural senses, exemplifying the shocking depiction of the pair's demise.

In her reading of *Bonnie and Clyde*, Liora Moriel refers to the construction of Clyde as either bisexual or homosexual in the film's original script. The topic of homosexuality was still unexplored by mainstream Hollywood in the 1960s, resulting in a change of the final script in which the writers abandoned the homosexual narrative and instead, constructed Clyde as impotent. Moriel argues that because the film narrative primarily concerns a man and a woman that the filmmakers 'bent and twisted the tale so it would fit some perceived [heterosexual] societal norm'[41] whilst still leaving obvious traces of homoerotic suggestion; these traces are particularly evident in the interactions between C.W. and Clyde. Moriel cites numerous occurrences of homoerotic interchange between the two male characters to support this idea. Whilst this illuminating discussion of the queer aspects of Clyde's character provides an interesting subversive reading of the film and of Clyde as an emasculated character, my discussion of the sound in *Bonnie and Clyde*, while focusing on the more subversive aspects of Clyde's character, reveals the idiosyncrasies in Bonnie and Clyde's heterosexual relationship rather than Clyde and C.W.'s homoerotic bond. Like *Easy Rider*, the music soundtrack of *Bonnie and Clyde* is used throughout and often underscores their ongoing journey. Yet, unlike *Easy Rider*, actual silence permeates the soundscape and suggests a divide in Bonnie and Clyde's relationship. Once Clyde's impotence is revealed, the couple are surrounded by silence or muted ambient noise which represents a distance between them, caused by a lack of intimacy.

Silence is a key aural motif in *Bonnie and Clyde* and is introduced at the start of the film when we see Bonnie alone in her bedroom. She appears frustrated and tortured – arguably sexually frustrated. Prior to this, her desire for Clyde is signalled formally through the merging of his photograph in the opening sequence, with a close up of Bonnie licking her lips, suggesting that her longing for Clyde will be a motivating force throughout the movie. The overwhelming silence surrounding Bonnie's frustration is broken with the sound of her punching the metal bars of her bed frame and slamming a drawer, abrasively puncturing the silence. Geoff King notes that the impression created here 'is one of restlessness, edginess and a palpable sense of sexual hunger or longing'.[42] Indeed, silence is used to construct Bonnie's current existence as void of any visual or audible activity, a vacuum temporarily filled by Clyde when they first meet and form an immediate bond. He fills the silence that surrounds her as they meet and chat about work, prison and robberies. Throughout this part of the film, we hear the ambient sounds of cars, music from a nearby radio and the wind blowing gently as they chat. However, once on the run with Clyde, the silence she first experiences is resumed and emphasises the 'gap' in their relationship caused by Clyde's impotence and thus linked to the emasculation and alienation of his character. From this point, we see the music soundtrack used in the same way as in *Easy Rider* and *The Graduate* – as a substitute for male silence. In the case of Clyde, the use of music is also linked to his inability to perform sexually.

The score of *Bonnie and Clyde* is vastly different to that of other films discussed in this chapter since it features bluegrass music[43] instead of the rock or pop tracks that feature in other soundtracks of New Hollywood films. The bluegrass song used for the main theme tune, 'Foggy Mountain Breakdown' (Scruggs, 1949), was insisted upon by Warren Beatty himself, being a fan of bluegrass in his high school days. According to Jack Ashworth, however, the success of the film and its soundtrack was such that it actually propelled bluegrass into the realms of popular music among young cinema audiences. He alleges the film's soundtrack 'helped imprint the banjo into the contemporary American consciousness'[44] while carrying a new set of connotations associated with rebellious youth culture. Neil Rosenburg similarly reflects on the impact of *Bonnie and Clyde*'s bluegrass score on young music consumers: 'It is significant that "Foggy Mountain Breakdown" was a pop music hit, for this reflected the fact that people buying the record were not country music consumers.'[45]

The bluegrass song 'Foggy Mountain Breakdown' is introduced in the scene following Clyde robbing the convenience store in Bonnie's hometown. Rosenburg comments that music of this kind is 'connected to the exhilaration of lawlessness, escape and travel'.[46] Indeed, the fast-paced, high-pitched banjo music embodies the breakneck speed of the car Clyde is driving as they make their getaway, but simultaneously signals Bonnie's sexual excitement at Clyde's use of his gun. Many critics discuss the phallic implications of Clyde's gun; for example, Robert Kolker states that by caressing his gun and urging him to 'use it', Bonnie is 'pressing the connection between repressed sexuality and the need for some physical action in which to sublimate it'.[47] This desire for physical action is also represented aurally through the film's soundtrack, which Rosenburg also highlights as carrying sexual connotations.[48] In this particular scene, the fast-paced, energetic music highlights Bonnie's frenzied arousal and excitement as she throws herself at Clyde while he is driving the car, kissing him passionately and emitting cries of sexual exhilaration, causing the car to career violently and eventually drive off the road.

This lively episode is immediately juxtaposed with a contrasting moment of silence. Michel Chion has noted about silence that it is 'the negative of sound we've heard beforehand . . . it is the product of contrast'.[49] Indeed the change in sound here marks a complete contrast in behaviour in the previously talkative Clyde, one which links silence with his emasculation. Once the car and music have stopped, Clyde forcefully pushes Bonnie away and limps out of the car as the couple are enveloped in diegetic silence. Here we are reminded of Clyde's earlier revelation that he is physically impaired through the self-mutilation of his toes whilst in prison; he then goes on to reveal his impotence, a further physical impairment. Clyde tries to explain to a perplexed Bonnie that he's 'not much of a lover boy' and that he views sex as pointless. This is a shock to Bonnie, and to the audience, since, as Bonnie puts it, for a man who has excessively flirted with her since their meeting he '[doesn't] have a thing to sell'. Clyde's previously flirtatious behaviour suggests that his sexual inabilities seem to be about physical incapability rather than his assertions about the futility of sex. Here we can begin to question the representation of masculinity as intrinsically linked to sexual (over) performance. This questioning is embodied aurally through the ensuing moments of silence that begin to proliferate the soundscape, especially when Clyde is alone with Bonnie. We are reminded of the silent frustration experienced by Bonnie in the film's opening, and despite finding a companion, silence and dissatisfaction prevail. This is augmented in a later scene, when Clyde, struck by Bonnie's loyalty to him, attempts (and fails) to make love to her. This awkward scene, underscored by no music and consisting only of the sounds of the bed sheets moving and Bonnie's heavy breathing in places, is eerily and uncomfortably silent; especially when one considers the generic norms in Hollywood for underscoring heterosexual intimacy, such as the inclusion of romantic, classical music.[50] Furthermore, Beatty's reputation in Hollywood as a charming lothario or 'lover boy' both on and off screen adds to the poignancy of this performance and its soundscape. This lack of diegetic and non-diegetic noise precisely conveys the sense of unease and tension between them and closeness which Bonnie so desperately craves, but which Clyde cannot deliver. These moments of silence contribute to the representation of Clyde as an emasculated character and to the sense of alienation surrounding him. The scene ends with him standing alone in the corner of the dark bedroom before turning to Bonnie and feebly reminding her, 'I told you I was not much of a lover boy'.

The aural spaces between our protagonists are later filled by the diegetic noise of C.W., Buck and Blanche. In a motel scene where the couple are in bed, Bonnie lies awake and the sound of loud, male snoring envelopes the soundscape. The camera soon reveals C.W. sleeping on a nearby sofa as Clyde opens one eye, revealing that the snoring must be coming from C.W. This aural cue, which takes place immediately after C.W. joins them, shows C.W. filling the silence between Bonnie and Clyde while preventing them from being physically alone together. The later arrival of Buck and Blanche to the sounds of the loud car engine with the horn blowing brings further noise to the soundscape. Buck and Clyde immediately create a sense of male camaraderie by whooping and shouting as they playfully punch and wrestle one another. Buck repeats 'c'mon, you can do better than that!' perhaps emphasising the familial idea that Clyde is expected to continually seek to assert his masculinity against his older, male sibling. This episode, featuring the sound of male banter, immediately follows Clyde's failed attempts to make love to Bonnie in the scene described above. Therefore, this physical and aural emphasis on his masculine attributes seeks to compensate for his perceived failure as a man in his relationship with Bonnie. Following the introduction of Buck and Blanche, Buck and Clyde retreat to have a 'man to man' talk. Interestingly, this is short-lived and also soon falls into silence, so much so that Buck resorts to emitting an arbitrary loud, long holler of 'woo hoo!', seemingly to simply fill the empty aural space that has now emerged between them. The latter shout is comically related to the beginning of their conversation where Buck enquired about Bonnie and Clyde's sex life, about which, Clyde obviously does not have much to say. Blanche adds yet another aural dimension with her exceedingly high-pitched voice and now, with five characters in the narrative, there is henceforth little chance for us to encounter Bonnie and Clyde's moments of silence.

Upon its release, *Bonnie and Clyde* provoked a divided response among audiences and critics. Maitland McDonagh notes a polarised response between the 'hip' and 'square': 'The hip loved it, the square squirmed about the violence and amorality of its portrait of a white trash couple on the run.'[51] The arrangement of the film's sound is also remarkably polarised. The soundscape moves from moments of extreme silence, discussed above, to the sudden, deafening sounds of gunfire. This allegorical arrangement can be partially explained by the structure of the narrative since, as one of the film's screenwriters, David Newman, points out,

> One of the motifs that run through the film is how this artificial family tries to live like a normal bunch, and, whenever they do, they become most vulnerable to attack: 'the laws' come riding in, guns blazing, and once again they are forced to abandon domesticity.[52]

The concept of polarisation is fundamental to the film's narrative structure, signifying the two different types of experiences undergone by Bonnie, Clyde and their gang – on one hand, moments of settled domesticity and, on the other, violence, death and lawlessness. These two extreme experiences are represented aurally through moments of quiet or silence and conflicting moments of loud gunfire, which Arthur Penn's sound department incorporated in the soundtrack at an increased volume, so much so that on the film's initial cinema release, projectionists worldwide, unaware of this intention, would try to lower the sound volume believing that the exaggerated sound was a mistake.[53] In linking this aural concept to the representation of Clyde Barrow, one may further shed light on the gender performance in the film: Clyde's lack of sexual potency forces him to reject these moments of quiet domesticity, which would traditionally inevitably involve procreation, opting instead for life on the run, aurally enveloped in loud gunfire. Much critical discussion focuses on the operation of Clyde's gun as a replacement phallus; read in this context, the extra loud noise of his gun seemingly emphasises his masculinity and compensates for his inability to perform sexually.

The most extreme examples of aforementioned polarised soundings occur during the police shoot-out scenes. As mentioned above, the addition of three gang members allows little opportunity for Bonnie and Clyde to be alone together and therefore less opportunity for the viewer to be reminded of Clyde's impotence. However, when Bonnie's frustration that there is '*always* someone in the next room!' causes a further silent rift in their relationship, the police shoot-out provides an ideal moment in which Clyde can showcase his masculinity by displacing sex with violence. The first police attack is preceded by a contrasting peaceful moment where Bonnie is reciting one of her poems to the group, until Clyde spots the police outside. Interestingly, it is diegetic sound that causes the police to attack as the mention of the presence of 'the laws' causes petrified Blanche to start screaming. The piercing sound of Blanche's terrified high-pitched scream fills the air and then the loud gunfire begins. Her wailing and crying continues throughout the gun attack and can be consistently heard over the sounds of multiple guns firing loudly and persistently. This moment in the film seems to present an aural attack on the audience's senses as the layering of gun noises, screaming, glass smashing and car engines merge to create a loud, disturbing soundscape. However, these exceedingly loud moments are the ones in which Clyde exerts his masculinity by firing back at the police and ensuring the safe escape of Bonnie and the gang. This climactic moment marks a breaking point in Bonnie and Clyde's relationship. Once they have escaped the police, Blanche's continual screaming causes Bonnie to echo the audience's sentiments by repeatedly shouting at Blanche to 'shut up!' This causes her and Clyde to argue about Blanche, at which point Bonnie berates Clyde about the lack of love-making in their relationship. Again, the acoustic implications are interesting here since it is really Blanche's hysterical screaming that causes this rift between them, rather than the gun attack. As Bonnie verbally attacks Clyde's impotence, he retreats from her as if he has been physically hurt by her words. One realises that it is in fact the level of noise that comes with the other three gang members that fills the aural gaps in Bonnie and Clyde's relationship, yet pulls the characters apart physically, leaving Bonnie feeling continually frustrated and lonely.

The second moment of climactic noise occurs during the second police shoot-out scene in which Buck and Blanche both get shot. Like the first shoot-out scene, there appears a polarisation of sound whereby the gang are quiet and restful; Bonnie, Clyde and C.W. listen to quiet, low-key tunes on the radio, while Buck and Blanche lie silently in bed. Suddenly, the police are rapping on the door and the sounds of loud, relentless gunshots echo through the soundtrack, later permeated with the sounds of Blanche screaming (although not as loudly as in the first instance, signalling her transition into the gang). The death of Buck and blinding of Blanche marks the acoustic climax of the film. Blanche's screaming is again prevalent on the soundtrack as her husband is loudly shot to death. The following scenes featuring C.W. Moss rescuing Bonnie and Clyde are once again permeated by silence.

The 'Foggy Mountain Breakdown' tune is used once again towards the end of the film when Bonnie and Clyde finally engage in sexual intercourse. Prior to this moment, Bonnie has read aloud her poem 'The Ballad of Bonnie and Clyde' which tells the story of their life on the run. Bonnie's act of writing down, reciting and finally publishing her love and admiration of Clyde cures his impotence. By emphasising his masculinity and heroism through words, she finally fills the empty aural space between them, leading to sexual consummation and putting an end to their lives on the run. Thus the construction of Clyde as an alienated male character is seemingly resolved towards the end of the film and is simultaneously underscored by the jaunty bluegrass music which has previously signalled movement and escape. However, the music also underscores the following scene in which the sheriff and C.W.'s father are plotting their demise. Therefore, this music signifies that their eventual physical intimacy (and the prospect of domestic life) is an overture to their deaths.

The notion of silence as a signifier of alienation is one explored in the soundtrack of *The Graduate*. Like *Easy Rider*, the choice of popular music to underscore the central protagonist spoke directly to young audiences. Paul Monaco argues that the soundtrack, written and performed by folk singers Simon and Garfunkel, 'lent a distinctive underpinning to the film's offbeat storyline'.[54] He maintains, however, that, despite the innovative style, it was used purely for conventional narrative purposes. Whilst the music throughout *The Graduate* does perform a narrative function, I argue that, like in *Easy Rider* and *Bonnie and Clyde*, the soundtrack in *The Graduate* also constructs Benjamin Braddock (Dustin Hoffman) as a silent, alienated male character through its frequent extra diegetic substitution for Ben's silence.

Posters advertising *The Graduate* in 1968 read: 'This is Benjamin. He's a little worried about his future,' a statement which encapsulated the sense of uncertainty many young people of the time indeed felt about their futures. The film follows Benjamin Braddock who, on graduating, is unsure what to do with his life. His affluent, middle-class parents would like him to apply to graduate school, yet Ben fills his days by aimlessly drinking beer, floating in the family swimming pool and embarking on an affair with a friend of his parents, Mrs Robinson (Ann Bancroft). However, upon meeting Mrs Robinson's daughter, Elaine, he falls in love with her. At the end of the film, Ben dramatically storms the church where Elaine is about to marry Carl Smith (Brian Avery), a medical student. He barricades the doors of the church with a cross, and the pair escape together on the first bus to arrive outside the church. They ride off together, seemingly having escaped the dull, conventional middle-class existence of their parents' generation.

The Graduate is often referred to as one of the first alienation films of the 1960s.[55] It was noted for its unusual aesthetics including extreme close ups, unusual camera angles, long takes and non-linear editing, all of which contributed to the creation of a world in which Ben doesn't quite 'fit'. In its acoustic arrangement, the non-diegetic performance of the Simon and Garfunkel soundtrack dominates the soundscape from the outset, often accompanying Ben's vacant stares. The diegetic sound in the early parts of the film frequently consists of dialogue by Ben's parents and their friends. Consequently, in the first half of the film, Ben barely has a voice and his silence is frequently supplemented by music or diegetic noise. This is evident through close analysis of the soundscape in the film's opening sequence, which sets the tone for a movie about the attempts of the older generation to dominate, and emphasises Ben's alienation.

The very first sound we hear in *The Graduate* is the persistent humming of the interior of an aeroplane, accompanied by an extreme close up of Ben's expressionless face. Whilst this noise lasts for only a few seconds, it nevertheless introduces us to our protagonist within an oppressive, restrictive environment and is the first example of Ben's silence being substituted with noise. The use of an extreme close up on his face contributes to a sense that he is trapped and alienated; the *mise en scène* representing him as a character that is closed in. The pilot's voice is then heard over the loudspeaker, announcing the plane's descent into Los Angeles airport. The calm, authoritative voice is clearly that of an older male and an initial aural representation of the conventional, patriarchal order of the generation of Ben's parents. His announcement is detailed with specifics about the journey such as the scheduled flight times and temperatures and ends with 'we have enjoyed having you on board, we hope to see you again in the near future'. This obviously obligatory statement is filled with hollow sentiment and is an aural introduction to the older generation as insincere and conventional. J. W. Whitehead observes the economic and monetary motivation behind this phrase, which, he says, is 'a mockery of polite social convention whose only sincerity is commercial: it is in the captain's economic interests to invite his guests to "join" him on some future journey'.[56] Throughout the announcement, the camera slowly pulls back to reveal Ben listening to the announcement; his lack of engagement with any of his fellow passengers and his blank stare further confirm the sense of alienation suggested from the outset of the movie.

The opening sequence then quickly cuts to Ben now walking through the airport and the non-diegetic gentle guitar strings of Simon and Garfunkel begin. We soon hear their famous lyrics 'Hello darkness my old friend . . .' as 'The Sounds of Silence' (1968) plays over the opening sequence. The song plays loudly over the long take of Ben standing on a moving walkway which lasts for almost two minutes, during which time we hear the song in its entirety and further announcements on a loudspeaker. Again an older male, robotic-sounding voice announces: 'Please hold the hand rail and stand to the right, if you wish to pass, please do so on the left'. This is repeated five times, each time interrupting, or talking over the non-diegetic music, thus suggesting the traditionalists' attempt to enforce dominant ideological rules on youth counter-culture, represented by Simon and Garfunkel and Ben himself. At this point in the film, we see Ben in total compliance with the request of the loudspeaker, dutifully standing on the right, not even thinking about passing either on the left or right. His blank facial expression and disaffected demeanour convey a sense of dissatisfaction with his current situation yet also a lack of motivation to rebel against it. Further loudspeaker announcements are heard at the baggage collection and the airport exit. Thus, the first three minutes of the film's sound diegesis are filled with the voices of faceless authority figures, to whom Ben abides, yet his deadpan expression denotes deep dissatisfaction with having to do so. This is augmented at the beginning of the next sequence with another close up of his anxious face as he sits silently in his bedroom, with only the sounds of the fish tank bubbling behind him. Again this moment of silence is interrupted by another faceless voice, that of his father – whom we do eventually see. Yet the aural similarities with the previous voices links Ben's father to the authoritarian, traditional values of the older generation. This aural construction is enhanced at Ben's graduation party where he is submerged in cries and calls from his parent's friends who coo over him whilst the camera remains in a close up of his face, creating the same air of claustrophobia as the opening scene in the plane. The words 'proud', 'track star', 'award', 'future' ring out above the din of general chatter and glasses clinking. The fact that no one of Ben's age is at the party demonstrates that the sentiment behind it (much like the earlier pilot's announcement) is a hollow one: this party is a chance for the Braddocks to showcase their 'star', highlighted by the voice of his mother who demands silence from everyone while she reads Ben's achievements aloud from his college year book. He escapes to his bedroom as her high-pitched voice pervades the soundscape, the viewer is left wondering if this passive, alienated young man is the same one of whom she speaks; his current disaffected behaviour does not denote someone who is a likely newspaper editor or head of the debate team. Herein lies the message behind the movie: Ben is not interested in debating, or even engaging, with this group of people. His disillusionment stems from their shallow, bourgeois predictable behaviour, and thus, he remains silent.

Ben's alienated silence continues to be substituted with non-diegetic music throughout the film until he meets Elaine. 'The Sounds of Silence' is repeated over a montage that depicts Ben's growing isolation from his parents and his continued affair with Mrs Robinson. However, his capacity to silently follow this meaningless pattern eventually reaches a climax at the culmination of the montage, when prior to having sex with Mrs Robinson, he demands, 'Do you think we could liven it up with a little conversation for a change?' This is the beginning of a transformation in Ben as the oppressive silence in which he is immersed becomes unbearable to him. Yet his subsequent attempts to find common ground with Mrs Robinson through conversation fail, only highlighting the stark differences between them. This is the first moment in the film that we hear Ben speak for an extended period, providing insight into the passion underlying his disenchanted exterior. It also reveals the unhappiness and discontent beneath the apparently gleaming surface of the bourgeois middle classes through Mrs Robinson's sad tale of her failed marriage. This provides direct motivation for Ben and Elaine to avoid a life like their parents – represented acoustically once they meet and Ben's silent alienation begins to disappear, instead replaced by noise and action.

From their first date, noise surrounds Ben and Elaine as the previously silent or ambient diegesis of *The Graduate* is now disrupted by the aggressive roar of Ben's car engine, the jazz music in the strip club, the cheering audience during the show and then Elaine's crying as she demands that Ben take her home. These loud, raw and aggressive sounds represent Ben's conscious efforts to dissuade Elaine from liking him, to displease his parents since the date was their idea. However, this sense of crude, acoustic release appears to have a somewhat cathartic effect, at once transforming Ben and breaking him out of alienated silence. Once the couple have reconciled, their amiable chatter fills the film's diegesis – a sound not yet heard in association with the younger generation. Simultaneously, loud music is played by the young people in the car parked next to them, which they block out by putting the roof up on Ben's car as we see him eagerly talking to Elaine through the car windscreen, but we do not hear him. This separation from the world of his peers means that he maintains his alienated character within the world of the film and emphasises his later assertions that Elaine is the only person in his whole life that he has liked or could stand to be around. Furthermore, though Ben breaks his silence from earlier in the film, the audience are still not privy to his dialogue and thus his seemingly new-found ability to express himself is kept from us and reserved entirely for Elaine.

This changes in the film's final sequence, depicting Ben at his most active and expressive throughout the film. As he searches for the church where Elaine's wedding is taking place, the loud sound of his car engine revving is an aural reminder of their first date and the ways in which their relationship has brought Ben out of his previously silent melancholy. We see him frantically driving from place to place, speaking to different people, demanding answers, using his voice to achieve his romantic goal, determined not to be silenced anymore. The fast-paced, staccato sound of guitars on the non-diegetic 'Mrs Robinson' (1968) track, which underscores the entire sequence, emphasises Ben's urgency. As his car runs out of fuel, so too does the music: slowing down and eventually petering out with the car. This moment signifies Ben's ultimate release from the silence enforced on him by the soundtrack, represented by his loud, deep anguished cries of '*Elaine!*' from the back of the church. Next we see a reversal of earlier privileging of the middle-class, parental voice in the diegesis as we see juxtaposed shots of both Mr and Mrs Robinson angrily berating Ben through gritted teeth, followed by a shot of Carl doing the same, yet we do not hear them. Their lips move almost comically, as if in mime, yet they now are silenced whilst Ben's repeated cries of '*Elaine!*' are heard loudly above the din of the church. Elaine cries '*Ben!*' in return at the top of her voice and the final moments in the church are filled with the sounds of Elaine screaming at her mother and Ben simultaneously roaring with determination as he angrily swings a large cross at the wedding party. This animated, irate character is in stark contrast with the silent graduate we met in the opening scenes of the film.

The closing sequence of Ben and Elaine riding on a bus is underscored by 'The Sounds of Silence' as in the opening sequence. This non-diegetic track once again forces Ben into silence, potentially suggesting that Ben has progressed no further from the beginning of the film. Yet, arguably, the lack of any authoritative voice within the film's diegesis here (unlike in the opening scene) represents Ben and Elaine's success at breaking away from bourgeois conventionality and the authoritarian older generation. The bus they are on is filled with passengers of their parents' age or older who silently glare at them, yet do not speak to them, and thus the repetition of the song with no diegetic intrusion seems to suggest that Ben and Elaine are embarking on a new journey or a new beginning. Furthermore, the announcement that interrupted the track in the opening scene was about following the rules which, in the movie's inauguration, Ben obeyed without question. Yet we have just witnessed Ben breaking several rules in order to fight for his relationship with Elaine, acting on impulse and emotion, precisely the actions which now separate him from his parents' generation. In his discussion of the hippie counterculture David Savran observes: 'The dominant culture prizes rationality, logic, the rule of law, sobriety ... [whereas] the counterculture celebrates the irrational, emotional, lawless, psychedelic, pre-industrial, impoverished, and transient'.[57] Whilst I am not claiming Ben Braddock to be a 'hippie' (as Geoff King points out, 'for all his escape from the world of his parents, he remains a rather "straight" individual'),[58] his lawless, rebellious behaviour aligns with him a representation of the rebellion of counter-cultural American youth.

In each of the films discussed here, silent, alienated male characters permeate the narrative, and as I have discussed above, silence is a sound motif that has frequently been aligned with male characters in classical Hollywood cinema. Yet the strategic juxtaposition of silence and sound in these films allows one to gain a more complex picture of gender norms and witness the interiority of our male protagonists. In *Easy Rider*, the carefully constructed music soundtrack tells us much about Billy and Wyatt without them having to relay it through dialogue. In *Bonnie and Clyde*, the silence surrounding Clyde is linked to his emasculation through lack of sexual ability, but is substituted by music and the loud sounds of gunfire as a form of compensation. The demise of these characters immersed in loud gunfire, however, could suggest that the blurring of complex gender boundaries explored by these films was still undergoing negotiation in the 1960s. In *The Graduate*, Ben is silenced by his dissatisfaction with the middle-class world of his parents, and this is augmented by the frequent non-diegetic music. Yet his immersion in silence eventually leads to his rebellion and the incorporation of loud, diegetic sound later in the film, including his emotional outbursts in the name of love.

The soundscape of each of these films, I argue, can be linked to an ideological shift in how we imagine masculinity whereby sound is used to construct meaning about the interiority of our male protagonists. This appears as a subversion of previous ideologies of glossy, studio-era films that rarely provide this interior insight – especially into male characters – and are instead overly concerned with surface appearances and upholding a sense of exterior perfection. Through the juxtaposition of soundtrack and silence, each of the films discussed here creates an alternative representation of masculinity that challenges dominant perceptions of 'maleness' found in preceding eras of American mainstream cinema. These representations are perhaps a more genuine portrayal of men during this period of social change in America. This aural depiction reveals male alienation to be a common plight of men and thus links the sound design of New Hollywood cinema to broader, ideological changes taking place in 1960s American society.

NOTES

1. Michael Ryan and Douglas Kellner, *Camera Politica: The Politics and Ideology of Contemporary Hollywood Film* (Bloomington: Indiana University Press, 1988), 17.
2. Paul Théberge, 'The interplay of sound and silence in contemporary cinema and television', in Jay Beck and Tony Grajeda (eds), *Lowering the Boom: Critical Studies in Film Sound* (Chicago: University of Illinois Press, 2008), 51.
3. Théberge, 52.
4. Lester D. Friedman, *Arthur Penn's Bonnie and Clyde* (Cambridge: Cambridge University Press, 2000), 2.
5. John Belton, *American Cinema, American Culture*, (New York: McGraw-Hill, 2005), 324.
6. Belton, 325.
7. Barry Keith Grant (ed.), *American Cinema of the 1960s: Themes and Variations* (New Brunswick, NJ: Rutgers University Press, 2008), 10.
8. Richard Maltby, *Hollywood Cinema* (Malden, MA: Wiley-Blackwell, 2003), 159.
9. Geoff King, *New Hollywood Cinema: An Introduction* (London: I. B. Tauris, 2002), 25.
10. Peter Biskind, *Easy Riders, Raging Bulls: How the Sex 'n' Drugs 'n' Rock 'n' Roll Generation saved Hollywood* (London: Bloomsbury, 1998), 20.
11. Barry Langford, *Post-Classical Hollywood: Film Industry, Style and Ideology since 1945* (Edinburgh: Edinburgh University Press, 2010), 107.
12. Langford, 115.
13. Grant, 18.
14. Notable examples include *The French Connection* (Friedkin, 1971), *Dog Day Afternoon* (Lumet, 1975) and *Taxi Driver* (Scorsese, 1976).
15. Paul Monaco, *History of the American Cinema, Volume 8, 1960–1969* (Berkeley: University of California Press, 2001), 107.
16. William Whittington, 'Sound design in New Hollywood cinema', in Graeme Harper *et al.* (eds), *Sounds and Music in Film and Visual Media: An Overview* (New York and London: Continuum International Publishing Group, 2009), 557.
17. Whittington, 559.
18. Langford, 115.

19. Peter Kramer, *The New Hollywood: From* Bonnie and Clyde *to* Star Wars (London: Wallflower, 2005), 12.
20. Brian Baker, *Masculinity in Fiction and Film: Representing Men in Popular Genres 1945–2000* (London: Continuum International Publishing Group, 2007), 2.
21. Baker, 4.
22. Method acting is a performance style that focuses on the actor's interiority. It relies on cultivating an aura of mood and emotion derived from the actor's own persona rather than stressing the interpretation of the language in the written script. See Virginia Wright Wexman, 'Masculinity in crisis: Method acting in Hollywood', in Pamela Robertson Wojcik (ed.), *Movie Acting: The Film Reader* (New York: Routledge, 2004), 127–44.
23. Harry M. Benshoff and Sean Griffin, *America on Film: Representing Race, Class, Gender, and Sexuality at the Movies* (Malden, MA: Wiley-Blackwell, 2004), 267.
24. John Beynon, *Masculinities and Culture* (Buckingham: Open University Press, 2002), 66.
25. David Savran, *Taking it Like a Man: White Masculinity, Masochism and Contemporary American Culture* (Princeton: Princeton University Press, 1998), 122.
26. Savran, 123.
27. Roger Horrocks, *Male Myths and Icons: Masculinity in Popular Culture* (Basingstoke: Macmillan, 1995), 76.
28. Horrocks, 77.
29. Baker, 131.
30. Robert Warshow, 'Movie chronicle: The Westerner', in Robert Warshow, *The Immediate Experience: Movies, Comics, Theatre & Other Aspects of Popular Culture* (Cambridge, MA: Harvard University Press, 2001), 105–24.
31. Steve Neale, Masculinity as spectacle: Reflections on men and mainstream cinema', *Screen*, v. 24, no. 6 (1983): 2–17.
32. Benshoff and Griffin, 254.
33. Steven Cohen and Ina Rae Clark, *The Road Movie Book* (London: Routledge, 1997), 51.
34. Cohan and Clark, 54.
35. Cohan and Clark, 54.
36. R. Serge Denisoff and William D. Romanowski, *Risky Business: Rock in Film* (New Brunswick, NJ: Transaction Publishers, 1991), 169.
37. King, 16.
38. Anahid Kassabian, *Hearing Film: Tracking Identifications in Contemporary Hollywood Film Music* (New York and London: Routledge, 2001), 3.
39. David Shumway, 'Rock 'n' roll sound tracks and the production of nostalgia', *Cinema Journal*, v. 38, no. 2 (Winter 1999): 36.
40. Murray Pomerance, 'Movies and the specter of rebellion', in Grant (ed.), *American Cinema of the 1960s*, 178.
41. Liora Moriel, 'Erasure and taboo: A queer reading of *Bonnie and Clyde*', in Lester D. Friedman (ed.), *Arthur Penn's Bonnie and Clyde* (Cambridge: Cambridge University Press, 2000), 150.
42. King, 12.
43. Bluegrass is a style of American country music that emerged in the 1940s featuring singers accompanied by acoustic instruments such as the fiddle, the mandolin, the guitar, the banjo and the bass. Bluegrass is often played at rapid tempos and features high-pitched, tightly arranged harmonies (see Neil Rosenburg, *Bluegrass: A History* (Champaign: University of Illinois Press, 2005), for more).
44. Jack Ashworth, 'Banjo', in Dennis Hall and Susan G. Hall (eds), *American Icons: An*

Encyclopedia of the People, Places and Things that have Shaped our Culture (Westport: Greenwood Publishing Group, 2006), 49.
45. Rosenburg, 265.
46. Rosenburg, 265.
47. Robert Kolker, *A Cinema of Loneliness: Penn, Stone, Kubrick, Scorsese, Spielberg, Altman*, 3rd edn (Oxford: Oxford University Press, 2000), 35.
48. Rosenburg, 265.
49. Michel Chion, *Audio-Vision* (New York: Columbia University Press, 1994), 57.
50. This sound convention might be related to the experiences of early sound film audiences, who accordingly, when watching scenes of intimacy and love-making without musical underscoring, reported a sense of awkwardness and embarrassment. See Buhler *et al.*, *Hearing the Movies*, 302.
51. Maitland McDonagh, 'The exploitation generation or: How marginal movies came in from the cold', in Alexanda Horwath, Thomas Elsaesser and Noel King (eds), *The Last Great American Picture Show: New Hollywood Cinema in the 1970s* (Amsterdam: Amsterdam University Press, 2004), 114.
52. David Newman, 'What's it really all about? Pictures at an execution', in Lester D. Friedman (ed.), *Arthur Penn's Bonnie and Clyde* (Cambridge: Cambridge University Press, 2000), 38.
53. Monaco, 107.
54. Monaco, 115.
55. Ryan and Kellner, 20.
56. J. W. Whitehead, *Appraising* The Graduate*: The Mike Nichols classic and its impact on Hollywood* (Jefferson: McFarland & Co., 2011), 71.
57. Savran, 115.
58. King, 16.

CHAPTER 4

Brothers in Arms: Masculinity and the Vietnam War Movie

Following the New Hollywood era, in which alternative depictions of masculinity began to pervade the screen, came a body of films that explored America's involvement in the Vietnam War. During the conflict itself, Hollywood produced only one film that dealt directly with Vietnam, *The Green Berets* (1968). The film starred John Wayne leading a team of Special Forces troops in a fight against the Vietcong. It was not well-received by critics and modern cinema audiences saw Wayne's portrayal of the ultra-patriotic Colonel Mike Kirby as wholly outmoded, and, according to David Savran, as 'embarrassingly out of place'.[1] The film's pro-war agenda did not sit well with the American public, many of whom were strongly opposed to US involvement in the Vietnam conflict.

The general perception of Hollywood at this time is that studios were reluctant to make films about Vietnam because the war was so publicly contentious. Furthermore, the industry itself was still in economic crisis and attempting to appeal to younger viewers, many of whom were largely opposed to America's involvement in the war. Drawing on Tom Englehardt to explain the impact of the Vietnam War on the American public, Steve Neale notes that the 'defeat and withdrawal from Vietnam in the early 1970s challenged the tenets of America's "victory culture" [and] ensured that its participation in the war remained deeply controversial'.[2] It was, therefore, a complex task to find effective ways in which to portray this conflict. The first solution was found in the mode of allegory. At this time, a number of successful films made attempts at portraying the underlying anxieties about the conflict through allegorical depiction and indirect association. For example, *The Wild Bunch* (1969) portrayed an unwinnable struggle between a group of ageing outlaws and a band of bounty hunters, *Deliverance* (1972) depicted a struggle between four Southerners on a river excursion and a group of in-bred folk living in the wilderness, and *Taxi Driver* (1976) featured the unstable, maladjusted war veteran Travis Bickle (Robert De Niro) struggling to re-adjust into civilian society.

It was not until the late 1970s that the film industry began to release pictures that directly depicted the Vietnam War. The most famous of these is probably Frances Ford Coppola's 1979 film *Apocalypse Now*, which follows US Army Captain Willard (Martin Sheen) on an assassination mission and features violent and brutal depictions of a dangerous war zone, peppered with helicopters and napalm attacks. From the perspective of film sound, the helicopter scene, accompanied by Wagner's 'Ride of the Valkyries' has become an iconic scene of the Vietnam War in film and of cinema more generally. James Lastra argues that the film itself 'stands for the emergence of modern, immersive sound design',[3] a concept I discuss in detail in the following chapter in relation to the blockbuster era. *Apocalypse Now* has been widely discussed by other scholars in terms of its use of sound, which is why I do not attend to it here.[4] Instead I explore the soundscapes of two other popular Vietnam War films, to demonstrate the ways that they use sound to challenge traditional perceptions of masculinity.

Stanley Kubrick's 1987 film *Full Metal Jacket* presents itself as a war film, which casts a retrospective look over America's involvement in the Vietnam War. The film makes general statements about the American military as an organisation structured around particular ideological beliefs and outmoded attitudes to masculinity. Importantly, it is a film that surreptitiously challenges this petrified gender profiling through its depiction of the training undergone by a group of young men in preparation for battle in Vietnam. This is further explored through the ways that the male characters cope in the midst of a war zone. Like *Apocalypse Now*, the film is highly discussed both inside and outside of academia, yet with very little focus on the film's soundtrack, which features pop music and synthesised sound. *The Deer Hunter* (1978) is an earlier film but one that explores the wider effects of war on men and their communities, hence I discuss these films in a non-chronological order. Patrick Hagopian has said of *The Deer Hunter* that it 'presented millions of Americans with a sympathetic image of troubled veterans in need of understanding'[5] and key to my discussion is the way that sound is used to represent masculinity and the acoustic world of the male characters. I will argue that these characters are frequently enveloped in sound until they reach combat in Vietnam, and henceforth find themselves embroiled in silence; but first I will discuss Kubrick's film.

The traditional concept of masculinity and its particular challenges in the 1970s is at the core of Stanley Kubrick's *Full Metal Jacket*. It is a film about Vietnam, but one which explores much more than the dynamics of war. The first part of the film follows the initiation and training of a group of recruits who all successfully become members of the United States Marine Corps. The narrative focus is placed on Leonard Lawrence, nicknamed Private Gomer

Pyle (Vincent D'Onofrio) – a slow, overweight and clumsy recruit who, after much bullying from drill Sergeant Hartman (R. Lee Ermey) and his fellow recruits, manages to pass basic training. Pyle then provides a grotesque finale for the film's first 'act' by shooting Hartman and then committing suicide by turning his gun on himself. The second part of the film takes place in Vietnam where Private Joker (Matthew Modine) – the sole character we recognise from the film's first half – is working as a reporter for the US military magazine *Stars and Stripes*. Battle soon breaks out and he and a platoon of Marines led by Private Cowboy (Arliss Howard) are thrown into combat: the Hue battle during the Tet offensive of 1968. The battle, however, is revealed to be between the platoon and a single enemy sniper, who is eventually shown to be a woman. The men kill the sniper and return to base singing the theme tune to *The Mickey Mouse Club* television show. Michael Klein calls the first part of the film a 'savage parody of the brutality of boot camp military indoctrination'[6] and argues that in the second part, when the men are tested in battle, they are 'panic-stricken, ill-disciplined, and decidedly unheroic'.[7] *Full Metal Jacket* is heavily critical of America's involvement in the Vietnam conflict and Klein is right to say that the recruits panic and lack discipline, for this is a film that explores the fears of men. In the first part of the film, the men fear not qualifying as Marines, which – as frequently re-iterated by Hartman – equates to them not qualifying as 'men'. In the second part of the film, during the combat scenes, the men fear death. Hence this film is not just critical of America's involvement in the Vietnam War, but critical of masculinity as a societal construct and the requirements it places upon men in terms of behaviours and achievement.

The fact that the film was made in 1987, twelve years after the exit of US troops from the Vietnam War, meant that Kubrick was making this film with the benefit of hindsight. The film is an adaptation of Gustav Hasford's 1979 novel *The Short Timers*. Hasford collaborated with Kubrick and Michael Herr to write the screenplay for *Full Metal Jacket*; Susan Jeffords notes that the film is therefore 'a re-writing of a 1979 novel with the participation of a 1968 author, produced in 1987'[8] and thus captures the full circuit of change that took place during these periods of time. Jeffords has identified the 1980s as a period in which images and narratives of masculinity were revived in order to reassert the ideological stability of patriarchal domination. She cites the advent of women's rights, civil rights, the 'generation gap' and social changes throughout the 1950s, 1960s and 1970s as causing a shift in the stability of patriarchy. In her discussion of *Full Metal Jacket* she sees the film as exemplifying a shift in attitudes between 1979 (the novel) and 1987 (the film), an attitudinal move towards remasculinisation. She argues that this is achieved through reinforcing a binary opposition between masculinity and femininity in the training of the recruits and in establishing a strong link between being a Marine and being a man. This link is also enforced through a rejection of anything that can be associated with femininity.[9] In my discussion of the soundscape of the film, I explore the merits of Jeffords' reading and enhance her interpretation by suggesting that with the rejection of femininity comes a rejection of the maternal, represented by the relationship between Joker and Pyle, which both confirms and contests this general assessment of the film.

The opening sequence of *Full Metal Jacket* arguably introduces the concept of remasculinisation and the rejection of the feminine. This iconic scene features numerous young recruits having their heads shaved in preparation for their basic training. The sight of the adolescents being sheared like sheep[10] appears degrading and highlights that each recruit is swiftly stripped of his individuality before becoming a Marine. The scene is underscored by a non-diegetic Country music track by Johnnie Wright entitled 'Hello Vietnam' (1965). The opening lyrics, 'Kiss me goodbye and write me while I'm gone, goodbye my sweetheart, hello Vietnam' introduces the recruits as subscribing to the patriarchal heteronormative ideology of having a girlfriend, yet also through following lyrics such as 'America has heard the bugle call and you know it involves us, one and all' emphasises that they must be prepared to reject this life amid the realm of women, and join up with fellow men in order to serve their country. Randy Rashussen observes that Kubrick's use of 'Hello Vietnam' is ironic because it implies a quick transition from civilian life to combat service while the film spends much of its time depicting the long and complicated process by which a civilian becomes a soldier, or as I argue, by which an adolescent boy becomes a man.[11]

As the song plays, piles of thick, youthful hair fall to the floor: the boys' rebellious and often feminine 1960s haircuts are eradicated in a matter of seconds, emphasising that fighting 'one and all' as a collective, male force involves the rejection of anything that could be considered feminine – including long hair. The steady upbeat rhythm of the music perfectly matches the editing in this sequence. Each haircut is on screen for exactly eight beats of music, before changing to the next shot. This highly organisational editing strategy means that the images of the men are choreographed to the music and links in with the formalised marching and chanting the men will engage in together throughout their training. Such formal audiovisual devices suggest subliminal military indoctrination from the film's outset. However, when compared with the shots in the scenes that follow, the shots here are less uniform – the boys are filmed from different angles and their hair is cut in different ways, sometimes from the side, sometimes straight across the head and by different barbers. The lack of uniformity within the *mise en scène* here suggests a lack of uniformity and cohesion between the recruits prior to entering the military. These shots also provide great contrast with the juxtaposing scene of their first day of training where they are lined up in neat rows, dressed in the same green uniform, stand by their identical bunks and when prompted, yell loudly in unison, 'Sir! Yes Sir!' The non-diegetic music instantly disappears when we cut to this scene, replaced by the loud diegetic sound of loud Drill Instructor Sergeant Hartman yelling insults at the recruits in his penetrating voice and cutting tone. Gilbert Adair notes that in this section of the movie, the language of the Corps is designed to trammel their humanity and curb their individuality: 'every utterance has to be bookended by the word "Sir", as in "Sir, yessir!" Even at that elementary level there exists neither exit nor escape – the possibility of reverie, of reflection, of open-ended communication, is sealed tight as a drum on both sides.'[12] As such, we hear very little dialogue from the recruits except for when they are yelling in response to Hartman. Thus the non-diegetic soundtrack provides insight into the minds of the men, demonstrating the challenges faced as they strive to become Marines.

The use of non-diegetic, popular music is not heard again until the second part of the film. Krin Gabbard and Shailja Sharma describe the music in *Full Metal Jacket* as an 'assortment of monumentally frivolous recordings from the mid-1960s' and argue that pop music is used 'to remind audiences that the soldiers, many of them still in their teens, are asked to give their own lives and to take the lives of others even though they are still very much a part of the adolescent culture represented by the pop tunes'.[13] If this is the case, the aural construction of the training sequence seeks to make us forget that these young men are part of a youth culture. The re-emergence of pop tracks during the Vietnam section later in the film highlights the alternative sounding used throughout the training sequence, which consists of fast-paced, military band music which is used to signify the progression of the recruits from, as Hartman calls them, 'maggots' into Marines. Thus I argue that this military music is linked to the formation of masculinity, and, as I discuss below, is absent from the soundtrack in moments where the masculinity of particular recruits is under question.

The first inclusion of military music occurs approximately ten minutes into the training section of the film. It accompanies several sequences showing the men climbing up ropes and various other training apparatus whilst Hartman barks insults at them; apparently his sole motivational technique. The music is fast-paced and mainly consists of percussive, staccato drumbeats, never entering into musical melody, implying that the men are still within the early stages of their training. Throughout this section, we see Private Pyle consistently failing to negotiate the training apparatus, unable to do one pull-up and being beaten to the ground during a wrestling activity with his fellow recruits. So whilst this sequence with its upbeat military acoustics demonstrates the achievements of the other men, it highlights Pyle's incompetence. Towards the end of the sequence we see Private Joker attempting to help Pyle, by holding him up and throwing his arm around him as the squad run through a muddy trench.

Returning briefly to Susan Jeffords, she argues that *Full Metal Jacket* explores the way in which the recruits are transformed from boys into men through a rejection of all things feminine, culminating in the silencing of the female sniper at the end of the movie. She asserts that Private Pyle is explicitly feminised and placed in contrast to the masculinisation of the recruits[14] and thus, his transformation is key to the remasculinisation project within the film. However, the aural construction of the film does not support this reading of the character: it reveals that it is in fact Private Joker who is feminised while Pyle is constructed as an infant in need of nurturing. This is initiated when Sergeant Hartman tells Pyle that Joker is his new squad leader, he adds: 'he'll teach you everything, he'll teach you how to pee!' Such vernacular demonstrates the maternal role to be taken on by Joker. The following sequence, accompanied now by slower-paced military band music, shows Joker teaching Pyle the necessary skills to become a Marine. The music gradually increases in speed as Pyle's skills steadily progress and we now hear the introduction of a familiar military melody, which will be repeated in later sequences. The tune becomes a leitmotif for the success of the squad in scenes featuring the whole group marching, symbolising their collective improvement. Unlike the previous training sequences, we now see Private Pyle marching in time with the other recruits and successfully performing drills with his rifle as well as navigating the training apparatus. We also see Joker teaching Pyle how to lace his boots and how to make his bed, and later on we see him dressing him. Such teaching is usually considered basic infant training to be undertaken by a child's mother, or primary carer. Joker speaks in soft, gentle tones, calling him by his real name, Leonard, unlike Hartman who calls him by his nickname mixed in with various other colourful insults. Joker uses phrases like 'thatta boy' to encourage him and his gentle aural approach is vastly different to the barking consistently heard from Hartman. Yet, despite Pyle's improved abilities at being a Marine, within the ideological constructs of patriarchy he is failing as a man, and so too is Joker by having to perform the role of Pyle's surrogate mother. Ultimately, the film suggests, this set up cannot succeed if being a man and being a Marine go hand in hand. Hence Pyle's failure seems inevitable, as adumbrated in the scene when Hartman discovers a smuggled doughnut in Pyle's footlocker and subsequently punishes the entire squad. The training sequences that follow this disruptive episode are not underscored by the previously used military music. The lack of non-diegetic accompaniment highlights the halt in progress being caused by Private Pyle's incompetence. His representation as infantile is reinforced by his sucking of his thumb while the squad is punished as well as by Joker's appropriation of a maternal role to Pyle. It is from this point in the film that the squad collectively forces both Pyle and Joker to break out of this transgressional, and transgender, mother-child relationship and to revert back to 'manhood', within the terms of the collective brotherhood represented by the Marine Corps.

There are three episodes in which composed (as opposed to pre-existing) music is used in *Full Metal Jacket*: the 'soap attack' on Private Pyle, his shooting of Hartman and himself, and the sniper scene at the end of the movie. Each of these episodes represents a challenge to Joker's masculinity. The composition of the music in these scenes configures each of them as a test that, should he fail, would compromise his masculinity in the diegetic world of the film. I would like to attend to each of them in detail here.

In the 'soap attack' scene, the non-diegetic soundtrack represents a distinct break in the aural construction of the film. Thus far, we have experienced pop music in the opening scene and regimented military music throughout the training sequences, and now a new type of music is heard. Accompanying the close up image of a bar of soap being carefully wrapped in a towel is low-pitched, synthesized non-diegetic music that creates the effect of deep, heavy breathing. The sound appears to 'inhale' and 'exhale' in a steady rhythm and the deep pitch creates a sense of a male group of people breathing in unison and, like predators, waiting patiently, ready to attack their prey. This menacing notion is supported by the predatory image of all of the men slowly creeping out of their bunks, with their soap bars wrapped in towels, moving towards Pyle, who is sleeping peacefully – like a baby. The light filling the room is a strong blue colour, creating a sense of horror and building a cold, sinister visual aesthetic to accompany the sounding. The soundscape also consistently features a very high-pitched metal sound, which inadvertently 'tings' every few seconds like a pin or bullet shell dropping on the hard floor, accentuating the diegetic silence and building the tension. This accentuated silence is broken as the men suddenly execute an organised strike on Pyle, with four men holding him down with a blanket and Cowboy holding a gag across his mouth. The men form a queue and run past his bunk, beating him one at a time with their makeshift weapons as he screams and cries out in pain. His sounding is infantile as he cries and sobs through the gag. The sounds of his cries mixed in with the bars of soap thudding down on his body pierce through the silence, emphasising his pain. Towards the end of the attack, we see that this episode is also an adverse punishment for Joker when Cowboy urges him to 'do it!' as he hesitates to hit Pyle. At this moment, Pyle's head, which was previously turned up to the ceiling, turns and he looks Joker in the eye as he thrashes him in the stomach several times with his soap – traditionally symbolising a maternal tool for cleaning an infant, soap is here used as a form of corporal punishment against his surrogate child. Unlike the other recruits, Joker hits Pyle six times – the other men hit him only once – his angry face expressing his frustration that despite his attempts to help Pyle, he is still not becoming a man or a Marine, and in doing so, is letting down the male group. As the attack plays out, the sinister breathing sounds continue to underscore the action and remains once the assault is over. The use of the eerie synthesised music and threatening breathing sounds is a jarring experience for the viewer, who has thus far identified and empathised with Joker's aiding of Pyle's development as a Marine. Here it is as if we are punished aurally for the pleasure we have found in this relationship. The non-diegetic sounds are now partially drowned out by Private Pyle crying out loud and shouting 'ooww!' at great volume while clutching his painful stomach and sobbing. Following this, we see a close up of Joker's face and the sounds of Pyle's crying is now enhanced with an echo as Joker puts his hands to his ears to block out the nightmarish sound. These actions and sounds symbolise him as a parent detesting to witness their child in pain, even whilst perhaps also acknowledging that their suffering is for their own good. Indeed, the result of this organised, internal attack is that Private Pyle then successfully completes his training, becoming 'a man', albeit a clearly mentally disturbed one, as demonstrated in the suicide scene, which I will now discuss.

The same non-diegetic underscoring is used in the scene where Pyle kills Hartman and then himself. Preceding this scene, Joker tells us through non-diegetic voice-over, 'the Drill Instructors are proud to see that we are growing beyond their control, the Marine Corps does not want robots, the Marine Corps wants killers'. This statement, of course, is entrenched with irony when applied to the final actions of Private Pyle. On the last night of training, when we hear the repetition of the non-diegetic 'breathing' music used in the soap attack scene, it immediately forewarns us that something sinister is about to happen, and that whatever is to happen is semantically and emotionally linked to the soap attack. In this scene, all of the men are in bed asleep, except Joker who is on duty, and is surprised to find Pyle in the bathroom with his rifle. Upon discovering him, a melody of non-diegetic synthesised notes is now incorporated into the soundscape. The notes are low-pitched and sound mournful, building a sense of sadness. The previously heard high-pitched metal sound is now played every few seconds, along with the low-pitched, slow paced 'breathing' sounds. This non-diegetic sounding creates a sense of foreboding which is heightened when Pyle becomes aware of Joker's presence and says 'Hi, Joker' in a deep, menacing, drawn out tone, vastly different from his higher pitched and more childish voice heard earlier in the film. He now begins to breathe deeply in time with the soundtrack, aligning his voicing with the menacing ambience created by the non-diegetic underscoring. The sense of diegetic silence is enhanced by the loud, echoed clicking sound of Pyle loading bullets into his rifle, before he gets to his feet to parody the rifle drills Joker taught him by spinning the rifle around before placing it on his shoulder. He starts fiercely reciting the previously heard Marine mantra at full volume: 'This is my rifle! There are many like it but this one is mine. . . !'

At this point, Hartman suddenly enters the bathroom and begins yelling at the two men. The sinister 'breathing' music meanwhile continues steadily and seems to symbolise Pyle's steady determination to be the predator in this scenario. Hartman's angry eruption at Pyle's audacity to confront him with a loaded weapon reinforces that he has but one mode in dealing with such situations – to shout insults: 'What is your major malfunction numbnuts? Did mummy and daddy not show you enough attention when you were a child?' At this reference to parental affection – which Pyle was receiving from Joker until the Marines put a stop to it (and Pyle might truly have not received enough affection from his parents) – Pyle now uses his weapon and blasts Hartman in the chest. The drill sergeant falls in slow motion to the sound of his own reverberating cry of pain, which is distorted and emphasised through echo. As he slowly falls, his loud, deep, echoed cry sounds the defeat of a mythic monster, incongruously romanticising the scene but also keeping the brutality of the act and what brought to it in the foreground; such sounding, however, evokes no sympathy for the killed. As Pyle now turns to face Joker, with loaded rifle still in hand, we are reminded of the soft approach used by Joker as he gently says, 'easy Leonard, go easy man . . .' a reminder that Pyle, as a Marine, is now a man, not a boy. Joker's approach seems to be successful and is indicated acoustically when Pyle slumps down on the toilet and the soundtrack too seems to 'slump' but now incorporates louder, major notes into the synthesised score, building a sense of sympathy and sorrow for Private Pyle. Yet the remaining presence of minor notes produces a musical dissonance and therefore an ambiguous sonic moment as we attempt to anticipate what will happen next. The music then suddenly builds to a loud crescendo as Pyle, without warning, swiftly turns the rifle around and shoots himself in the mouth. The loud music, the bang of the rifle and Joker yelling 'no!' combine to create a climactic audible moment, which is met visually with the image of Private Pyle sprawled on the toilet, surrounded by blood and bits of his brain and skull, his facial expression denoting pain and suffering. High-pitched, non-diegetic synthesised strings remain as Joker looks at the two dead bodies. We are not privy to a view of Hartman, just Joker's point-of-view of Pyle, thus the sympathetic, poignant music is reserved entirely for him and for Joker's sorrow at the loss of his surrogate child.

In the Vietnam-based part of the film, the atmosphere changes from a strict military regime to the men apparently at war, yet largely appearing bored and restless. This section of the film is paradoxically far more light-hearted as we see the Marines in Vietnam with not much to do except make jokes and tease one another. This joviality is emphasised by the use of non-diegetic upbeat, popular music, symbolising the youth of the soldiers and also maintaining a good-humoured atmosphere even in brief moments of battle or where we witness the death of Vietnamese people. It is not until the end of the film, when men from Cowboy's platoon begin to lose their lives that the atmosphere changes. It is in this section that we see the Marines and their masculinity tested and when it becomes clear that Sergeant Hartman's training might not have prepared them for the inhumanity of war.

During this episode, Cowboy suddenly finds himself squad leader after their previous leader is blown up by a landmine. The role of squad leader – a much-coveted position from the Marines' training days – now becomes a fearful station of pressure and responsibility, a real test of manhood that could result in death. The lack of surprise or any slight emotional reaction from the Sergeant on the radio in response to the death of the previous leader is disturbing as we simply hear 'okay, you're senior NCO Cowboy, you're in charge'. Cowboy is clearly scared and nervous, yet Joker's reassuring words 'I'll follow you anywhere, scumbag' is a reminder of the bond they share from training and the ethos drilled into them by Hartman: 'the Marines are a brotherhood, every Marine is your brother'.

With Cowboy in command, the troop continues on their journey. Silence and intermittent ambient sound heightens the tension and builds a sense of fear. Every ambient sound in their environment is noticeable, so that when we see Cowboy walking through the street of derelict buildings, we also hear his feet clinking through layers of rubble. We can hear fire crackling and the sounds of smoke billowing from behind him – a low, bass-like, breathy sound, the type of sound which has previously signalled death in the soundscape. Likewise, every click of every gun and every soldier's smallest movement is heightened on the soundtrack. Accentuated silence, we have seen, is a quintessential part of the sound design of *Full Metal Jacket*. Christine Lee Gengaro has observed that Kubrick's strategic use of silence in *2001: A Space Odyssey* (1968) allowed audience members to make up their own minds about the emotional content of scenes. Highlighting the affective function of music, she notes that 'we, the audience don't have music to help us decide how to feel'.[15] The same could be said for these scenes in *Full Metal Jacket*, where we are left to gauge our own feelings about watching the young Marines engaging in warfare. The look of fear on the men's faces is instead where we can take our cue about the emotional impact of these silent scenes. Yet, perhaps there is a further, symbolic function of this strategic approach to sound design: the diegetic silence not only emphasises every move made by every soldier, but highlights the enforced vocal silence of each character, since speaking aloud could lead to being killed by the enemy. The enforced silence here could furthermore symbolise the silencing of a generation of young people, who felt their voices were unheard when protesting about America's involvement in the Vietnam War, or the cultural 'silence' regarding the conflict more generally throughout the 1970s and 1980s.

The city in which the Marines now find themselves is a still, quiet location, almost deathly silent, and every noise they make can be heard. This heightened sounding underscores the sheer level of destruction caused in Vietnam's cities since we hear the Marines walking through ruined buildings that continue to crackle and burn. The tension gradually rises as the sounding suggests that anything could be waiting in the quiet stillness, waiting to pounce. This effect is emphasised by point-of-view camera shots that pan alongside the soldiers from within the buildings, suggesting that they are being watched. In the distance, ambient sounds of gunfire can be continually heard, emphasising that a full-scale battle is taking place around them.

When Eight Ball (Dorian Harewood) enters the block of buildings, the sounds of his movements are equally heightened on the soundtrack, at which point we find out – via a point-of-view shot – that there is an enemy in the midst, waiting to pounce. As we see Eight Ball from the sniper's position, a great distance away, the camera pans up and a gun slowly appears on the left side of the screen. Every slight hand movement is heard as the sniper grips the gun and takes aim. As Eight Ball raises his hand to signal to the other men that the area is safe, the sniper unexpectedly shoots him in the leg. He cries out in pain and falls to the ground in slow motion, blood spurting from his wound. Immediately the Marines respond with a barrage of loud, heavy gunfire. The loud, abrasive sound fills the previous silence like a communal protest from the men as one of their brethren is wounded. A close up of Animal Mother's (Adam Baldwin) angry face, with gritted teeth, swearing as he shoots, creates a sense that all the men have been hypothetically hit by the sniper. Their collective anger is represented through loud, raucous gunfire, reaching its crescendo as three loud bazooka rockets hit the buildings in front of them. Amid this reaction to the shooting of Eight Ball, Cowboy calls them to cease fire and questions if anyone saw a sniper. Their negative replies confirms that this collective firing was a knee jerk reaction, a venting of anger against the sniper, rather than tactical firing, aimed at bringing the sniper down. When the sniper shoots Eight Ball again, he cries out loudly in pain and the scene replicates that of Hartman's killing: the echoed sound, coupled with slow-motion camera movement, imparts a mythic quality to the act of killing. This shot also emphasises the skill of the shooter, who appears to be able to shoot Eight Ball in places on his body that will not kill him, at this point serving to merely anger the Marines more than anything else. Again, the Marines respond with heavy firing, simultaneously yelling in disdain. As Doc Jay (John Stafford) enters the fray to rescue Eight Ball, he meets the same fate and again the men respond with heavy fire. When Cowboy is then hit, three of the men – including Joker – comfort him while Animal Mother and another Marine again vent their anger by shooting in futility at the sniper, as if unable to face up to the loss of Cowboy in any other way. Gilbert Adair compares the visual aesthetics of these shootings to the shootings in Sam Peckinpah's *The Wild Bunch* (1969), which 'pioneered the notion of romanticizing or sentimentalizing the bloodier forms of carnage through a self-consciously "sublime" deployment of slow-motion; and recurrent images . . . of blood spouting from a rash of freshly drilled bodily orifices'.[16] The shooting of Cowboy is again indicated by a point-of-view shot that zooms to focus on him as he speaks on the radio. The shot that hits him echoes and therefore seems to ring out about five or six times as he crashes to the ground in slow motion, before two of the Marines fill the air with the sound of rifle fire and the other four men carry Cowboy out of harm's way. The visuals here arguably romanticise this carnage. But the heightened, echoed sounds of the men in pain and finally the sounds of Cowboy choking on his own blood also emphasise the horrific reality of the Vietnam War and the fear experienced by the men when faced with death, while at the same time making this naturalistic representation functional on a mythic scale: this rampage is both site/time specific and universal.

As the squad enters the building in which they know the sniper is hidden, non-diegetic music is suddenly introduced on the soundtrack. Unlike all other scenes in the Vietnam section of the film, which were underscored with pre-existing pop records, this non-diegetic music was created for this particular scene (and was composed by Stanley Kubrick's daughter).[17] It is low-pitched and sounds like it was played on a wind instrument, producing an eerie, squeaky whistling noise. The music also features soft, deep, rhythmic drumming. The lengthy, low-pitched notes are drawn out while the percussion remains soft but constant, like a heartbeat. The Eastern and almost tribal sound of this music emphasises that the men are entering the lair of the Vietnamese enemy – the closest we have seen our protagonists to encountering actual warfare. As this music plays, the camera tracks alongside the men, passing behind pillars, signifying that a predator is lurking and that they could be being watched. Amid this music, we also hear the staccato high-pitched metal sound used in the Private Pyle scenes from the first part of the film – an aural reminder of previous harrowing experiences faced by Private Joker that ended in death. Animal noises that could be exotic birds or insects are then introduced, suggesting the type of sounds one might expect to hear in the jungle, not in a Vietnamese town, highlighting that the men are on unknown, foreign terrain. Again, the ambient sounds are heightened – fire crackling, footsteps, the creaking of weaponry as the men move around – emphasising the diegetic silence. The music stays at a constant, quick tempo, accentuating that the men are working quickly – perhaps on limited time – and also highlighting the sense of a racing heartbeat within the sound mix. Moving beyond the ways in which these sounds build fear and tension about an unknown foreign terrain, this music is later revealed to be linked to the female sniper, since it is only heard during her presence within the diegesis. Thus the soundtrack here seems to exoticise her, accentuating her 'otherness' since she is not only

Vietnamese, but also female. The inclusion of the high-pitched musical tones associated with Pyle here, further stresses not only her femaleness and otherness, but also the threat she poses to the male group hero.

It is Joker who discovers the sniper, at which point the acoustics abruptly change. He takes aim and attempts to shoot, but his gun jams; his fumbling alerting the sniper to his presence. As she suddenly turns around, the shot plays out in slow motion: braided pigtails can be seen skimming gently through the air showing that this is not just a female, it is a young girl. The sniper is roughly the same age as the two prostitutes seen earlier in the film, further linking to the exoticisation of young, Vietnamese women by American troops. Now a high-pitched alarm sounding tone is heard, perhaps signalling Joker's, and the audiences' alarm that the sniper is female and that he is now unarmed against her. As this alarm sound continues, the sound of her gun quickly firing echoes through the soundtrack along with a fast-paced drum that sounds like a heartbeat. The sniper moves towards Joker, continually firing loud shots as he panics and his gun slips through his fingers and drops to the floor. Reaching for his handgun, he hides behind a thin pillar as the sniper shoots at him. However, we now hear the loud, rattling sound of machine-gun fire and the sniper is shot down by Rafter Man (Kevyn Major Howard), whilst Joker quakes with fear. Once he has shot the sniper, Rafter Man checks the rest of the room to ensure there are no more soldiers, confirming that Cowboy's assertion of suspected 'strong enemy forces' was incorrect since they amounted to being just one (albeit very skilful) sniper. The tribal-style music continues whilst he is checking, suggesting that further foreign enemy presence is a possibility. Once he confirms that there is only one sniper, this music stops, indicating that the threat of foreign enemies has passed. All that can be heard now are the diegetic sounds of fire crackling and burning and the heavy breathing of the sniper, as she teeters on the brink of death while the men move to stand over her. Her heavy breathing is reminiscent of the breathy soundtrack used twice in the training section of the film and is linked to Joker's hesitation as he morally struggles over his decision to shoot her. The same synthesised music from these previous scenes is now incorporated into the soundscape and combined with the diegetic sound of the sniper desperately pleading, 'shoot me' again and again. The volume of the music gradually builds as we see a close up of Joker's face and hear the sniper's repeated pleas. We hear a gunshot and the sniper's voice is silenced, the camera remains on Joker's face as the Marines now utter sounds of admiration that Joker has shot the girl, indicating that they now consider him to be a real man. The voices echo as the camera remains on Joker's expressionless face while he looks at the dead girl. His blank facial expression suggests that, in fact, he has been paradoxically de-masculinised by this event and that far from being a 'heroic' act, this was more of a mercy killing, to relieve the girl of her painful suffering.

Thus we get the sense that his masculinity is no more reinforced now than it was before he killed the sniper, leaving the audience to question the strive for 'manhood' that is explored throughout the narrative.

The revelation that the sniper is female is, of course, a shock to the Marines and also to the audience, based on the assumption that during the 1960s and 1970s, engagement in warfare was solely a male prerogative. Yet here we see a young girl, skilled at shooting, managing to accurately target and kill soldiers from great distances, a feat we never really witness from any male character in the film, except for Private Pyle in the training sequence. Here we could draw an aural similarity between Pyle and the young Vietnamese soldier, who each present a threat to the masculine world and 'brotherhood' of the Marine Corps as represented in *Full Metal Jacket*. Both characters, when displaying their skills with a weapon, take a quiet, considered approach to warfare that is the complete opposite to the loud, raucous chorus of (generally untargeted) gunfire that we see and hear from the Marines.

The closing scene where the Marines sing the theme tune to *The Mickey Mouse Club* television show is a rather unexpected ending. The troops return to base loudly singing in unison, while Joker's non-diegetic voice-over closes the film. The first lyrics sung are 'we play fair and we work hard and we're in harmony' which seems to summarise the approach of the collective male in the war sequence. As the song continues, the camera tracks alongside Joker, Rafter Man and Animal Mother. Their faces are expressionless and as they sing and march with their rifles in hand, this moment is reminiscent of the 'this is my rifle, this is my gun . . .' chanting that the men engaged in with Sergeant Hartman in the first half of the film. Nonetheless, the singing of *The Mickey Mouse Club* theme tune is nostalgic and linked to childhood, imbuing this final scene of the film with a sense of regression, or a painful reminder of innocence and childhood through song. Having experienced death, fear and bloodshed, these soldiers do not appear as men, but as boys. Similar to the way in which non-diegetic popular music is used throughout the second part of the film, this pop culture reference reminds us of the youth of many of the soldiers involved in the war. Through having the soldiers collectively sing this well-known song from a 1950s television programme, this message is foregrounded and notions of masculinity and gender expectations that have arisen throughout the film are summarily revisited.

Collective singing is a key sound motif in Michael Cimino's 1978 Vietnam War film *The Deer Hunter*. Like in *Full Metal Jacket*, the ideological figuration of masculinity is overtly questioned in this film when the male characters are presented with the harsh and terrifying experience of war. Despite being released nine years before *Full Metal Jacket*, *The Deer Hunter* and its treatment of gender are best explored after the former film because the amount of the conflict featured in Michael Cimino's film is actually minimal; rather, the film focuses on the wider effects of war on men and their communities. This more complex image of conflict yields an even more multifaceted soundscape.

The film begins in Clairton, Pennsylvania, where a group of young male friends finish their night shift at a steel mill. Three of them – Michael (Robert De Niro), Nick (Christopher Walken) and Steven (John Savage) – are leaving for Vietnam the following day, after Steven's wedding that evening. Michael, Nick and three friends go deer hunting after the wedding and Michael kills a deer in one shot. Next we see the three men under attack in Vietnam and then captured by Vietcong soldiers who force them to play Russian roulette. Michael engineers their escape but they are split up when being rescued. Unable to find Nick, Michael returns home and begins a relationship with Nick's girlfriend, Linda (Meryl Streep), but later discovers that Nick is regularly seen at a gambling house in Saigon and returns to Vietnam to bring him home. Seemingly not recognising Michael at first, Nick enters into a game of Russian roulette with him at the gambling house. Pressing the gun against his head, Michael says 'I love you' and shoots, surviving this round. Nick utters the words 'one shot' before pressing the gun against his own head and firing a bullet into his brain, killing him instantly. The film finishes with Nick's funeral and his group of friends singing 'God Bless America' at their local bar.

This film is particularly interesting in terms of representation of masculinity because it invests much of its diegetic time in establishing the strong bonds of friendship between the male characters, and in particular between Mike and Nick. From the outset, the men are depicted as a strong male group, but a group wholly different to the men featured in *Full Metal Jacket*, whose relationships are forged when joining the military. These come across as lifelong friendships, established without ideological imposition or ordering, and music, dialogue and sound effects are key in establishing this idea of friendship and maintaining it throughout the film. While it could be said that in *Full Metal Jacket* ideology (and an ideology of conflict) establishes relationships among men as a kind of enforced camaraderie, here the comparable ideology destroys them.

One of the distinct and perhaps disconcerting narrative features of *The Deer Hunter* is the abrupt shifts in location throughout the film. The narrative begins in Clairton where the main characters are introduced as part of a close-knit Russian-American community. This section of the film lasts for just over an hour before abruptly switching to scenes of warfare in Vietnam and then back to Clairton after about forty minutes. Towards the end of the film the location changes once again to Vietnam, before the film's culmination in Clairton. Robin Wood highlights that the thematic imagery used in these vastly different sections ties the alternate locations together. Key images such as helicopter blades rotating and blasts of fire are repeated in each section, as is the notion of killing a deer in 'one shot'; the last is then reconfigured in the

Russian roulette scenes that continue to permeate the film henceforth and lead to Nick's suicide.[18] These, however, are also sequences that foreground sounds that are abrasive, violent and mechanical. It is in this way, too, that the film's soundscape becomes of equal importance in creating a sense of continuity throughout the somewhat broken narrative.

As hinted above, the key continuity upon which the diegesis of *The Deer Hunter* is premised is that of friendship and the apparently lasting – if ultimately most painfully tested – ties between the characters. Popular music, exemplified in the 1967 Frankie Valli hit record 'Can't Take My Eyes Off You', is introduced early in the film. Utilised to demonstrate the bond between the men in the initial narrative stages, the song is re-introduced later in the film as an acoustic reminder of this bond. The film also noticeably makes use of classical guitar music, male choral singing, ambient sound and sound effects; all of these have been carefully brought together and reconstructed to create a diverse and interesting film soundscape. From the perspective of gender, from the film's outset, the combination of music, voice and sound effects create a sense of an overtly male-dominated, close-knit community from where our three protagonists hail. On occasion, this closeness acoustically transforms into its extreme, a feeling of claustrophobia, as sounds are frequently layered over one another, making it difficult to hear dialogue. In this way, many parts of the film are seemingly naturalistic and build a sense of the male group and bonds of masculinity: strong but also oppressive. Furthermore, these combined sounds are often incredibly loud, presenting an aural world of the male characters that verges on rowdiness. Enveloped in the deafening sounds of the steelwork factory, other male voices and overpowering diegetic music, the men seem to be aurally entombed in a world that consists of constant noise.

This sound representation is interesting when compared with the other films focusing on masculinity discussed in this book, which frequently present men as either silent, or part of a silent world. As discussed in Chapter 3, Wyatt and Billy barely talk to one another throughout *Easy Rider* and depictions of chattiness or the art of conversation seem to have traditionally been reserved for female characters in classical Hollywood cinema – the women of screwball comedy being a notable example. Yet, in *The Deer Hunter*, we see male characters introduced as chatty and lively and furthermore as only interested in talking to other men, while the world of women in this film is represented as lonely and silent. Let me demonstrate this point with a detailed discussion of the opening scene of the film.

The film's sound life begins with gentle, classical guitar music playing over the opening credits featuring a black background and white lettering.[19] It is a high-pitched, slow-paced tune with a steady rhythm that conveys a sense of calm to the opening of the film. This is an unexpected start to a so-called war film since it creates a mood of romance or melodrama and, in traditional mainstream Hollywood filmmaking, connotes femininity. This musical underscoring is perhaps our first hint that this is not to be a typical war film (the scenes of war itself make up approximately 40 minutes of the 182-minute film) and points to the fact that, rather than focusing on the battleground, the narrative of this film will instead explore relationships and the potential effects of war on communities.

As the title sequence fades to black, the music fades into silence. When the screen fades up, we see the first shot of Clairton – the film's main setting – is grey, dreary and foggy. The loud diegetic sounds of roaring machinery replace the gentle, non-diegetic music from the title sequence and are more in line with what we expect to hear from the opening scene of a war film. Yet as a truck rumbles across the screen and the camera zooms in on the large steelworks we can soon see that we are not in a war zone, but in the small, industrial town of Clairton. The scene changes to take us inside the steelworks, where flames rage and the sounds of the machinery hammering and whirring consume the soundscape. We see several men in protective clothing undertaking various tasks involving molten metal. They attempt to shout over this abrasive, loud noise but are forced to signal to each other in order to get their message across. The visual and aural information combined tells us that this is a harsh, unforgiving domain of sweaty, dirty, manual labour and furthermore establishes this type of work and this workplace as exclusively male. From the film's outset we are drawn into a world of men, male experience and rather extreme depictions of masculinity.

Outside the factory, the camera now begins a slow pan down the side of a huge chimney, briefly capturing a glimpse of blue sky in the otherwise grim landscape. A whistle or alarm sounds in the diegesis, signalling the end of the working shift, but is combined with a non-diegetic orchestral string sound in a minor key. This strategy is deployed throughout the film and was deliberate on the part of director Michael Cimino, who often instructed the film's composer, Stanley Myers to compose the non-diegetic score in the same key as sounds heard in the diegesis. This was undertaken accordingly to create a jarring, desolate experience[20] and indeed, the viewer is not quite sure if this sound is coming from within the world of the film, or is an emotional signifier solely for us, created by non-diegetic underscoring. The minor key of this orchestral sound creates a feeling of sadness and ambivalence but we are unsure if the men in the film can hear it or are even aware of it, creating sympathy for these characters who are oblivious to the tragic turn the narrative will take. Such sounding in these moments seems to break down the barrier between us and the world of the film, at once merging the two worlds and allowing meaning to flow between the two. However, these breakdowns are frequently re-established as we now hear a third layer of indistinguishable sounds of the men talking and laughing, and this is met visually with the closing down of heavy lift doors as if to now visually and aurally distance us from the diegesis once again. The film cuts to the locker room where our vision is further obscured by locker doors and the backs of other men and the sound is muddied by the hissing of showers and several men talking at once, emphasising the insularity of this diegetic space.

The camera settles on Michael and Nick making their way through the crowded, noisy room. As they do, their fellow workers shake their hands, pat them on the back and hug them. The men talk simultaneously and loudly over one other, making it hard to distinguish what is being said, but wholly establishing this as a world of male banter, camaraderie but also of genuine fondness for one another. The fact that we cannot hear much of what is said creates a sense that their world is cliquish and we, the viewer, are not a part of it. All in all, this introduction establishes a world of male banter and physical overfamiliarity as the men frequently touch one another, while shouting greetings or goodbyes. Two naked men in the showers shake Michael's hand as he passes, with a sense of normality, establishing a sense of close physical bonds that exist between the men in this film.

As Michael, Nick and their three friends, Steve, Axel (Chuck Aspegren) and Stan (John Cazale), leave work, they playfully hit one another, wrap their arms around one another and jibe one another, enhancing the close physical bonds between the men established in the scenes inside the steelworks. The camera maintains its distance in these scenes but the dialogue is heightened on the soundtrack, giving the audience audible access to the male group but not physical proximity, re-affirming the insular world of these men. This male camaraderie rather obviously carries notions of homoeroticism (an aspect of the film that is highly discussed by other scholars)[21] but as the men now joke about Steve's impending wedding night, this extends to an imagined group sex scenario with Stan saying if he needs any help to call on him. Nick then comforts apprehensive Steve by gently saying 'we'll be right there, we'll be with you, all of us'. The fact that Steve would clearly rather be hunting with his male friends than spending the evening with his new wife reinforces a binary opposition between the male and female world in this film. Throughout this scene we continue to hear the ambient sounds of other men chatting and laughing around them and horns sounding at the steelworks. Thus the sound motifs linked to representations of masculinity in this film appear to be ambient male voices, and the sounds of machinery or industry. In short, these men are constantly surrounded by noise of some sort or another and are frequently in conversation with each other, even if the words are somewhat semantically meaningless, consisting of banter and jokes.

In contrast, the world of women in the film is strangely silent. Angela the bride-to-be is depicted alone and worried in her wedding dress with no one to talk to except herself in the mirror. As she paces the floor of her bedroom, we hear the rustling of her wedding dress and her whispered words as she repeats 'I do' under her breath, signifying her nerves about her impending marriage. At the end of this short sequence she rests her hands on her stomach and turns to view her side profile. This silent action suggests that this marriage is due to her being pregnant rather than her love for Steve or a desire to be married. Meanwhile, the next scene cuts to Steve's mother frantically appealing to the priest in the church for an explanation as to why her son is marrying this girl (who is 'not so thin'). Despite her anguished pleas, she is met with silence from him while he busies himself in the church, preparing for the wedding. This seems to further emphasise the binary opposition between male and female characters in the film and the lack of communication between them. In a following scene, Linda is introduced to us alone and frantic in a kitchen, preparing a meal for her violent, drunken father. This further delineates women from men in the film as they are frequently restricted to the domestic realm of the kitchen and is emphasised visually by the four women carrying a huge, four-tiered wedding cake through the streets of the small town.

Returning to the men, the sounds of camaraderie in their world get louder as we now see them at the bar, where the loud banter continues and we see a further use of sound to demonstrate the physical and emotional bonds between them – music and collective singing. As the men play a game of pool, we hear the introduction to 'Can't Take My Eyes Off You' playing loudly in the bar. The music is more than just background music, at once taking over the diegetic world of the film. Each male character responds to it by either singing along or, in the case of Nick, performing a small shimmying dance move with his pool cue. Subversive male desire is indicated through each man joining in at various points and then having the camera cutting to another member of the group. For example, Stan stands up out of his seat to loudly sing 'I wanna hold you so much!' and an eye-line match in the following cut suggests this is directed at Mike. Mike is meanwhile taking a pool shot, and after he successfully pots a ball he extends his arm, momentarily suggesting he is inviting Nick to dance, yet Nick merely slams some money in his hand, having lost a bet. The words of love and desire in the song become ironic when the camera fixes on Steve, who looks nervous and upset. He says to Stan, 'this is it . . . this is really it . . . here I go!' conveying his ambivalent feelings about his impending marriage to Angela where the words in the song should perhaps be striking a chord with how he should feel about his wife-to-be. Instead this sequence conveys the love between the men and, at times, conveys their homoerotic tendencies. The high volume allows most of the words and phrases in the song to be clear to the film audience and any dialogue uttered by the men is difficult to hear, thus we take our sematic cue from the song lyrics. As the song builds, the words 'if you feel like I feel, let me know that it's real' ring through the diegesis and Nick's dancing becomes more animated. He starts to sing 'bah dah, bah dah' in readiness for the chorus, as does Stan and on the final loud brass note, even Mike (who has thus far not participated) gives in and loudly sings 'baaah!' while stomping his pool cue on the floor. This climactic moment builds to all of the men singing together 'I love you baby! And if it's quite alright, I need you baby . . .' with gusto and spirit that reinforces the warmth and friendship between them. The camera shot changes to one that frames Nick, Stan, Steve, Axel and the bar-owner John (George Dzundza) singing and drinking, they throw their arms around one another, clearly enjoying this celebratory moment and John even kisses Steve roughly on the cheek. At this moment, Steve's mother bursts into the bar and drags Steve out, causing great amusement for the men and strengthening the binary opposition between the world of men and women in the film. Ian Inglis argues that the song functions as 'a vehicle through which group cohesion can be ritually maintained in the face of potential and serious invasions – their departure from the factory, their imminent transfer to Vietnam, the marriage of one of the group, the hostility of Steven's mother'[22] – and he points out other moments in the film in which the male group participate in communal singing, such as when they are in Mike's car on the way to the hunt, and when they return with the killed deer. This sense of ritual is key to the film, but in considering how these sounds relate to representations of masculinity I believe these moments are important in establishing the close bonds between the male characters and affirming the level of comfort and security they feel when around one another, and as part of a wider community.

The insular world of these men is reinforced also at the wedding, where throughout the ceremony the camera focuses on Michael, Stan and Axel nudging one another and giggling while religious choral music is heard around them. The wedding reception is a loud and raucous affair, featuring lots of Russian dancing and singing. Men dance with women and men alike, suggesting sexual subversion or less concern with the boundaries of gender and sexuality, or simply is an indication of Russian culture when men would traditionally dance together. Steven's dancing here is particularly lively and memorable, as he performs the famous crouching and leg kicking moves of the Cossack Hopak dance, a Ukranian folk dance where the male moves often verge on acrobatics. This lively scene, to audiences who know the film, is tinged with sadness and foreboding when one considers the fact that Steven finishes the film as a triple amputee in a wheelchair, a shadow of his former self, estranged from his wife and seemingly stripped of his masculinity. The wedding reception room features a large, prominent banner that reads 'Good Luck Michael, Nick, Steven' rather than one about the newlyweds and when the wedding singer makes his only announcement throughout the evening it is about the three men and their impending departure to Vietnam, rather than Steven and Angela; he then promptly breaks into a reprise of 'Can't Take My

Eyes Off You'. When the song begins it is largely ignored by the men at first, but as it continues it seems they cannot resist joining in and dancing to the song that brought them so much joy in the earlier bar scene. While the reprise of this song does not have the impact it has in the bar scene, its purpose seems to be to remind us of that moment and the song represents the bonds of male friendship, reinforced by them dancing together to it here.

When (after roughly an hour of screen time) the film does cut to scenes of war in Vietnam it is rather a shock to the viewer. The expected tropes of war films leads us to imagine scenes involving the men meeting the next day, travelling together, meeting their new comrades and easing us gently into battle. There are no such opportunities with this film, which cuts from a gentle scene of the men listening to John softly playing Chopin on the piano in the bar to a shot of Mike, covered in blood and laying on the ground while explosions and helicopter blades ring out around him. This harsh cut emphasises the way that men were thrown into war zones with which they were unfamiliar and unprepared for, and the diegetic sound here increases the sensation of shock and disorientation. The sudden introduction of the harsh, diegetic sounds of war emphasises that Mike has been extracted from the warm, protective sphere of Clairton, with the sounds of the steelworks, collective singing and male banter. This sense of shock is about to get worse in the following scenes when Steven, Nick and Mike are captured and imprisoned by members of the Vietcong army.

Here we see and hear a distinct change in the way that the men communicate as they are imprisoned below the hut where other prisoners are being forced to play Russian roulette. Mike assumes the role of protector as he gently comforts Steven, who finds this situation unbearable. Every time a gun is loudly fired, Steven cries hysterically and physically gags, breaking down in tears, shaking and barely able to speak. Mike holds him and stands close to him, he speaks to Steven in quiet whispers, consoling him, telling him to 'shake it out' and think of home, reinforcing the sense of comfort and security of Clairton. As we see the two men now, they are totally different from the carefree individuals we met at the start of the film and the banter that once existed between them has given way to stammering and tears. Whereas the diegesis in the first part of the film features the reassuring sounds of male laughter and singing, we now hear loud gunfire, the sound of blood trickling through the floorboards and the Vietcong captors shouting as they demand for the next prisoners to be brought up.

The aural figuration of the Vietcong captors emphasises their 'otherness', much like the sniper in *Full Metal Jacket*. When the men speak, they do so in a loud and curt manner, at once onomatopoeic, but no attempt is made for a Western audience to understand their words as no subtitles are provided. The aural coding and abrupt manner is clear, these Eastern 'others' are meant to be read by the audience as being malevolent and bloodthirsty. When Steve is forced to play Russian roulette, he breaks down in tears after aiming the gun at himself and narrowly grazing his head with a bullet when he does finally shoot. His captors laugh loudly at his cowardice, making mere sport and entertainment from the mortality of young men and increasing our view of them as savages. The noise from the Vietcong men increases when Mike and Nick enter a game and up the odds of death by insisting they put three bullets in the gun. The tension is increased as the Vietnamese men constantly shout at Nick and Mike, jabbing them with their guns prompting them to scream, cry out and swear in anger. These scenes are excruciating to watch, especially when compared to the first part of the film that was full of careless frivolity. As the film continues, our two protagonists Mike and Nick escape, but are drawn apart, only to be reunited in a tragic ending that leads to Nick's death.

The final scene of the film, following Nick's funeral, is in complete aural contrast with the film's opening section, which is based in Clairton. Instead of loud, raucous talking and laughing as heard previously in John's bar, the characters silently shuffle around each other, re-arranging chairs and tables and the whirring sound of Steven's wheelchair can be heard dimly in the silence, reminding us that Nick was not the only victim of war in this narrative. The characters exchange nervous glances and are clearly not sure what to say, as if the death of Nick has drained the life from the rest of the male group. The female characters are likewise awkward and silent: Linda attempts to break the uneasy silence by offering to help John with the breakfast, which is a confused medley of coffee, beer and eggs. Angela attempts to make conversation: 'it's been such a grey day . . .' but the other characters look at her almost with contempt, suggesting that fruitless discussion of the weather is wholly inappropriate on this sad occasion. Meanwhile in the kitchen, while preparing the eggs, John suddenly breaks down in tears, seeming to externally convey the emotion the rest of the group is feeling, yet are unable to express in front of one another. Alone cooking the eggs, tears run down his cheeks and he shakes while sobbing into a handkerchief. While cooking, John then begins to hum and sing a familiar melody. The camera cuts to a shot of Steven and a slight smile appears on his face, the following shots of Linda and Mike reveal the same and the group seem to relax upon hearing the sound of John singing. His deep, baritone voice seems to represent a sense of 'normality' as expressed earlier in the film via communal singing and breaks the tension in this fraught scene. As John enters the room with the eggs, Linda begins to hum along with him and then starts singing 'God Bless America' with him. Gradually, the other characters join in and eventually the whole group are singing.

As the friends join in singing one by one, the song rings out in the soundscape, building a sense of irony and confusion, since surely America's involvement in the Vietnam conflict has caused the death of their friend. Yet as Robin Wood has observed about this unusual moment, 'the tone of the singing never becomes confident or affirmative'.[23] Rather, the tone is submissive, resigned and sounds of defeat. To me, this collective singing can be semantically linked to the Green Beret's brief comment on Vietnam at Steve and Angela's wedding: when asked about the conflict, his brief response is 'fuck it'. This acute phrase is the closest thing to a political comment on the film's narrative and seems to summarise and express a sense of loss, confusion but also resignation about America's involvement in this war. It also suggests that the reality and terrible consequences of the Vietnam conflict are simply too horrific to attempt to put into words.

By the group engaging in communal singing, it reinforces a sense of friendship and camaraderie as witnessed earlier in the film. Yet there is also a suggestion that life will not be the same for them due to the feeling of detachment in this performance, when compared with the jovial singing heard elsewhere in the film. The fact that two women are now a part of this chorus is significant and could suggest that the previously silent world of women in this film has seeped into the world of men. Conversely, we could question if the loss of Nick has led the men in this narrative into listening and thinking, rather than frequently talking over one another, as heard in the early parts of the film. This might suggest a heightened socio-political awareness as the group have faced the realities of war, either personally like Mike and Steven, or by feeling the wider impact of war on men and their communities, like the rest of the group. Thus it seems the death of their friend has broken the characters out of their somewhat parochial, small-town 'bubble' that previously immersed them in noise and consequently a state of ignorance. Yet this heightened political awareness and perhaps more mature outlook on life is arguably futile since it is also clear that these characters are without agency or the means to act on this new outlook on life. Their realisation of this lack of agency is underscored at the end of the film via the collective singing of 'God Bless America' and thus might lead us to conclude that this communal singing is their way, like the Green Beret, of saying 'fuck it'.

The fact that both *Full Metal Jacket* and *The Deer Hunter* end with large groups of men singing together is interesting and points to other areas in this book where I discuss the apparent difficulties men experience when articulating their thoughts and feelings. As discussed in Chapter 3, male characters are frequently depicted as either silent or verbally inept so perhaps singing is a compromise between the two. However, in both examples, the songs that are supposed to represent and fortify their bond are either, in the case of *The Deer Hunter*, patriotic, or in *Full Metal Jacket*, linked to childhood or perhaps to capitalism and patriarchy through the song's association with Disney. Their ultimate meaning is overdetermined, though, and their continued presence in the ears of the audience invites both the corroboration of their apparent ideological position and their ironic comment on the films' narratives.

The sound design of *Full Metal Jacket* is diverse, ranging from orchestral military music to synthesised scores and an intense focus on detail to the diegetic sounds of war. The links between the representation of gender and the meticulously designed soundscape of the film are clear when analysed as a whole. The use of strong, ordered military music in the first half of the film is linked to the notion of 'becoming a man' and is reinforced through the complex visual aesthetics featuring the men training and marching. The sounding of the relationship between Joker and Pyle emphasises their subversive bond, mainly through speech and quiet ambience. This obstructs the group goal of being 'men' (and enemies to relational tenderness) and is subsequently represented via the composed synthesised sounds that accompany the Marines' efforts to quell this damaging relationship. The use of pop music records in the second half of the film signals the youth culture to which the young Marines belong, which, in many cases, they would never re-join once the war had ended. This point can also be made about the pop music in *The Deer Hunter*, which also represents the bonds of friendship in the male group. As well as music, the layering of male voices and machinery in the early parts of the film create an acoustic 'bubble' that surrounds the characters, strengthening the sense of an insular existence and gesturing towards their naivety before entering the conflict in Vietnam.

The film's loud soundscape changes when the men enter warfare and ultimately leads to the male characters falling silent, much like the Green Beret at Steve and Angela's wedding, who has no way of articulating his thoughts on Vietnam, other than to say 'fuck it'. The prevailing use of silence in *Full Metal Jacket* and *The Deer Hunter* is important for highlighting the terrors of war and for symbolising a group of men who were in fact 'voiceless' throughout the period of the Vietnam War. In *The Deer Hunter*, silence is a sound trope that is initially reserved for the female characters, for example, Linda, who finds it difficult to express her feelings about traumas in her life such as her alcoholic father or the death of her fiancé Nick. This sound convention is unusual when considering my findings so far in this book, which are that Hollywood movies seem to frequently depict women as chatty and loquacious. A further departure from this representation is the female sniper in *Full Metal Jacket*, who preys on the Marines in silence, and defeats them with her deft shooting skills. Unlike Linda in *The Deer Hunter*, the sniper seems to laugh in the face of gender preconceptions and offers yet another alternative approach to representations of gender and warfare.

NOTES

1. David Savran, *Taking It Like a Man: White Masculinity, Masochism and Contemporary American Culture* (Princeton: Princeton University Press, 1998), 194.
2. Stephen Neale, *Genre and Hollywood* (London: Routledge, 2000), 123.
3. James Lastra, 'Film and the Wagnerian aspiration: Thoughts on sound design and the history of the senses', in Jay Beck and Tony Grajeda (eds), *Lowering the Boom: Critical Studies in Film Sound* (Chicago: University of Illinois Press, 2008), 123.
4. For readings of music and sound in *Apocalypse Now*, see Lawrence Kramer, *Music and Meaning: Toward a Critical History, volume 1* (Berkeley: University of California Press, 2002); Vincent LoBrutto, *Sound-on-Film: Interviews with Creators of Film Sound* (Westport: Greenwood Publishing Group, 1994); for a discussion of silence in the film, see Stan Link, 'Going gently: Contemplating silences and cinematic death', in Nicky Losseff and Jenny Doctor (eds), *Silence, Music, Silent Music* (Aldershot: Ashgate, 2007).
5. Patrick Hagopian, *The Vietnam War in American Memory: Veterans, Memorials, and the Politics of Healing* (Amherst: University of Massachusetts Press, 2011), 68.
6. Michael Klein, 'Historical memory, film, and the Vietnam era', in Linda Dittmar and Gene Michaud (eds), *From Hanoi to Hollywood: The Vietnam War in American Film* (New Brunswick, NJ and London: Rutgers University Press, 2000), 29.
7. Klein, 29.
8. Susan Jeffords, *The Remasculinization of America: Gender and the Vietnam War* (Bloomington: Indiana University Press, 1989), 170.
9. Jeffords, 173.
10. A sheep shearer was in fact used to cut the men's hair in this scene because a human hair trimmer could not cut quickly enough for the pace that Kubrick desired.
11. Randy Rashussen, *Stanley Kubrick: Seven Films Analysed* (Jefferson: McFarland & Co., 2005), 287.
12. Gilbert Adair, *Hollywood's Vietnam: From 'The Green Berets' to 'Full Metal Jacket'* (London: William Heinemann, 1989), 173.
13. Krin Gabbard and Shailja Sharma, 'Stanley Kubrick and the Art Cinema', in Stuart Y. McDougal (ed.), *Stanley Kubrick's 'A Clockwork Orange'* (Cambridge: Cambridge University Press, 2003), 100.
14. Jeffords, 174.
15. Christine Lee Gengaro, *Listening to Stanley Kubrick: The Music in His Films* (Lanham: Rowman and Littlefield, 2012), 99.
16. Adair, 182.
17. Gabbard and Sharma, 100.
18. Robin Wood, *Hollywood From Vietnam to Reagan and Beyond* (New York: Columbia University Press), 247.
19. The theme tune is entitled 'Cavatina' and was composed by Stanley Myers and performed by guitarist John Williams.
20. Charles Schreger, 'Altman, Dolby, and the Second Sound Revolution', in Elisabeth Weis and John Belton (eds), *Film Sound: Theory and Practice* (New York, Columbia University Press, 1985), 351.
21. See Wood, *Hollywood from Vietnam to Reagan*; Ian Inglis, 'Music, masculinity and membership', in Steve Lannin and Matthew Caley (eds), *Pop Fiction: The Song in Cinema* (Bristol: Intellect Books, 2005); Stella Bruzzi, *Men's Cinema: Masculinity and Mise-en-scene in Hollywood* (Edinburgh: Edinburgh University Press, 2013); Christine Gledhill,

'Women reading men', in Pat Kirkham and Janet Thumin (eds), *Me Jane: Masculinity, Movies and Women* (London: Lawrence and Wishart, 1995), 73–93.
22. Inglis, 67
23. Wood, 258.

CHAPTER 5

Subversive Sound: Gender, Technology and the Science Fiction Blockbuster

This chapter considers the representation of gender in the late 1970s and 1980s in the so-called blockbuster era, focusing specifically on the science fiction genre. The aural dimension of these types of films immediately conjures up ideas of space, technology and other worlds and thus potentially appear as acoustically distinct from the experimental or avant-garde nature of New Hollywood or the loud, pervasive sounds of weaponry, shouting and male camaraderie in war films, which, as previously discussed, explored alternative representations of masculinity in mainstream US cinema. Financially, the most successful American films to emerge in the post-New Hollywood era were Hollywood blockbusters. These films, which were popular from the late 1970s onwards, saw a return to classical movie formulas and genres which, according to some scholars, also saw the re-emergence of strong male heroes and passive female characters and thus a noticeable return to binary representations of gender.[1] Scholars such as Benshoff and Griffin consider this was a cultural backlash to the growing independence of women in the 1970s. But the new depictions of gender in films of this period seem also to veer away from simplistic, binary views of gender that characterised the negotiation of rigid heteronormative ideologies in the US cinema of the 1950s. This chapter explores the previously unattended to subtleties of the soundscapes of these films, which has led to discoveries of some subterranean subversions of traditional representations of gender.

Much previous discussion about the representation of men and women in films of this era emphasises the conservative political climate in which such texts emerged. The election of ex-movie star Ronald Reagan as President of the United States in 1980 (and his subsequent re-election in 1984) led to the emergence of an ideology that recalled the sociological structures of the 1950s; a so-called era of patriarchal family values. In his role as president, Reagan frequently capitalised on his Hollywood, tough-talking cowboy persona to maintain his popularity with voters.² Susan Jeffords argues that he constructed himself as a strong, father figure to America,³ believing that this was what the country wanted after a previously liberal government and an apparent loss of family values. Reagan's political standpoint on this matter is arguably present in the most popular films of this era, such as the *Star Wars* and *Indiana Jones* trilogies, which feature a strong, patriarchal worldview dominated by male characters. Later examples, such as *Rambo II* (1985), *Commando* (1985) and *Die Hard* (1988), feature overtly masculine characters single-handedly defeating their respective enemies and invariably saving their weak female counterparts. Conversely, David Gauntlett has pointed out that in many of the big, successful blockbusters of this period, strong female characters were also present, even if they were not at the forefront of the narrative. Indeed, we do not need to search too far in popular film to find such characters: notable examples include Princess Leia (Carrie Fisher) in the *Star Wars* trilogy, Ellen Ripley (Sigourney Weaver) in the *Alien* series, Sarah Connor (Linda Hamilton) in *The Terminator* (1984) and even Karen Allen (Marion Ravenwood) in *Raiders of the Lost Ark* (1981) who, as Gauntlett has observed, is 'not simply a "love interest" for the hero, but is a spunky, assertive and intelligent character in her own right'.⁴

This chapter focuses on two highly successful films from this so-called blockbuster period. Through a brief exploration of the soundscapes of George Lucas's *Star Wars: A New Hope* (1977) and a more in-depth discussion of James Cameron's *Aliens* (1986), I explore alternative representations of male and female characters and their gender (or beyond gender) inscriptions. These films were selected for this discussion since *Star Wars*, as an early blockbuster film, marks the beginning of this highly successful period in film history. Perhaps more importantly, the sound design of the film is a marker of the alternative sounding strategies utilised for constructing the aural universe of the science fiction film; as I will discuss below, *Star Wars* marked a change in the way sound was conceived in the science fiction genre. *Aliens*, released nine years later, represents the generic developments that took place throughout the blockbuster era since the film is often considered to be a generic hybrid of war, action, horror and science fiction. Furthermore, with regards to depictions of gender, the legacy of Princess Leia as a feisty science-fiction female is taken up and continued by the female protagonist Ellen Ripley in *Aliens*. The sound design constructed around her marks general developments in sound technology, as well as presenting new ideas about contemporary representations of gender.

Some critics argue that Hollywood became formulaic and overly commercialised in the 1980s, and many would contend that it remains so. For example, Mark Crispin Miller and Richard Schickel criticise the apparent commercialism of blockbusters, arguing that they 'marked a blurring between the movies and advertising, with the artful complexities of narrative and character development being sacrificed to the selling of tie-in products (Miller) or the refining of "concepts" (Schickel)'.[5] Yet the rise in independent filmmaking throughout the 1980s conversely demonstrates the diversity that existed outside of mainstream cinema, which was partly also driven by the increase in home entertainment. This also led to major Hollywood studios distributing independently produced films in order to satisfy the needs of the home cinema consumer.[6] At the same time, much independent filmmaking signalled the continued existence of a liberal counter-culture in American film. John Belton argues that 'the Reaganite cinema that dominated the early 1980s seemed to spawn an oppositional cinema that set forth a dramatically different image of America in the late 1980s'.[7] For every big-budget blockbuster that seemed to perpetuate the dominant ideals of the right-wing conservative Reagan era, there was a film that displayed marked scepticism about them. For example, Barry Langford has observed about *Jaws* (1975) that the film presented a 'reauthorization of a conservatively conceived middle-class patriarchal masculinity, embodied by the father, husband and lawman Chief Brody (Roy Scheider)'.[8] In contrast, Belton highlights filmmakers such as David Lynch, whose film *Blue Velvet* (1986) and television series *Twin Peaks* (1989–91) were heavily critical of small town, middle-class America, depicting a world of corruption and brutality.[9] Thus, it is important to underscore that blockbuster movies were not the only output of Hollywood during the 1980s. Stephen Prince is arguably correct when he claims that 'the pictures produced in this era reflect a healthy mix of perspective, style and intended audiences. Filmmaking during the period was decidedly heterogeneous.'[10] In this chapter, I demonstrate that the same heterogeneity to which Prince refers here is also present in big budget blockbusters, which are far more ideologically complex cinematic texts than some scholars have previously asserted.

From the perspective of sound, blockbuster films such as *Jaws*, *Star Wars* and *Raiders of the Lost Ark* saw the return of the lavish classical orchestral score familiar in the classical Hollywood era, as well as the technological enhancement of sound effects. *Jaws* is often cited as the first New Hollywood blockbuster,[11] partly due to the alternative cinema release strategy implemented by Universal Studios. Due to the audience's familiarity with Peter Benchley's novel from which the film was adapted, and the intense television marketing of the film prior to its release (instead of utilising the usual road show format), Universal Studios block-booked cinemas throughout the country. Thus *Jaws* was exhibited simultaneously in theatres throughout America, it was the first 'event' film and was highly anticipated by cinema audiences. This, of course, is now standard practice, and Michael Allen has observed that this mode of 'saturation' release, led to high-sell, short release patterns which buried all but the most resilient or overhyped film.[12]

It is perhaps easy to forget that part of the 'hype' surrounding the release of *Jaws* was created via the film's soundtrack. Integral to the impact of *Jaws* was its use of eerie, atmospheric music to signal the presence of the shark, creating huge tension and fear among audiences, even causing people across America to be too frightened to swim in the sea.[13] The low-pitched, two-note theme tune has now become infamous in relation to both the film and sharks generally, and would have been familiar to audiences via the film's television promotion before they even stepped into film theatres. Thus the use of a signature theme tune allowed filmgoers to attribute ambivalent meaning to the film's acoustic underscoring prior to viewing the film itself. Such prominence given to the tune also signalled the newly important role that film music played in this era of cinema. *Jaws* became a signature film in the body of early Hollywood blockbusters that feature famous music soundtracks. Indeed, on hearing the theme music to blockbusters such as *Star Wars*, *E.T. The Extra-Terrestrial* (1982) or the *Indiana Jones* series, mainstream cinema viewers are highly likely to recognise the films from which they came. This revival of the 'big' musical score – customarily associated with classical Hollywood – decisively contributed to the inauguration of blockbuster films.

Sound in film was undergoing as many changes as the film industry itself, both technologically and artistically. In 1975, when *Jaws* was released, despite the existence of multichannel technology in the form of Dolby Stereo, many theatres had not undergone the expense of upgrading their sound systems. The implications of new saturation release pioneered by the initial screenings of *Jaws* meant that the simultaneous showing of the same film in different theatres made obvious to audiences those venues with more basic sound equipment. It was in 1977, with the release of *Star Wars* in Dolby Stereo, that the advantages of multichannel sound became most apparent. When the revenues of cinemas with an upgraded, Dolby sound system became significantly higher than those with a monaural system, audience behaviour convinced virtually all theatres to invest in the improved sound reproduction offered by Dolby.[14] At the beginning of 1978 there were 700 cinemas in America with Dolby Stereo, but during that year the number increased by 500 per month.[15]

The evident increase in the audience's awareness of the merits of multichannel sound technology is indicative of an era in which home entertainment, in the realm of both film and music, was on the rise. The arrival of VHS (Video Home System) and cable television into the homes of many Americans fuelled an interest in film and sound alike. Throughout the 1980s, the number of US households with a VHS increased from 2.5 per cent to 66 per cent and sales of video cassettes increased by a staggering 6,500 per cent. The number of homes subscribing to cable television between 1980 and 1990 increased from 9 million to 42 million.[16] Buhler *et al.* argue that, more than any other technical transformation, the advent of home video fundamentally changed the ways audiences

TECHNOLOGY AND THE SCIENCE FICTION BLOCKBUSTER 129

interacted with and so also understood film, transforming films, in the most direct ways, into commodities and film audiences into consumers.[17] Where film sound is concerned, the advent of home cinema sound systems allowed film audiences to potentially recreate the public viewing space of the cinema, yet in the privacy of their own homes. This signals the viewers' heightened awareness of the importance of high quality sound equipment and the strategic placing of 'surround sound' equipment in enhancing the cinematic experience.

The aforementioned technological advances and a change in audience viewing patterns meant that film sound in American cinema was not just undergoing significant modifications, but was also becoming more important in the entire filmmaking process. When Buhler *et al.* note that 'before Dolby, the sound track remained of secondary concern',[18] they are highlighting a particular circumstance in film production: namely, that prior to the changes of the 1980s, sound had by and large been a technical consideration in the post-production stage of filmmaking. In the 1950s, 1960s and first half of the 1970s, sound departments were heavily reliant on the film studio's sound libraries, which were usually consulted only once filming was complete. Thus the initial aesthetic imagining of studio-made films prior to Dolby was biased towards the visual features of film, with sound conceived as somewhat of an 'add on'. The integration of Dolby Stereo as an industry standard did not just guarantee greater sound quality and allow for strategic placing of speakers; it also created the potential for a soundtrack with a far greater density of sound, giving filmmakers the opportunity to incorporate more complex sound effects within the sound mix – something that had not been explored in earlier cinematic periods. As I have discussed in previous chapters, musical accompaniment and the voice tended to dominate the soundscape of classical Hollywood cinema, often serving narrative purposes. My discussion of New Hollywood sounding in Chapter 3 highlights new artistic approaches to sound and some of the technical changes that were taking place throughout the late 1960s and early 1970s, such as postproduction manipulation of sound recorded on location. Yet this experimental movement, which was often referred to as 'sound montage', was relatively short lived, giving way instead to concepts such as 'sound design' and the 'sound designer' which signalled a move away from the avant-garde influences of the European New Wave and art cinema.[19]

The term 'sound design' is widely acknowledged in film sound theory as being coined by Walter Murch to describe his approach to the construction of the soundtrack in Francis Ford Coppola's *Apocalypse Now* (1979).[20] The term denotes the artistic overseeing of the layering and interaction of sound effects, music and voice, as well as the creation of new sounds. It also refers to the ways in which sound is 'physically' located using multichannel equipment comprising five different speakers, demonstrating the increased potential for a heightened visceral experience for film audiences.

Once the technological capabilities of Dolby surround technology had become apparent, the Dolby company found themselves in need of filmmakers who would utilise its creative potential. Gianluca Sergi notes that, in the late 1970s, even when films were recorded in Dolby Stereo, filmmakers were often unaware of the ways in which the technology could be employed to its full, more creative capabilities. A few titles such as *Tommy* (1975) and *A Star is Born* (1976) were released in Dolby Stereo but, according to Sergi, they did not showcase what the technology could really do. He argues that Dolby was in need of a 'special' kind of movie and a new kind of filmmaker – 'someone who understood technology and its potential and was not afraid of using it'.[21] Fortunately for Dolby, in creating the soundtrack for the *Star Wars* trilogy, these needs were met by the filmmaker George Lucas and the sound engineer Ben Burtt.

It was the release of *Star Wars* in 1977 that demonstrated the full technological capabilities of Dolby Stereo, causing it to become an industry standard in both filmmaking and film exhibition. The film also set a new precedent in sound design, being one of the first films to be conceived visually and audibly at the same time; as reported, George Lucas had a distinct idea of what he wanted the film to 'sound' like as well as its visual aesthetics. He gave sound designer Ben Burtt one year to collect the myriad of sounds that would create the *Star Wars* universe. In doing so, according to William Whittington, Burtt 'reshaped the lexicon of Hollywood film sound'[22] whilst also working against established generic conventions for sounding in science fiction films. William Whittington highlights that the sound in *Star Wars* introduced multifaceted sound design through the creation and layering of new sounds that would be used for the creatures, weapons, spaceships and ambient sound within the film's diegesis. Furthermore, multichannel sound technology allowed the strategic deployment of sounds within the cinema space, creating new spectacles and sensations for the audience during their viewing experience. In his writing on the cinematic space and the cinematic ear, Thomas Elsaesser notes the ways in which such considerations can create an affective, bodily experience for the spectator:

> A focus on the ear and sound directly emphasizes the spatiality of the cinematic experience . . . while many traditional approaches treated the spectator in the cinema as someone solely concerned with looking in a rational-agent, goal-oriented way, and of processing information in objective fashion, the ear shifts the focus to factors such as the sense of balance and spatial sensibility . . . a bodily being enmeshed acoustically, spatially and affectively in the filmic texture. Technological developments such as the tremendous improvements of sound technology since the 1970s must also be a part of the discussion, giving 'voice' to theoreticians whose reflections focus primarily on cinematic sound.[23]

This enhancement of the spectator's bodily experience undeniably allows for a wider scope of gender-related meanings to be generated by cinema sound. In my analysis, this wider scope of meanings attached to gender and sound can be perceived as being transferred in a way that was all encompassing for the film audience, immersing them in sound, vision and potential meaning.

William Whittington highlights that Lucas' previous box office failure, *THX 1138* (1971), which was influenced by avant-garde filmmaking, caused him to conceive *Star Wars* as a mainstream, commercial work with its roots firmly placed in the classical Hollywood realm of myth and romanticisation. The film's soundscape was meticulously designed, including the tiniest details such as the different sounds needed for individual spaceships, guns, lasers and light sabers. Whittington notes that the soundtrack was constructed through innovative editing and re-recording techniques, which created an impression of authenticity, but also of being highly theatrical – it '[emphasised] the abstract concepts of faraway locales, creatures and vessels'.[24] Lucas and Burtt wanted an organic, familiar soundtrack for the film, to create a sense of a 'used future', full of rusty, dented spaceships that do not always work properly. Ben Burtt accomplished this sound design through experimentation with, and the manipulation of, everyday sounds. For example, the rumble of the huge, imperial war ship in the opening scene was created through manipulation of the pitch and frequency of the sound of a broken air conditioner. This Foley approach, using sounds that would be familiar, yet not quite recognisable to audiences (because displaced from their regular setting), reflected a new way of sounding the science fiction genre; previously, sound in science fiction had been inspired by artificially produced sounds and heavily reliant on studio sound libraries.

The sound design of *Star Wars* also consciously incorporated the film's overarching theme of the struggle between good and evil to generate new layers of meaning. For example, spaceships belonging to the evil Empire are frequently linked to frightening shrieking or howling sounds, whereas the Rebels' aircrafts are more 'junky sounding'[25] and would pop and sputter like an old car or sometimes completely break down. The light saber of Darth Vader (David Prouse/James Earl Jones) is regularly sounded in a minor key, whereas Ben Kenobi's (Alec Guinness) is given a C major chord. Ben Burtt himself notes: 'When they get together, they don't really harmonise very well.'[26] Such aural disharmony adds to the dramatic tension between the characters but also points to the ways in which some principles of classical music composition were used to add meaning to sound effects in the *Star Wars* world. This motif-based sounding, famously used in the nineteenth century by opera composer Richard Wagner, allows audience identification with not only the film's characters, but also with the spaces they inhabit within the film's diegesis. This is based on the repetition or development of these motifs and also the contrast between them and the motifs of characters or domains with which they are associated. Whittington notes that such innovative techniques in sounding had a huge influence on the soundtrack in future blockbusters: 'The quality of these effects established a new tradition and attentiveness to even the smallest detail of image-sound relations in the Hollywood blockbuster. These factors would be key in establishing the lexicon of sound design in this new era of filmmaking.'[27]

For the purposes of this discussion, it is noteworthy that the representation of the strong, independent character of Princess Leia in *Star Wars* signalled the advances in female liberation aided by the women's movement in the 1960s and 1970s. Despite being the only main female character in a male-dominated narrative, Princess Leia is not only at the core of the rebellion against the Galactic Empire, but she also often dictates the actions of the male characters as part of the Rebel uprising. The music motifs that underscore this character in the film are illuminating in this respect: she is symbolically aurally constructed through strong, commanding orchestral scoring, previously reserved for male heroes. Furthermore, being in the midst of warfare throughout most of the film, she is aurally immersed in the sounds of shooting, explosions and spaceships, aligning her with the male-centred action that otherwise dictates the narrative.

The film begins with her ship coming under attack by the Empire. Leia's possession of information about the Empire's powerful space station, the Death Star, reveals a weakness in the station's defences, which she implants in the droid R2-D2 (Kenny Baker), who is then purchased by the family of the film's main protagonist, Luke Skywalker (Mark Hamill). Skywalker is enlisted by Jedi master Obi-Wan Kenobi to deliver R2-D2 to Leia's father; they embark on their journey across the galaxy with the aid of pilot and smuggler Han Solo (Harrison Ford) and the wookie Chewbacca (Peter Mayhew). Before delivering the plans, they also rescue Princess Leia from the clutches of Darth Vader and then join the Rebel Alliance in an attack on the Death Star. With help from Han Solo, Luke utilises the powers of The Force to destroy the space station, defeating the Empire and being rewarded for his bravery in the film's culmination.

Princess Leia is visually introduced when we see her placing the stolen data inside the droid R2-D2. Gentle, disparate notes play on the orchestral soundtrack, creating an air of mystery about this (so far) unknown female figure. Being the character in possession of this particular piece of information heightens her importance in the narrative, and her determination to ensure this data reaches her Rebel comrades allows them to ultimately defeat the enemy. Thus we see the resourcefulness and bravery of a female character being integral to the outcome of the movie. Indeed, as one of Vader's aides comments, the princess would rather die than give up information that would

TECHNOLOGY AND THE SCIENCE FICTION BLOCKBUSTER

harm her Rebel friends. Later on, Darth Vader himself observes that her resistance to the 'mind probe' they use on her is 'considerable', emphasising Leia's mental strength and resistance.

Her narrative importance is actually indicated acoustically before she appears on screen, when we see her name emerge on the scrolling text in the film's opening sequence. The first two paragraphs of prose explain the civil war between the Rebels and the Empire, the third one announces: 'Pursued by the Empire's sinister agents, Princess Leia races home aboard her starship, custodian of the stolen plans that can save her people and restore freedom to the galaxy.' Words such as 'pursued' and 'sinister' suggest her bravery in the face of those who hunt her. The fact that she 'races' home suggests a character with agency, and the fact that it is 'her' starship highlights a sense of power, responsibility and ownership, while 'her' people are clearly valued by the princess, as is their freedom. Such expression in this short written passage conveys the sense of a female character who is dynamic and daring and who has integrity. This set of meanings is reinforced by the powerful, orchestral, non-diegetic music underscoring the words. Just before the words 'Princess Leia' appear on the screen, the music, which had previously featured a soft, romantic leitmotif that becomes associated with Luke Skywalker, slows down in tempo, only to swell again and increase in pace and volume as her name appears. Similar strong, brassy orchestral moments are often allied with Leia, while softer, romantic stringed themes are often linked to Luke, particularly in the early stages of the film when he is represented as boyish and immature. When Princess Leia appears onscreen and her presence is underscored with romantic, stringed themes, these moments are usually subjectively focalised from the position of Luke. She is represented through this acoustic 'point-of-view' on multiple occasions – from her frequent appearances as a hologram, to the moment he rescues her and she lays suggestively on a bench in her prison cell. Such episodes, represented visually and acoustically through Luke's perspective, emphasise the princess's attractiveness, and the romantic aural construction of these moments suggests Luke's boyhood 'crush' on this mysterious princess. But, upon being rescued, the princess actually becomes 'one of the boys', rather than a stereotypical rescued damsel, and this is replicated on the music score, which is brassy and forceful. Such musical coding suggests subtle subversion of gender roles and their expected aural representation, as we hear what could be classed as strong, masculine music linked to Leia and soft, feminine sounding linked to Luke.

This repositioning of traditional gender roles is acoustically reinforced at the beginning of the film. As the Imperial ship closes in on Princess Leia's starship, the effeminate droid C-3PO (Anthony Daniels) – a more palpable example of subversion of gender – says the first spoken words of the film: 'We're doomed! There'll be no escape for the Princess this time!', emphasising that this is not the first Imperial entanglement in which Leia has found herself. Again, before we even meet her, the film's soundscape is providing key information about her being an intrepid female character. A further key function of the soundscape in these early stages of the film (which features mainly non-diegetic music and sound effects) is creating fear surrounding the character of Darth Vader, a narrative circumstance that in turn emphasises the bravery of Leia when she fearlessly challenges him. As the Rebel ship prepares for the Empire attack, loud, deep orchestral bassoons signal the evil presence of the Empire. Loud, rumbling drumbeats are introduced and a sinister, steady breathing sound can be heard as C-3PO fearfully questions, 'what was that?' The look of fright in the eyes of the men expresses their fear of the unknown, and as the door of the ship is seared open, a loud explosion and billowing smoke fill the screen, through which several stormtroopers emerge to the short, sharp piercing sounds of their laser guns firing. The strong enemy forces quickly defeat Leia's soldiers and strong, deep brassy notes announce the arrival of Darth Vader. This musical leitmotif has become synonymous with this infamous character who is configured to be an embodiment of evil. This is coupled with the eerie sound of his lengthy mechanical breathing – which is now heightened on the soundtrack – culminating in the sounding of a truly terrifying 'baddie'.

When faced with this frightening villain, Leia fiercely challenges him, and her first words of the film are: 'Darth Vader! Only you could be so bold!' Her voice is strong and controlled, her words are well articulated and her attitude towards the menacing presence of Darth Vader is defiant. Her speech throughout the film is comparable with the fast-talking actresses discussed in Chapter 1 and she is often heard delivering amusing one-liners to her surrounding male characters. Han Solo, who she condescendingly refers to as 'fly boy', is frequently on the receiving end of her verbal quips. On angrily informing her that he takes orders from one person only, himself, she coolly comments: 'hmm, it's a wonder you're still alive . . .' and on seeing his worn out, yet beloved spaceship, the Millenium Falcon, she jokes, 'you came in that thing? You're braver than I thought!' In these moments, Solo appears more affronted by Leia's curt insults and the sounds of sharp female vocals than he does by the Empire's attempts to kill him.

This discussion of the links between sound and gender in *Star Wars* reveals that this 1970s film, for all its inscription in traditional ideological frameworks, did have its finger on the pulse of an emerging epoch in which perceptions of masculinity and femininity in American society were shifting. The strong orchestral tones associated with Leia, her snappy dialogue and the sense of agency about her character was perceived as subtly subversive. Diana Dominguez has observed that Princess Leia was 'a woman who was outspoken, unashamed, and, most importantly, unpunished for being so'.[28] Indeed, her commanding role is accepted as 'the norm' within the narrative. By contrast, the romantic scoring is frequently associated with Luke, and partly with his adolescent desires for Leia. His voicing too can be described as high-pitched, verging on 'whiney', as he protests against his uncle being overprotective. Luke's journey from Padawan (apprentice) to Jedi Master over the course of the three films can be described as his path to manhood, and indeed we see his aural representation becoming more 'masculine' as his character develops.

This subtle subversion of gender representations demonstrates the ways that the science fiction genre has historically depicted male and female characters and has the capacity to challenge gender expectations. When the first *Alien* film was released two years after *Star Wars* in 1979, it was a film that also placed a strong female character – Ellen Ripley (Sigourney Weaver) – at the centre of the narrative. In this film, when one of the crew aboard the Nostramo spaceship is impregnated by an alien, Ripley establishes herself as the voice of reason by her calls to quarantine this individual. She is ignored by her male superiors before the alien kills the rest of the crew, one by one, leaving Ripley to defeat the alien and become the film's sole survivor.

The image of Ripley, gun in one arm and young Newt (Carrie Henn) in the other, is an iconic image from James Cameron's 1986 sequel, *Aliens*. For many film scholars, throughout the entire *Alien* series, Ripley symbolises strength, power and the intelligence that outsmarts not just alien creatures, but also most of her male counterparts. Thomas Doherty notes: 'The striking element in Ripley's image as a woman warrior is not just her grace under pressure but that her grace under pressure is set in relief against so much male cupidity and incompetence.'[29] This element of her character is set in place in the first film, and the sequel is where we really see her as a warrior as she battles against the alien queen to secure the safety of herself and her surrogate daughter.

The second instalment in the quadrilogy begins where the first film finished, with Ripley floating through space in the Nostramo ship. On being discovered, she relays the events of the first film to her superiors, who dismiss her story of aliens as nonsense since, fifty-seven years after her encounter, there are colonists residing on planet LV426, where Ripley encountered the aliens in the first film. However, on suddenly being unable to contact any of the colonists, Ripley is enlisted to assist a team of space Marines to investigate. When arriving on LV426, the colonists are discovered trapped in an alien nest, in which they are to be impregnated by alien 'facehuggers'. The Marines also discover Newt, a young girl who becomes a surrogate daughter to Ripley, eventually calling her 'mommy'. A battle ensues between the Marines and the aliens, who gradually wipe out the Marines, leaving just Ripley, Newt, Hicks (Michael Biehn) and the cyborg Bishop (Lance Henriksen). The final showdown takes place between the alien queen and Ripley, who defeats the queen by donning a large metal exoskeleton in the form of a forklift power-loader. In a narrative repeat from the first film, she forces the alien into the airlock, blasting it into space and rescuing Newt, Hicks and Bishop.

Much discussion of the *Alien* quadrilogy focuses on the transgression of gender boundaries since the prime aim of the alien is to lay its eggs within humans, regardless of gender. Amy Taubin highlights the precedent set by this series of films in terms of the representation and understanding of the sexes, as well as that of predictable gender behaviour: 'when the baby alien . . . burst from John Hurt's [male character's] chest, it cancelled the distinction on which human culture is based'.[30] But Cameron's film, I argue, performs even more: part of the quadrilogy's agenda is to question the fixedness of the notions of masculinity and femininity as such and highlight what recent feminist theory has called 'constructivism' of gender through an engagement with performativity not unlike the one I explored at the end of Chapter 1. In the following revisiting of a range of key scenes from the 1986 sequel *Aliens*, I investigate the ways in which sound is linked with gender and gender construction. This analysis focuses on the bodily transgressions of the aliens and their visceral aural representation. I also consider the dual operation of the sound of technology/machinery in the film as it becomes a marker of gender construction: the negative sound associations related to weapons and guns and routinely linked with the film's masculine characters, and positive meanings imparted on the representation and the sounding of machinery, most frequently linked to the character of Ripley.

The soundscape of the first film in the series, *Alien*, features many formal conventions associated with the horror genre. Accordingly, the director Ridley Scott insisted that the film's soundtrack emphasises terror and deliberately builds a sense of foreboding in the first half of the film.[31] William Whittington's in-depth analysis of the sound design in the inaugural film reveals the way in which one such complex combination of musical score, sound effects, Foley and ambient sound can be rendered disturbing because it utilises the familiar musical codes of the horror genre.[32] For example, moments of extreme silence are suddenly punctuated with loud orchestral outbursts on the soundtrack featuring alarming minor chords. This classical formal sound technique, frequently used in the horror genre, has the effect of building so much fear in the audience that when the alien is finally revealed, tension is at breaking point. Whittington also refers to the 'complex weave of human and mechanical noises',[33] which merges science fiction, horror, sound and body, creating what he refers to as 'audio-biomechanics': 'on the sound track, Foley and ambiences are infused with issues related to organic unity, anthropomorphism, and gender'.[34] This approach to sound is transgressive in its merging of human and machine on an aural level, in addition to the animate-inanimate fusion happening on the visual level. This merging of boundaries between, specifically, genders, and, more generally, human and machine, is furthered in Cameron's *Aliens* where the sounds associated with gender are played with and subverted, leading us to question the validity of prescribed gender roles in this futuristic setting where particular 'male' or 'female' behaviours are disregarded by human and alien alike. In this sequel, the female character, Ripley, is frequently allied with technology — visually, thematically and aurally. This alliance is not unusual in the realm of science fiction, yet is worthy of exploration since Ripley is the only character in the film not only to be consistently linked to technology, but also to be set in opposition to the realm of the biological and to regard it as nightmarish. In this discussion, through exploration of the sound essence of her characterisation I argue that this transgressive representation of Ellen Ripley in *Aliens* constructs her as a cyborg.

In her socialist-feminist 1984 'Cyborg Manifesto', Donna Haraway theorises on the position of women in a postmodern, technical age; she argues that all women are cyborgs. She highlights that previous social-feminist analyses are problematic in their use of Marxist, psychological, feminist or anthropological modes of analysis. This is largely due to a tradition in 'Western' science and politics, referred to by Haraway as 'the tradition of racist, male-dominated capitalism'[35] which emphasises societal oppositions and the social pre-construction of distinct borders and boundaries between organisms and machines. Haraway conversely champions the notion of taking pleasure in the contemporary confusion of such boundaries, specifically highlighting the ways in which these boundaries have now eroded in what she believes is a post-gender, utopian age. She identifies three key ways in which these borders have been breached: through the closer links between humans and animals; closer links between humans and machines; and closer links between the physical and the non-physical world. Haraway's 1984 manifesto is contemporaneous with the *Alien* film series, and, in particular, it narrowly precedes Cameron's *Aliens*. Therefore, in the film *Aliens*, Ripley's construction as a cyborg not only corresponds with Haraway's manifesto, but is augmented through the movie's sound design.

The first key area Haraway delineates concerns the dissolution of boundaries between human and animals. Haraway explains that at one time human and animal worlds were distinctly separate due to apparent lack of language, tool use, or social behaviour within the animal kingdom. Now, thanks to technological advances in scientific research, this boundary has eroded and has allowed for greater interaction between animals and humans. At the end of *Alien* and the beginning of *Aliens*, we see Jones, the ship's cat given a distinctly human name, sleeping in the pod with Ripley. The cat is Ripley's sole companion and the frequent sounds of purring it emits (signalling contentment) in Ripley's presence in the early parts of the film denote the intimate relationship between them. Furthermore, the cat's aurally emphasised presence demonstrates an allegiance between humans and animals. It is important to note, however, for the purposes of this argument that the erosion of boundaries between human and animal does not extend to creatures that are not of this world – that is, the aliens. Whilst Haraway's manifesto embraces an egalitarian approach to gender, animals and technology, aliens are still 'alien' in Cameron's film and thus the boundary between Ripley and the aliens is still very much in place. In fact, it is accentuated in the sound design of the film which reinforces the organic, visceral features of the aliens, emphasising their 'otherness'.

The organic, visceral sounding of the aliens represents exactly that which Ripley detests and is also represented through her nightmares in the first act of the film, which I discuss below. In her analysis of the *Alien* series, Catherine Constable argues that the aliens are frequently constructed in a way that forces Ripley, and the audience, to confront the abject horror of the body's insides.[36] She asserts that humans are represented as sterile and scientific – an interpretation which is not so much opposed as subsumed under my own argument that we should treat Ripley as cyborg due to her visual and aural alignment with technology and her becoming mother to a daughter through non-biological means. All of these qualities in Ripley are in binary opposition to the alien(s), which, in turn, frequently transgress the boundaries of the body and threaten to disrupt the symbolic order. The sounds of the aliens are introduced from the opening scene and the allocation of the motif of visceral sounding to the aliens is established from the beginning.

The film opens in a visually understated manner with simply the names of the cast appearing in white, capital lettering on a completely black background, symbolising the dark, vastness of space. But the soundtrack underscoring this minimalist visual moment is decidedly complex, featuring several layers of sounds. Firstly, a low, quiet noise like wind blowing can be heard very faintly. The use of a sound linked with harsh weather evokes horror genre conventions and immediately creates a sense of ambivalence. Next, a very low-pitched, brassy orchestral sound is introduced, it gets louder and then gradually fades away as light, fast percussive, metallic sounds are introduced intermittently. They start beating three times successively, sounding like footsteps running on metal flooring, or like a heartbeat, yet the fact that there are three each time makes the sound simultaneously unidentifiable and hard to pin down, yet also partially recognisable. This creates an immediate impression of ominous tension and captures a sense of foreboding of the unknown, lurking in the darkness of space on the screen. Next, the film title 'Aliens' gradually emerges in thin, electric blue, capital lettering, whilst the volume and pitch of the layered sounds now begins to swell and dramatically increase, growing very loud and at once linking these strange sounds with the alien creatures themselves. As the word 'ALIENS' appears, the letter 'I' from the word now begins to glow brightly and then gradually expands like the pupil of a cat's eye. As it expands, the accompanying noise simultaneously crescendos, becoming extremely loud and the soundtrack is filled with an instrumental screaming noise, underscored by a loud, rattling cymbal dramatically reverberating. The sound is extremely disturbing since it sounds like a scream, but also like the call of some terrifying monster. As this sound builds to screaming point, the 'I' from the word continues to expand until it fills the screen as it goes white. This takes place only seconds into the film, yet the dramatic changes in volume on the soundtrack with such strange noises and a mutating letter within the word immediately instils a sense of fear and foreboding within the audience, highlighting the terrifying prospects that lurk within the unknown world of the alien. The fact that it is the 'I' in this word that suddenly opens, revealing this cacophony of chilling sounds, is interesting since it signals what I believe is the main issue the film sets out to explore: that of subjectivity, or identity. The alien is certainly not part of the world of the symbolic, yet it is a catalyst for what other characters in the film arguably experience as they struggle with their identities – Ripley as hero and surrogate mother, Vasquez (Jenette Goldstein) as masculine warrior attempting to 'fit in' with the men, or the young nervous marine Hudson (Bill Paxton) attempting to do the same.

As mentioned above, this alien sounding is established from the opening sequence in the movie and re-emerges frequently throughout the film, forcing the characters and audience to confront the prospect of otherness both visually and audibly. This sounding of 'otherness' is repeated several times throughout the movie and adds to the sense that the alien creature transgresses, or encroaches upon, human boundaries. When the Marines and Ripley arrive on the planet LB426, the oppressive sounds of loud, torrential rain fill the soundscape, causing the Marines to have to shout over it. The distressing effect caused here is increased when the noisy exterior scenes are frequently juxtaposed with the quiet, safe, interior scenes comprising Ripley and the Lieutenant as they wait for the Marines to secure the area. Here we see the alien creatures again allied with sounds linked to the harshness of nature; in the opening scene, low-pitched, eerie sounds of the wind blowing are used and in this scene, heavy rain signifies the presence of something unknown. Again this technique has frequently been used in the horror genre and signifies the ways in which the construction of soundtracks can also transgress generic boundaries. As the Marines enter the colony building, we see the ways in which the aliens physically disrupt the human-built structures through the melting of metal constructs with their acid blood, indicating that humans, too, may be penetrated in a similar way. The observation of the effects of this posthuman alchemy is linked with the sound of the rain since it is through holes created by the alien blood that rain now seeps in from the outside world.

We also see the visceral sounding of otherness invading scenes that we initially regard as 'safe'. So, in the early part of the film, when Ripley has been rescued and is recovering in hospital, the image and sounds of cleanliness, science and technology are comforting and reassuring. These sounds are ambient in this scene and they include the rustling of the clean, starched white bed sheets and nurses' uniforms, the comforting beep of machinery monitoring Ripley, as well as the gentle humming of the sliding doors when Burke enters to visit Ripley. The nightmarish aspect of the scenario is introduced aurally through the sudden fading down of Burke's voice and fading up of non-diegetic orchestral music playing minor chords. The notes begin to spiral downwards, indicating falling and suggesting that Ripley's mental state is plummeting. Jones the cat suddenly hisses loudly, his face and teeth filling the screen visually, symbolising the break in rapport between Ripley and her beloved pet, moving the protagonist away from the safe realm of the cyborg and into the unknown world of the visceral as her loud, sharp breaths and the sound of her heartbeat permeate the soundtrack. Chaos ensues as her flailing limbs now begin to damage the technology around her, which has previously signalled safety and aligned her to the realm of the cyborg. A glass smashes loudly, equipment crashes to the ground and several medical staff attempt to hold her down while her stomach begins to move. She cries 'kill me!' emphasising that she would rather be dead than become a transgressive, biological mother to an alien. For those familiar with the first film, the sight of an alien about to burst forth from Ripley's abdomen prepares us for the impending abject sight and we ready ourselves for gory bloodshed. A sudden cut to Ripley bolting upright in bed, covered in sweat reveals to us that this was merely a dream. Yet this nightmare has a lasting impression and establishes the alien as a threat to the symbolic order, providing further insight into Ripley's alignment with the realm of the cyborg and her wish to remain so.

Returning now to Haraway's theory, we can further ascertain why Ripley is allied with the realm of the cyborg. Haraway's second key area of boundary breakdown concerns the attenuation of the boundary between human and machine: while once humans were merely operators of machinery, late twentieth-century machinery evolved to work simultaneously with humans, eroding boundaries between natural and artificial, mind and body. Throughout *Aliens*, Ripley uses technology for survival, from the opening scenes where she is cocooned in a spacecraft, to her later use of a tank and forklift loader that aid her defeat of the aliens. She frequently regards technology as an alternative weapon to the guns used by the Marines, which often fail to protect them, and which I discuss in more detail below. Ripley's frequent alliance with technology and machinery represents the subversion of boundaries between human and machine, further confirming her status as a cyborg.

This affiliation is established early in the film when she is discovered sleeping in a chamber on the Nostramo, the spaceship from the first film – effectively where we 'left' her at the end of *Alien*. We see Ripley surrounded by and immersed in technology, being kept alive by the capsule, which is

TECHNOLOGY AND THE SCIENCE FICTION BLOCKBUSTER 141

represented as protective, housing her through fifty-seven years of hypersleep, along with Jones the cat. Technology here is represented as Ripley's saviour, especially when we later hear that the chances of her being discovered were a mere one in a thousand. When we first see the exterior of the tiny spaceship floating in the vastness of space, James Horner's orchestral score accompanies the scene. The piece is reminiscent of a tinkling lullaby, played on very high-pitched strings. The melody begins by being played in gentle harmony, creating a sense of splendour about these vast images of space. Yet as the camera gradually moves in closer to the ship, minor notes are introduced and the score begins to move down the musical scale, creating an increasing sense of aural disharmony as we get closer to the ship, suggesting ambivalence. This musical theme is continued as the accompanying notes now begin to move quickly down the musical scale, still in minor key, creating a spiralling sense of descending or falling as we finally see a shot of Ripley lying motionless in the capsule. At this point, there is suddenly another slight change in the music as major notes are now re-introduced. This creates a sense of positivity about her character, yet the remaining presence of deep minor notes creates an overwhelming sense of ambiguity and foreboding about her surroundings. The capsule in which Ripley sleeps is coated in ice and as the light catches it, it sparkles and creates softness around her image as she sleeps peacefully, looking remarkably like a fairy-tale princess – indeed, she is referred to as Snow White by the Marine, Vasquez, later in the film, and the classical orchestral score now creates a convincing fairy-tale ambience. This feeling of peace and tranquillity is abruptly disturbed, however, as the sudden intrusive sounds of technology monitoring Ripley and the approaching salvage ship are introduced. These sounds punctuate this classical aural moment, drowning it out and bringing us firmly into a postmodern era that sounds of staccato, high-pitched beeping and computer scripts gently running. As the Nostramo is slowly raised up and attached to the salvage ship, a thoroughly unpleasant, ear-splitting sound of the metal door of the ship being seared open fills the soundscape. Thus the very loud arrival of salvage men ripping into Ripley's peaceful world, and her forced awakening is represented as menacing, reinforced by the now deep, low-pitched notes and echoing footsteps that accompany their entry into the Nostramo. Three men enter the dark ship clad in space suits and masks, the sound of their deep breathing could be mistaken for multiple Darth Vaders and the sound gets louder as they approach Ripley, building the tension. As one of them wipes the ice from the capsule with a harsh, scratching sound, Ripley can now be seen sleeping peacefully. Simultaneously, a short, classical harmonious tune plays on woodwind from the moment we see her face, conveying a sense of excitement through recognition to viewers of *Alien*, reinforced by the slow pan to reveal Jones the cat also sleeping peacefully. This moment of excitement, which is enhanced by the music that underscores it, is immediately cut short upon the revelation that she is alive, which is met with dismay by the salvage crew as the leader announces 'there goes our salvage guys' immediately signalling the male, capitalist edge that runs throughout the movie. This comment also foreshadows Ripley's attempts later in the movie to prioritise human safety over the 'dollar value' attached to modern technology; for although she values technology, she values its usefulness in aiding human survival above all. In this early scene in the film, we clearly see the life-saving sounds and images of technology allied with Ripley, whereas the sounds of loud, destructive technology or weaponry are affiliated not just with men, but with male corporate greed.

This eroded boundary between human and machine can be linked to cyberfeminist arguments about the ability of machines and technology to negate gender boundaries and highlights what Butler has argued to be their fundamental constructedness in performative acts. Judy Wajcman refers to the work of Sadie Plant in her exploration of the link between women and technology in the 1980s. Plant argues that technological innovations during this period resulted in a power shift from men to women due to the erasure of the importance of physical capabilities: 'Automation has reduced the importance of muscular strength and hormonal energies and replaced them with demands for speed, intelligence and transferable, interpersonal and communication skills'.[37] Nowhere is this aspect of technology made clearer in *Aliens* than in the scenes of the film featuring Ripley in the loader, which give her small, feminine frame a powerful tool that puts her physically on (or above) par with the strong, masculine Marines.

The loader forms a mechanical exoskeleton around her body, giving her increased physical strength. The use of Foley sound effects when she first uses the huge machine demonstrates her aural and physical allegiance with, indeed extension in, this large, complicated apparatus. As she climbs into the enormous machine and locks in each body part, the loader makes a corresponding thumping or clicking noise that signifies the stability and power of the machine. The sounds of the machine whir continuously, so that when Ripley is in the loader she is physically secure and surrounded aurally by the gentle, reassuring sounds of the machinery suggesting stability, strength and also high technical capability as she becomes one with the machine. As she successfully lifts the first items (much to the disbelief of her male onlookers), she is accompanied by the mellow whirring sound of the moving machinery. In terms of the film's diegesis, the scene serves to prove to the Marines Ripley's strength, courage and knowledge of using a machine that will ultimately become a weapon. From a sound perspective, this is a marker-scene, one that installs a difference in the sounding of machines and weapons; for the scene is juxtaposed with those which seek to visually and aurally fetishise the guns used by the Marines. There are moments throughout the film where – in line with

Haraway's theories of boundary breakdown – we see Ripley immersed in the sounds of warfare, as she becomes a sort of honorary Marine and at one point rescues the platoon from annihilation by the alien creatures, yet when she is featured alone, technology is her natural ally.

Related to this scope of aurally imparted meanings is Haraway's third area in her breakdown, that between the physical and the non-physical, which is highlighted through frequent human interaction with machines, or what Haraway defines as 'quintessentially microelectric devices'. Haraway notes that such devices 'are everywhere and they are invisible'[38] and it is their invisible pervasive presence that crucially shapes our world and ourselves. Throughout the *Alien* quadrilogy, viewers are auditorily made aware of technology's capabilities for invisible signalling, emitting electromagnetic waves and the miniaturisation and portability of technology, which Haraway argues has changed our experience of mechanism. The humming of (sometimes visible sometimes invisible) machines contributes to Ripley's sounded identity and her aural alliance with such technologies.

The application of Butler's theory of performativity and Haraway's discussion of cyborgs here allows for a more positive reading of Ripley's characterisation than that pursued in previous feminist readings, which either described her as an archaic mother[39] or emphasise her apparent re-inscription into a patriarchal role of wife and mother at the movie's culmination. Viewed through the lens of the three key aspects of Haraway's cyborg manifesto and Butler's theory Ripley, I argue, emerges as a postfeminist cyborg that constructs and at times even shifts its own gender identity through performative acts.

Since *Aliens* is a sequel, it is a film that viewers experience with certain expectations concerning narrative, character and theme already in place. Whereas Ridley Scott, director of the first film, conceived *Alien* to be a hybrid between science fiction and horror, James Cameron, director of the 1986 film, imagined the sequel as a generic hybrid between science fiction and action or war films. Cameron has frequently remarked that he conceived of the Marine's mission to LV426 to defeat the aliens as a representation of the Vietnam War, in which 'a high-tech army confident of victory over a supposedly more primitive civilization found itself mired in a humiliating series of defeats that added up to an unwinnable war'.[40] I follow Cameron in my exploration of the sounds associated with the Marines and their technological weaponry as relaying an ideological comment about overconfidence in weapons and the besmirching of alien cultures.

Ripley's nightmarish perceptions of the aliens, based on her prior encounters with them in the first film is set in binary opposition to the overconfidence of the space Marines, whose naive beliefs in the capabilities of their weapons sets them up to fall. The sound of weaponry is frequently heard alongside sounds of masculine banter and thus masculinity and weaponry become aurally linked. Early in the film, the introduction of the Marines emphasises their male camaraderie and their interaction creates a stereotypical portrait of the masculine military that is exaggerated and borders on caricature. Such representation emphasises the military personnel's narrow-minded beliefs that being in possession of a gun offers invincibility and also creates a sense of unease in any audience members who have seen the first instalment of the film series. On arriving on LV426, the Marines are initially informed that they are on a rescue mission but their spoken language (e.g. 'there's some juicy colonists' daughters we have to rescue from their virginity') puts them in the traditional position of the group male hero; the film self-consciously emphasises the affiliation of such traditionally conceived group character with misogyny and sexism that, as we see from a close up of Ripley's facial responses, is wholly out-dated in this postfeminist period. The possibility of transgressing gender boundaries is, however, immediately explored in the dialogue heard from the Marines. Hudson is represented as the young, inexperienced and often 'wimpy' character. For example, when they first reach the spaceship he complains the floor is cold on his bare feet. He then asks the muscular female marine Vasquez 'have you ever been mistaken for a man?' as she does pull-ups on a nearby metal bar, flexing her muscles. She replies, 'no, have you?' much to the hilarity of the other male Marines. Then the men reminisce about sexual encounters they have had with 'the Octurians', to which one of them remarks 'yeah but yours was male'. One of the black Marines replies, 'it doesn't matter when it's Octurian' suggesting the uneasy intertwine between discursively represented/constructed sexuality and racial, or species, identity. This banter takes place before an episode when the android, Bishop, performs a knife trick on Hudson's hand to the sound of his high-pitched, ascending screaming, and the laughs and guffaws of the other Marines. This short episode first introduces stereotypical jocular behaviour from the male group hero in which they assert their masculinity, yet frequently jibe one another about potential homosexual preferences or transgender appearance. As such, their establishing banter is aimed to represent their attempts to assert their masculinity, yet it is instilled with the intimations of gender transgression, and, more pointedly, repeated glosses on the performativity of gender. Ripley's obvious indifference to this male performance (shown via facial expression alone) is indicative of her knowledge that merely being (or acting) male and in possession of a gun is not enough to defeat these creatures, who, in addition, anyway have no regard for the humanly defined and practiced boundaries of gender. Here the notion of gender performativity is evident in the early stages of *Aliens*. While the dialogue heard from the Marines is based on traditional notions of gender, it continually moves beyond the notion of sexual difference and begins the process of exposing gender as a social construct. The science fiction, futuristic setting here seems to allow for such explorations with the notion of gender, which appears to be wholly out-dated in this undefined, futuristic time frame.

In a later scene, as the Marines prepare their weapons to go into battle, a deep, ominous orchestral tune plays on the soundtrack, like the one during the film's opening, and each click of every gun is loudly accentuated. Unlike the gentle whirring of the machinery in previous scenes, this sound is staccato, high-pitched and aggressive. Military drum beats are now introduced non-diegetically on the soundtrack as Vasquez and Drake perform a pre-battle tribal ritual movement – a performative act that can now also be recognised as constructing their masculinity – which will further corroborate traditional 'masculine', or machismo, sounding of war: the intertwine of drums, guns and battle sounds. When the Marines are moving through the alien's lair, the sheer size of their weapons seems accentuated through the frequent shots of Vasquez, who is physically smaller than the other Marines, but represented as the toughest (and, in terms of performative acts, most 'masculine') of them all. Yet, her naive belief that her large gun will protect her from the aliens is one that her character perpetuates throughout the movie, until her death. These episodes of stalking the aliens with oversized guns are accompanied by eerie, high-pitched instrumental non-diegetic sounds, creating tension within the audience. The episodes of battle, on the other hand, are marked by the sound of weaponry. But the representation-sounding of masculinity and weaponry in *Aliens* emphasises that being in possession of a fully loaded, high tech weapon is not enough to defeat an alien – just as the male banter is nothing more than a performance. Yet the implication throughout is that it makes the Marines feel overtly 'masculine'; indeed, the size of the weapons and the loud sounds emitted by them gives them visual and aural prevalence within the narrative. Ripley's final defeat of the alien queen using the strong sturdy loader instead of a gun points to James Cameron's views that over-reliance on weaponry and brute force is not an intelligent way to engage in warfare.

One noise that is, however, key to the diegesis and is the leitmotif of such episodes is the sound of the tracking device. The latter emits a frequent, fast pulsing sound, contrasted with that of the weapons. The tracking device sounding is a good example of the ways in which the sounds of technology are soft, muted and gentle when compared to the harsh and staccato sounds of the guns. Paradoxically, the sound of the tracker is a source of comfort as it warns the characters when an alien is approaching, yet also a source of fear for exactly the same reason. Here we see Ripley and the Marines using invisible technology to assist them in their mission, which I have linked earlier to Haraway's theory about the transgression of boundaries between humans and technology. The world charged with such devices, Haraway suggests, becomes one of microelectronic politics, and the latter has intrinsic, if indirect, links to the discourses of race and power.[41] No wonder, then, that precisely such technology proves key to defeating the aliens, and is particularly effective in helping Ripley find Newt before she battles with the alien queen. Yet, the Marine's over-reliance on their weaponry is what leads to their downfall. This particular device bridges the 'masculine' sounding of weaponry/support weaponry and the soft ('feminine practice') sounding of technology in productively unresolved ways. Just as this device could be seen as a helpful piece of technology associated with peaceful female performance, it can also act as a marker of, or support for, 'masculine practice-performance' (success in a battle).

As discussed at the beginning of this chapter, the vast developments in sound technology provided a new wealth of opportunity for sound design in films of this era. The movies discussed here provide key examples of the ways in which big budget movies, which some might perceive as formulaic or homogenous, are subtly able to challenge complex ideological notions related to gender. These subversions are often evident in the film's sound design. The incorporation of a strong female character, with associative masculine scoring and sound effects in *Star Wars*, provides an early example of the ways in which sound and gender can be combined to challenge traditional views of masculinity and femininity as social constructs. The same could be said for the sounding of Ripley in *Aliens*, which overtly challenges preconceived and dated perceptions of masculinity and femininity. Her frequent alliance with the sounds of technology emphasises that a postfeminist cyborg performing masculine acts negates traditional notions of gender.

The cult success and continued popularity of both the *Star Wars* and *Alien* film series, which both maintain their inclusion of strong, female protagonists (and subsidiary characters), demonstrates the pleasure experienced by film viewers in observing strong, independent, quick-witted females onscreen. Furthermore, it demonstrates the success of films that show female characters who subvert gender conventions and effortlessly take on masculine behaviours, challenging preconceived notions of masculinity and femininity. These ideas are related to the strive for gender equality advocated by the second wave feminist movement throughout the 1960s and 1970s. Moving this discussion forward and into the realms of postfeminism, I now examine a selection of female performances in contemporary 'chick flicks' to determine the ways in which speech, dialogue and bodily sounds might challenge contemporary notions of femininity in a more playful and self-reflexive manner than demonstrated by the protagonists discussed in this chapter.

NOTES

1. Harry M. Benshoff and Sean Griffin, *America on Film: Representing Race, Class, Gender, and Sexuality at the Movies* (Malden, MA: Wiley-Blackwell, 2004); Helena Vanhala, *The*

Depiction of Terrorists in Blockbuster Hollywood Films 1980–2001: An Analytical Study (Jefferson: McFarland & Co., 2011), 112.
2. Benshoff and Griffin, 287.
3. Susan Jeffords, *Hard Bodies: Hollywood Masculinity in the Reagan Era* (New Brunswick, NJ: Rutgers University Press, 2004), 5.
4. David Gauntlett, *Media, Gender and Identity: An Introduction* (London: Routledge, 2002), 51.
5. Helen Hanson, 'Professional investigators and femme fatales in Neo Noir', in Helen Hanson, *Hollywood Heroines: Women in Film Noir and the Gothic Film* (London: I. B. Tauris, 2007), 139.
6. Stephen Prince, 'Hollywood in the age of Reagan', in Linda Ruth Williams and Michael Hammond (eds), *Contemporary American Cinema* (London: Open University Press, 2006), 229.
7. John Belton, *American Cinema, American Culture* (New York: McGraw-Hill, 2005), 376.
8. Barry Langford, *Post-Classical Hollywood: Film Industry, Style and Ideology since 1945* (Edinburgh: Edinburgh University Press, 2010), 154–5.
9. Belton, 376.
10. Prince, 235.
11. David A. Cook, *Lost Illusions: American Cinema in the Shadow of Watergate and Vietnam 1970–1979* (Berkeley: University of California Press, 2000), xvi.
12. Michael Allen, *Contemporary US Cinema* (Harlow: Pearson Education, 2003), 21.
13. Harry Witchel, *You Are What You Hear: How Music and Territory Make Us Who We Are* (New York: Algora Publishing, 2010), 52.
14. Buhler *et al.*, *Hearing the Movies; Music and Sound in Film History* (Oxford: Oxford University Press, 2010), 372.
15. Charles Schreger, 'Altman, Dolby, and the Second Sound Revolution', in Elizabeth Weis and John Belton (eds), *Film Sound* (New York: Columbia University Press, 1985), 354.
16. Hanson, 139.
17. Buhler *et al.*, 375.
18. Buhler *et al.*, 377.
19. William Whittington, *Sound Design and Science Fiction* (Austin: University of Texas Press, 2007), 93.
20. See interview with Walter Murch in Vincent LoBrutto, *Sound-on-Film: Interviews with Creators of Film Sound* (Westport: Greenwood Publishing Group, 1994), 83–100.
21. Gianluca Sergi, *The Dolby Era: Film Sound in Contemporary Hollywood* (Manchester: Manchester University Press, 2004), 24.
22. Whittington, 93.
23. Thomas Elsaesser, *Film Theory: An Introduction Through the Senses* (New York: Routledge, 2010), 131–2.
24. Whittington, 98.
25. Whittington, 108.
26. Whittington, 109.
27. Whittington, 111.
28. Diana Dominguez, 'Feminism and the Force: Empowerment and disillusionment in a galaxy far, far, away', in Carl Silvio and Tony M. Vinci (eds), *Culture, Identities and Technology in the 'Star Wars' Films: Essays on the Trilogies* (Jefferson: McFarland & Co., 2007), 116.
29. Thomas Doherty, 'Genre, gender, and the *Aliens* trilogy', in Barry Keith Grant (ed.), *The*

Dread of Difference: Gender and the Horror Film (Austin: University of Texas Press, 1996), 195.
30. Amy Taubin, 'The *Alien* trilogy: From feminism to Aids', in Pam Cook and Philip Dodd (eds), *Women and Film* (London: BFI, 1994), 94.
31. Mervyn Cooke, *A History of Film Music* (Cambridge: Cambridge University Press, 2008), 459.
32. Whittington, 155.
33. Whittington, 150.
34. Whittington, 152.
35. Donna Haraway, 'A cyborg manifesto: Science, technology, and socialist-feminism in the late twentieth century', in Amelia Jones (ed.), *The Feminism and Visual Culture Reader* (London: Routledge, 2010), 588.
36. Catherine Constable, 'Becoming the monster's mother: Morphologies of identity in the *Alien* series', in Annette Kuhn (ed.), *Alien Zone II: The Spaces of Science Fiction in Cinema* (London: Verso, 1999), 184.
37. Judy Wajcman, *Technofeminism* (Cambridge: Polity Press, 2004), 63–4.
38. Haraway, 590.
39. See Barbara Creed, *The Monstrous-Feminine: Film, Feminism, Psychoanalysis* (London, Routledge, 1993).
40. Stephen Mulhall, 'Making babies: James Cameron's *Aliens*', in Stephen Mulhall, *Mulhall On Film* (London: Routledge, 2002), 65.
41. Haraway, 53–4.

CHAPTER 6

Girl Talk: The Postmodern Female Voice in Chick Flicks

The image on the front cover of this book is from the 2011 film *Bridesmaids* and depicts the film's female characters embarking on a bachelorette party. This type of exclusive, female-only event or rite of passage frequently features in postmodern 'chick flicks' and in this final chapter, I revisit my discussion of the female voice in mainstream cinema to explore the aural representation of women in contemporary chick flicks. In examining this category of films, it is clear that they have some evolutionary links with the screwball comedy genre discussed in Chapter 1. This is evident in the female characters we encounter in modern chick flicks who, like their screwball predecessors, are often strong, confident and quick-witted, engaging in verbal battles to achieve their 'happily ever after' either with their lead male character or with fellow female characters, or sometimes with both.

Films that have come to be defined as chick flicks tend to be, according to Suzanna Ferriss and Mallory Young, 'commercial films that appeal to a female audience'.[1] As Ferris and Young explain in their in-depth analysis of contemporary women at the movies, chick flicks frequently span numerous genres including romantic comedy, melodrama, thriller or the female friendship movie. However, the narratives, themes and ideology from which they have evolved make chick flicks more than just simply movies for women and not for men, as I will demonstrate in this chapter. These films frequently portray a complex representation of modern females and female chick flick protagonists are often hard-working, intelligent, professional women and working mothers. In line with postfeminist notions of having the freedom to choose,[2] and unlike previous second wave agendas that rejected femininity, women in postfeminist chick flicks revel in the pleasures of womanliness, embrace consumerism, thrive on the notion of 'having it all' and do not hold back when it comes to verbalising their experiences of contemporary womanhood.

Angela McRobbie has posited that postfeminism can be explored as a 'double-entanglement' between the co-existence in society of neo-conservative values related to gender, sexuality and family life and the process of liberalisation in regard to choice or diversity in domestic and sexual relationships.[3] This apparent tension between second wave feminist concerns with the strive for gender equality and with postfeminist female choice in contemporary society is a common narrative theme in the films discussed here. As Michele Schrieber has observed in her discussion of the postfeminist romance film, this tension is frequently woven through the narratives of contemporary chick flicks: 'there are still traces of political feminism's forward momentum toward equality for women woven with a shift backward toward women's embrace of more traditional conceptions of individualised femininity'.[4] In this chapter I discuss *Sex and the City: The Movie* (2008), *Bridesmaids* and *Bachelorette* (2012). The films were chosen for their varied depictions of modern women, ranging from characters who are successful professionals, working mothers or failed entrepreneurs. The latter two films feature women of different ages, body type, socio-economic backgrounds and all three feature a narrative involving a (heterosexual) wedding. Diane Negra has argued that while some postfeminist texts leave 'open spaces' that may facilitate spectator negotiation, the overwhelming ideological impact of an accumulation of postfeminist cultural material leads to a reinforcement of conservative norms as the 'best choices' in women's lives.[5] In the case of the films discussed here, this idea is reinforced by the narrative culmination in a wedding, a stable signifier of patriarchal ideological conservative norms. Yet I argue that by examining the voices of the characters in these films, the 'open spaces' referred to by Negra reveal alternative dialogues, choices and meanings that exist for women in postfeminist societies, who even while opting for 'conservative norms', such as marriage, are free to redefine the boundaries of the choices they make. Furthermore, these 'open spaces' can reveal much to us about the varied issues and experiences faced by contemporary females and the relationships between modern women, which is at the heart of these contemporary films.

Much previous scholarly discussion of chick flicks points to the emergence of 'chick culture' in the United States and Britain in the 1990s, highlighting the release of Helen Fielding's novel *Bridget Jones's Diary* as a starting point. The book was released in 1996, and by 2001 when the film version was released it had sold over 2 million copies in the UK, over 8 million copies worldwide, and it had been translated into 38 languages.[6] (The film broke box office records when released in the UK, making nearly £7 million in its opening weekend and has since grossed in excess of £280 million worldwide.)[7] This cultural trend saw chick culture expanding and sees it continuing to proliferate today with various other 'chick' cultural products such as magazines, blogs, music and female-centred television programmes. The emergence and substantial success of these types of texts arguably demonstrates a heightened recognition of the importance of representing contemporary women in, in particular, British and North American societies. Ferriss and Young note that many of these cultural products, through their association with capitalist consumption and commercialism, emphasise the important economic power held by women during the 1990s and early 2000s – a period of global economic boom.

In this discussion, my focus falls on the subgenre of female friendship movies, since a large number of successful contemporary chick flicks explore female relationships rather than male-female heterosexual partnerships. In the case of the film *Bridesmaids*, when released it was actually referred to as a 'sistermance' or 'womance'[8] movie by some film critics in recognition of the narrative focus on female friendship. Such films lower the significance of the male-female relationship, which is frequently featured yet arguably inconsequential in narrative terms in comparison to the representation of the bonds between women. This is also comparable to the popular subgenre of male-centred buddy movies from the 1980s and 1990s referred to in Chapter 4 of this book, and the more recent burgeoning of the 'bromance' genre since the late 2000s, which includes popular films such as *Superbad* (2007), *The Hangover* (2009) or *21 Jump Street* (2012). Female friendship films have had a long history of popularity in American cinema and the successes of contemporary films such as *Muriel's Wedding* (1994), *Clueless* (1995), *Mean Girls* (2004), *Miss Congeniality 2* (2005), *Sex and the City: The Movie*, its 2010 sequel, *Bride Wars* (2009), *Bridesmaids* and *Pitch Perfect* (2012) demonstrates the on-going popularity of female-centred narratives. Typically featuring an almost all female cast, these films are popular for their candid portrayals of modern women and their relationships with each other. Karen Hollinger maintains that the female friendship film is not a particularly recent phenomenon. With reference to films such as *Julia* (1977), *Nine to Five* (1980), *Desperately Seeking Susan* (1985) and *Thelma and Louise* (1991), she highlights the marked presence of female-centred movies during the 1970s and 1980s in what she argues was a 'newly created cycle of films specifically addressed to a female audience'.[9] She argues that the female friendship film is actually a subgenre of the woman's film and is therefore a multifaceted film genre with a long cinematic history that begins with the sentimental melodramas of the 1930s and 1940s. But there is a fundamental difference between the films Hollinger interprets as earlier epitomes of the female friendship genre and the chick flick. Whereas these earlier films frequently aimed to subtly subvert the inherited generic conventions of heterosexual behaviour (*Thelma and Louise* and *Desperately Seeking Susan* are key examples cited by Hollinger), contemporary chick flicks instead take the subjects of heterosexuality or homosexuality and rather than subverting them, treat them in a far more playful and light-hearted manner.

These charted developments demonstrate the ways that genre conventions associated with women's films and melodrama have transformed over time. The resulting female friendship subgenre has evolved as filmmakers have found new ways of adapting a popular genre for new audiences, in line with social changes linked to gender and the dimensions of female friendship. An interesting case in point in this discussion is the 1939 film *The Women*, a fast-paced screwball comedy featuring an all-female cast including Norma Shearer, Joan Crawford and screwball star Rosalind Russell. The film was re-made into an all-female chick flick in 2008 and, like the original version, explored the complex dynamics of female relationships. Both versions feature a narrative about the breakdown of a marriage but focus on the reconciliation of female friendship between the protagonist and her best friend. The 2008 (updated) version features notable narrative changes and thematic re-workings to ensure its contemporary relevance, such as the quest for protagonist Mary Haines (Meg Ryan) to forge a successful career as an independent fashion designer while helping her preteen daughter face issues such as body image, updating *The Women* in a postfeminist context.

In a more general vein, Roberta Garrett argues that the influx of contemporary chick flicks is in fact a postmodern resurgence of the classical woman's film. Despite the apparent absence of female-centred films during the New Hollywood and blockbuster eras and the success of male-centred action and sci-fi genres throughout the 1980s, Garrett notes that 'the "chick flick" has steadily clawed its way back into popular consciousness'[10] and that this reincarnation of the woman's film features an undeniable employment of postmodern form. Garrett highlights: 'What distinguishes the new woman's film from previous female-orientated forms is the integration of certain aesthetic, formal and thematic concerns that, in other contexts, have been identified as postmodernist.'[11] These aesthetic features include allusion to previous cinematic codes and conventions, and narrative self-consciousness and irony. Postmodern cinema is often considered to be 'playful' and self-knowing, featuring anti-realist distancing devices, and the prominent use of cinematic allusion. In reference to the work of Fredric Jameson and Jean Baudrillard, Val Hill notes the intensification of the exterior surface in postmodern cinema and critical emphasis on the reflexive nature of postmodern cinematic texts: 'The film and its audience "know their own histories". The pleasure of the text spills over into the audience's knowledge of other films, other performances, other musics: the referent becomes part of the treasure house of signifiers that constitute popular culture.'[12] My examination of postmodern chick flicks shows that this element of 'self-knowing' is not only obvious, but that it also shapes the form of these films. The films I discuss here are very aware of the tradition of female films from which they have evolved, and this drive to self-reflexivity permeates their soundscape. It is for this reason that female voices in contemporary chick flicks are highly performative in the way in which they embody meanings and ideas related to the characters, always interpreting a few or a whole range of other female voice performances.

Michel Chion has noted that since the 1970s, the voice in Hollywood cinema has become a formal dimension that involves a far higher level of creativity when compared to classical cinematic voice conventions. He refers to films such as *The Exorcist* (1973), where the terrifying voice of Regan (Linda Blair) highlighted to audiences and actors alike that the voice in cinema is 'stuck on' and can be non-naturalistic. He says that, in film, 'there is no "natural" voice; every voice is a construction and forms a particular composite with the body. Each actor can take on different voices according to the demands of the role.'[13] He cites other examples of actors significantly changing their voices to match a performance, such as Dustin Hoffman as Ratso in *Midnight Cowboy* (1969), Marlon Brando as Don Corleone in *The Godfather* (1972) and Robert De Niro as the young Don Corleone in *The Godfather, Part II* (1974). Examples of actresses changing their voices for performance are widespread in chick flicks. Notable examples include Reese Witherspoon's high-pitched 'dumb blonde' character Elle Woods in *Legally Blonde* (2001), Meryl Streep as the deep-voiced, softly spoken Miranda Priestley in *The Devil Wears Prada* (2006) or Sandra Bullock's snorting tomboy Gracie Hart in *Miss Congeniality* (2000). This performative and creative element to voice in mainstream cinema can be linked to the idea that many of the female characters we encounter in chick flicks are overwhelmingly stereotypical, representing a particular 'type' of woman, perhaps a different version or choice available to women in postfeminist societies. This ties in with Jean François Lyotard's theories in *The Postmodern Condition: A Report on Knowledge* (first published in France in 1979). In this manifesto, he proposes that in postmodern society, Western, grand narratives (or metanarratives) have collapsed and have been replaced by a multitude of micronarratives. It could be argued that these micronarratives explore the narratives of diverse communities and social groups instead of the dominant white, middle classes. Therefore, the varied voice performances in postmodern chick flicks might be seen to allow for greater representations of varied female types, challenging previous aural representations of the classical female voice in film.

Unlike the voices heard in screwball comedies, which I discuss in my opening chapter, voices heard in contemporary films are highly mediated by advanced technology. This circumstance affects the ways the voice sounds: the female character's contemporary sounding can carry a wider range of inflections than the recorded voice in the early days of sound film, which did not capture the range and textures of voices as today's sound technology can. Thus it can convey a greater sense of characterisation and arguably paradoxically serve to reinforce contemporary female stereotypes in an aural capacity. For example, such technology could capture inflections in a female voice that suggest a heightened emotional state, as discussed below in relation to *Bridget Jones's Diary*. Arnt Maasø notes that the modern mediated voice 'clearly communicates a wealth of information other than mere semantic and referential meaning, such as attitudes, emotions, and closeness and distance in relation to other subjects in communication'.[14] In his analysis of the mediated voice, he highlights that the laws of physics related to sound and human interaction are largely suspended in contemporary film. For example, an intimate softly whispered voice can be mediated by a microphone and loudspeaker to enable its broadcast into a room full of people, creating a unique sense of familiarity or intimacy among audience members whilst speaking to them all simultaneously. Thus important parameters in the relationship between body and voice in everyday life are open to technological manipulation and aesthetic choice in mediation.[15] Michel Chion notes that contemporary multichannel sound equipment such as Dolby allows for a greater depth of sound relating to voice, giving the voice a direct, close, and palpable physical presence, entirely changing the way we perceive it. He concurs with Massø's notion about the intimacy of the voice by stating that such technology 'focuses finer attention on vocal texture, subtle variations of timbre, vibration of vocal chords, resonances'.[16] Maasø's empirical research demonstrates that mainstream Hollywood movies display a much more personal vocal register when compared with other filmic modes of production, such as television programmes or advertising. Also he notes that the vocal intimacy of Hollywood becomes much more personal than what would be possible in 'real life' or unmediated scenarios in interpersonal communication, noting, 'much of this is presumably due to great control over the recording situation, and what I also suspect is an underlying ideology (or tradition) of vocal intimacy'.[17] Female friendship movies often feature sentimental narratives and the portrayal of close or confidential female camaraderie, such as the *Sex and the City* films and *Bridesmaids*, which I discuss below. Therefore, the vocal intimacy of the mediated female voice is highly significant in this context. An important effect of such structuration of sound in the contemporary female friendship genre is also linked to the film's reception. These films are often enjoyed socially by groups of women in communal environments so the creation of intimacy through sound manipulation is key to the audience response to the movie and its characters.

Voice-over is often used to create this sense of intimacy and is frequently featured in chick flicks. This sound-narrative proclivity may be related to its possible descent from melodrama. Women's films are particularly prone to using voice-over narration in order to allow the audience to properly 'know' the female protagonist, as observed by Sarah Kozloff.[18] This allows the character to express her thoughts and feelings extra-diegetically, a classic example being the 1948 film *Letter from an Unknown Woman*. Furthermore, the literary tradition from which some chick flicks (like melodramas) have descended might also explain the frequent presence of the female disembodied voice in the form of first person narration. Michel Chion refers to the filmic voice that has not been 'tied' to an image as the *acousmêtre*. He highlights the power of this voice that is heard but not seen, likening it to the archaic stages before birth or early months of life 'during which the voice [of the mother] was everything and it was everywhere'.[19] This notion is interesting when applied to the female disembodied voice as it appears in contemporary chick flicks. In what follows I explore the power relations of this so-called acousmatic voice to explore the effect of the disembodied female in its representation of contemporary women.

The book and film *Bridget Jones's Diary* is frequently cited as the phenomenon that established popular chick culture. Since it is technically a British-made film, I am not including it in my wider discussion, but feel it important to discuss it here briefly due to its popularity and for arguably establishing some of the chick flick filmic conventions discussed later in this chapter. The female voice plays an important role in the film's soundscape since Bridget Jones (Renée Zellweger) narrates her diary to the audience as the film plays out. Thus we are in the privileged position of hearing the events entirely from Bridget's perspective. Bridget is thirty two, single and desperate to find 'Mr Right'. After embarking on an affair with her playboy boss Daniel Cleaver (Hugh Grant) and getting her heart broken, the final minutes of the film eventually see her united with human rights lawyer Mark Darcy (Colin Firth). One of the pleasures of the film is Bridget's comical voice-over which often narrates the exact words that film audiences might have read themselves in the book. Bridget narrates her actions, gives her opinions, states her aspirations and at particular points in the film, tells the stories of her friends and family.

The voice-over of Bridget Jones does not carry Chion's acousmatic qualities since we see Bridget narrating herself on screen from the films' opening; a formal strategy that Chion refers to as 'the I-voice'. This is the voice that separates from the body, and returns at certain points in the narrative as an *acousmêtre* to 'haunt' the past tense images conjured by its words.[20] He notes that the I-voice creates a unique bond with the film viewer due to the use of the first person singular narrative and also due to its forward placement on the soundtrack.[21] He describes this closeness as 'a certain sound quality, a way of occupying space, a sense of proximity to the spectator's ear, and a particular manner of engaging the spectator's identification'.[22] Thus the I-voice is a powerful means by which to personally engage with audience members and, in Chion's terms, seems to consume the viewer in the aural space of the film. Chion again makes the link between the disembodied I-voice and the maternal since as he says, the voice of the mother frequently articulates things, makes sense of the world, narrating and explaining it to the infant child. Thus, in Chion's terms, we can see the voice-over as an innately female and specifically a matriarchal storytelling device that comes with the power of communicating the world and aiding our understanding of the diegesis of the film.

The world of Bridget Jones is one that often requires explanation. The popularity of the film and book was often attributed to Bridget's apparent normalcy and uncanny representation of 'desperate singletons' in their thirties. Imelda Whelehan notes that key to the success of the novel was the lack of distance between the fiction and the audience's own experiences:

> The pull of Bridget for many seems to be that she tortures herself with diets, self-help relationship advice, and finds herself constantly wanting: yet at the same time she seems to be aware that these obsessions *are* obsessions and trap her in a vicious cycle of perceived inadequacy and self-loathing.[23]

Therefore, the inner thoughts of Bridget, conveyed through voice-over, are essential in portraying this fully-rounded, and apparently realistic character, with whom audiences had already identified in the book.

The voice of Bridget Jones, due to its heightened placement on the soundtrack, creates an immediate intimacy between her character and the audience. This type of sounding allows us to hear the subtle inflections in her vocal tones and creates the sense that she is speaking in close proximity to the audience. At the start of the film, her voice is deep and throaty, almost croaky, and tinged with sadness as she introduces us to her world in which her general existence is fairly unhappy. Her first words in the film are softly spoken and between each phrase of speech she hesitates, as if recalling a memory that is emotionally difficult: 'it all began ... on New Year's Day ... on my thirty second year of being single. Once again I found myself on my own and going to my mother's annual turkey curry buffet.' The exaggeration of her years as a singleton suggests a melodramatic sense of perpetual loneliness about her character and as Bridget navigates her parents' festivities, her gentle voice-over gives us her whispered personal insights that she cannot air within the diegesis. So when she says hello to Uncle Geoffrey (James Faulkner), her voice-over brightly says: 'actually not my uncle. Someone who insists I call him Uncle while he gropes my arse ...' These insights are often rather amusing, and create a sense of Bridget's world inside her head, or a version of Bridget that she is only comfortable to reveal to us through her whispered thoughts.

As mentioned above, these extradiegetic insertions are often the main source of comedy in the film. Yet due to the close aural proximity of Bridget's voice, we often feel she is whispering directly in our ear with her frequently 'broken' sounding voice, which creates a sense of realism and makes the voice more embodied. Arnt Maasø notes, 'when a voice is close we hear more of the lower frequencies, because of the so-called equal loudness contours in psychoacoustics . . . whereas a voice becomes "thinner" and more high-pitched when heard from a distance'.[24] So Bridget's close, lower frequency voice creates a sense of her physical presence, allowing for audience identification and empathy. Importantly, the fact that Bridget is given the power to narrate her entire story, a specific micronarrative concerning young, single, British women and the pressures of postmodern society, suggests that she is in total control of the account as it plays out. This is important given the overwhelming female audience identification with the character of Bridget, who is frequently portrayed as slightly pathetic, but who attempts to takes charge of her own story by setting out to achieve her goals with regards to her career and weight loss, even if her love life is out of her hands.

Like *Bridget Jones's Diary*, the *Sex and the City* movies have their origin in chick literature. The television show, which first aired in the US in 1998, was based on Candace Bushnell's book of the same name and has become a worldwide success. The four main characters, Carrie Bradshaw (Sarah Jessica Parker), Charlotte York (Kristen Davies), Miranda Hobbs (Cynthia Nixon) and Samantha Jones (Kim Cattrell), hit the big screen in 2008, two years after the culmination of the TV series. The film sees Carrie marrying her on-off love interest, 'Mr Big' or John James Preston (Chris Noth). However, when he jilts Carrie on their wedding day, the film demonstrates the bonds of friendship between the four girls as they support Carrie through this crisis. Interestingly, the film's main narrative follows a screwball comedy style 'remarriage' between Carrie and 'Mr Big' who, after several months apart, eventually marry at the film's culmination.

The four characters in *Sex and the City* represent different versions of womanhood[25] and although the television series narratives took the characters in different directions and through varied experiences, the stereotypes surrounding their characterisation remain in the film. Carrie, the professional writer, is a witty, funny, creative and philosophical character. Kim Akass and Janet McCabe have observed the postmodern link between the *Sex and the City* protagonist and screwball comedy heroines: 'Carrie is cut from the same mould as her screwball predecessors, with her sharp witty dialogue and pratfalls. Just as she is aware of how the representation works, the series rearranges and adds to conventions of these generic forms.'[26] Thus Carrie's performances are very aware of the meta-cinematic history of the character type she embodies and arguably, this idea is heightened in the movie. Miranda, 'the serious one', is a cynical, corporate lawyer and mother; Charlotte, previously an art gallery manager but now a happily married, full-time mother of an adopted daughter, is 'the romantic one'; Samantha is 'the sexual one' and as manager of her own PR company, a hardened, successful businesswoman.

In her detailed discussion of the television series, Deborah Jermyn highlights the ways in which the show continually foregrounded female discussion of postfeminist women's issues. She refers to the recurrent 'chat and chew' scenes showing the four main characters eating and discussing a key issue that would be explored in that episode via Carrie's newspaper column. Each of the four characters would express a different perspective on the same topic, representing a range of female views on contemporary issues. Carrie's subsequent 'think-and-type' scenes amalgamated her different friend's perspectives and would present her own views on the matter. Jermyn claims that the show

> became a kind of shorthand through which to articulate a particular cultural moment among a generation of 'postfeminist' television audiences, each week condensing a whole series of contemporary preoccupations surrounding femininity, feminism, sexuality, consumerism, and women's lifestyle choices into its thirty minutes of screen time.[27]

Akass and McCabe similarly foreground the importance of adept female discourse throughout the television series. They note that 'smart one-liners and pithy commentaries characterize the dialogue between the chums'.[28] This previous scholarly attention to dialogue in the television show highlights the importance of female voice in the world of *Sex and the City*. My following discussion of the different types of voice in the film (including paralinguistic voice performances, such as screaming) demonstrates a crucial mode in which voice performance transmits meaning about postmodern female stereotypes.

In a similar vein to *Bridget Jones's Diary*, *Sex and the City* is always narrated by Carrie Bradshaw. To return to Chion's framework, Carrie's acousmatic (bodiless) voice is present at the start of every television episode, and at the start of both films. Carrie's voice is arguably a postmodern one since film viewers are likely to be aware of Carrie Bradshaw's iconic status within the world of *Sex and the City* as well as with the actress Sarah Jessica Parker's off-screen status as star, fashion icon and celebrity mother. So despite the disembodied voice, we know exactly who is speaking. Chion argues that the not-yet-seen voice

> possesses a sort of virginity, derived from the simple fact that the body that's supposed to emit it has not yet been inscribed in the visual field. Its *de-acousmatisation*, which results from finally showing the person speaking, is always like a deflowering. For at that point the voice loses its virginal-acousmatic powers, and re-enters the realm of human beings.[29]

Chion's view of the powerful and almost pure, unspoiled essence of the unseen disembodied voice when applied to the female voice-over in postmodern chick flicks, where the actresses featured are well known in the 'real world', suggests they are unlikely to possess this 'virginal' status. Instead, as audience members, we often already bring a set of associations upon hearing the sound of Carrie's voice since she is inscribed in the visual field of the series and of the world outside of the series, making her seem more 'real', rather than some sort of unknown heralded virgin goddess, as Chion's theory might suggest. Instead, Carrie's voice is very much a part of the aesthetic of the movie, even when she narrates a piece in which she does not appear, she seems part of the narrative, rather than 'floating' above it. These narrations frequently appear throughout the film in moments of intimacy for other characters, for example when her voice-over tells us that Charlotte and Harry 'made love four times that night'. This exemplifies another aspect of female voice in chick flicks by demonstrating the personal discussions that take place between the four friends.

Sex and the City: The Movie opens with a musical 'mash up' of the jazz score used in the opening sequence of the TV programme, and Fergie of the *Black Eyed Peas* singing 'Labels or Love' (2008). The voice-over of Carrie Bradshaw immediately ties the song lyrics to the visual essence of New York by saying that every year, women in their twenties come to New York 'in search of the two L's: Labels and Love'. This introduces a double-edged theme that runs throughout the movie linked firstly to consumerism and secondly to idealism and perhaps naivety. Carrie's lively, confident voice-over carries authorial strength, linked to her profession as a writer and perhaps as the voice of experience since, as we are repeatedly told, she is forty one in the film. Carrie's voice is soft, evenly-pitched and frequently in rhythm with the sequence that she speaks over so that, despite being disembodied, she seems completely inscribed in the fast-paced cadence of the opening of the movie. The intonation and performative aspect of her speech is directed straight at the listener and gives the film a sense that it could actually be a visual enactment of words being performed at a book reading, perhaps making us question the temporality of this voice. This literary sense at the film's outset is heightened by the frequent use of wordplay, alliteration or rhyme that is henceforth performed by all four characters throughout the film, creating a constructed, non-naturalistic feel to the voice and dialogue. In the opening minutes of the film we are presented with a 'recap' of the four main characters, reminding us where we left them at the end of the television series. This features the non-diegetic voice of Carrie and various diegetic interjections from the characters, confirming her description of their characterisations.

Interestingly, before she embarks on this summary, the first diegetic intrusions come from other, unknown, women in the film, such as a girl violently beating a man with her handbag whilst screaming at the top of her voice: 'you're married? I fucking hate you . . .' This diegetic vocal interjection in the opening sequence prepares us for a movie that does not intend to hold back its expression of aggressive, forthright female attitudes both verbally and physically, especially when the cause of any upset is a man. In fact this moment foreshadows exactly what Carrie does to Big with her wedding flowers when he jilts her on their wedding day. This scene comes immediately before the first moment in the film where we see the four female friends together, walking and talking, surrounded by the tall buildings of New York, imbuing the film's opening with a sense of female solidarity and friendship.

As the opening sequence continues, Carrie introduces the other three main characters as her 'salvation' and 'meal ticket' emphasising female friendship as a means of emotional support but also, for her, as a means of earning a living as a professional writer and linking to the neo-liberalist thread that runs through these films. The non-diegetic voice-over is interspersed with diegetic snippets of speech from each character, building a picture of each. So the first words uttered from Samantha (whose main interest is introduced as sex) are 'oh my god, look at this . . .' as an attractive man walks past them on the street. Her high-pitched voice and New York accent portray an 'everywoman' aspect of her character, yet whose stereotypology is centred on her overt, liberated sexuality. This snippet of speech confirms her overly forward tactics where men and sex are concerned and introduces the notion of the objectification of men in the series, especially as all four women turn to admire him. However, on a comedic or ironic note, he walks up to another man and kisses him, introducing the notion of homosexuality which is also prevalent throughout the movie and TV show and perhaps links to Carrie's words about the difficulties of finding love in New York City, where men and women openly explore 'alternative' sexual lifestyles. As the sequence continues, Charlotte is introduced as the romantic character who believes in true love. In an exasperated, rather child-like high-pitched tone we see a snippet from a previous TV episode where she cries: 'I've been dating since I was fourteen, I'm exhausted! Where is he?' Further diegetic dialogue demonstrates her girlishness as she gushes with excitement at converting to Judaism to marry Harry (Evan Handler) and her emotional reactions when discovering she cannot have children and subsequent adoption of a baby. Miranda is introduced by Carrie as 'a disciple of tough love'; her first diegetic words, spoken flippantly in a detached and deeper voice than the other characters are 'bye! Great sex' indicating her lack of emotional involvement in sexual encounters. Her key life events are having a baby, marrying Steve (David Eigenberg) and moving to Brooklyn, which is frequently figured throughout the movie as a sacrifice to her professional status as a lawyer. In Carrie's rendition of her own story, she speaks of her love for 'Mr Big'. It is here that there is a noticeable change in Carrie's voice as it gets softer and breathier, conveying the clichéd notion of finding true love after years of searching. The sequence ends, however, by noting that after all those years, it is her female friends that she cherishes, thus emphasising female camaraderie as being of key importance throughout the film.

This sense of female solidarity is exemplified in the 'chat and chew' scenes

– noted by Deborah Jermyn as a trait of the television show – and which are also frequent throughout the movie. These scenes feature fluid conversational interaction between the women, which enhances their character types through voice performance. The dialogue between the characters in such scenes, I argue, is frequently unnatural and unrealistic. This view opposes common discourse about the television show, since the show was heralded for its realistic depiction of 'girl talk' and frank discussions about real women's issues. While I do not disagree that the content of these discussions represent a realistic depiction of commonly discussed topics in women's real lives, I argue that the constructed nature of the dialogue, which commonly features wordplay and innuendo, is unrealistic, although highly amusing and entertaining. For example, during one lunch early on in the film, at Charlotte's insistence that the word 'sex' be omitted from the conversation, lest it be repeated by her daughter Lily (Alexandra/Parker Fong), Carrie – true to her creative characterisation and inspired by Lily's colouring books – suggests they use the word 'colouring' instead. What follows is an amusing, metaphorical conversation about sex in which Samantha proudly and loudly proclaims: 'Well! I can't colour enough! I could colour all day, every day if I had my way, and I would use *every crayon in my box*!' Here her high-pitched voice and New York drawl confirm the characterisation introduced by Carrie. She is often constructed as a very excessive character, both in appearance and behaviour, so when Carrie, rolling her eyes, firmly and humorously replies, 'we get it! You love to colour!' it seems to acknowledge this exaggerated ostentatiousness that is key to her characterisation. This also sounds in stark contrast to Charlotte's delicate, softly voiced disclosure of how often her and Harry 'make love'. Her decision to adopt these words instead of the colouring metaphor likewise confirms her status as the romantic character since, for Charlotte, sex with her husband represents their love for one another. Carrie ends this conversation by telling her friends in a quiet, yet dramatic tone: 'when Big colours . . .' she pauses, looking around dramatically, 'he rarely stays inside the lines', which provokes raucous laughter from the women and neatly ends this short scene with an example of Carrie's trademark snappy wordplay.

As well as the sounds of female interaction and conversation, *Sex and the City* frequently features non-verbal expressive sounds that create further meanings about the characters. An aural similarity between some of the films mentioned in this chapter resides in a sound that I am terming 'the engagement scream'. This is the noise commonly emitted by women in chick flicks immediately following the announcement that their friend or friends are engaged. Such voicing is not always necessarily limited to the news of engagement, but the scope of meanings it conveys is most frequently related to rejoicing in friendly congregation. I have observed that a number of other chick flicks (*Bride Wars*, *Legally Blonde*, *Miss Congeniality*) use this sound in response to exciting events that occur within the narrative. It has thus become, I argue, a somewhat clichéd expression of female enthusiasm. Michel Chion notes that 'since the cinema first discovered women screaming, it has shown great skill in producing screams and stockpiling them for immediate and frequent deployment'.[30] Chion believes that the cinema works like a machine in order to elicit screams from females at precise moments within the narrative. Chion does not stipulate what 'type' of scream is elicited, whether of pleasure or terror, but the aural similarities between the two, I argue, and the prevalence of female screams of pleasure that populate mainstream cinema allows this theory to be equally applicable. Furthermore, I suggest that rather than the cinema working to elicit screams from females, here we see the female scream being appropriated and used within the realms of female friendship to express excitement.

In *Sex and the City*, one such scream marks the turning point in the film's narrative where Carrie gets swept up in the world of wedding planning. It is Charlotte, the romantic, who, when hearing that Carrie and Big have decided to get married, immediately emits a long, high-pitched scream in the middle of a busy restaurant, causing the room to fall suddenly into silence. She fills this silence by standing and announcing Carrie's engagement to the entire room, loudly gushing: 'she's just got engaged, and she's been going out with the guy, for *ten years*!' As she speaks, her voice gets high and squeaky with excitement and the crowd of strangers, the majority of whom are women, loudly congratulate Carrie with their own high-pitched cheering and clapping, implying a collective female grievance with the notion of the man who is unwilling to wholly commit. Thus the function of this scream seems to be in provoking a shared empathetic response across the character-viewer divide, taking collective female experiences beyond the film's diegesis. Chion argues that the female scream embodies a fantasy of the auditory absolute, saturating the soundtrack and deafening the listener. So Charlotte's scream at first seems to express excitement beyond words, suggesting that female fervour cannot be effectively articulated through language. This high-pitched vocal expression can also rather be described as disruptive in the way in which it saturates the diegetic soundtrack. As explored in the opening chapter of this book, female voice has historically been perceived as disorderly and unmanageable, dating as far back as Aristotle, thus Charlotte's scream arguably operates as a subversive, incomprehensible expression of female excitement. Furthermore, because a scream moves beyond the realms of language, it can be recognised, and perhaps identified with, by global audiences demonstrating the ways in which female communication can move beyond language. Such meanings attached to this voicing are maybe counterintuitive in their representation of complex female expression, especially when compared to the more sophisticated verbal representations that exist elsewhere in the film and in others discussed here. Significantly, in *Sex and the City*, Charlotte's outburst finds retort in Miranda's comic and sober response that she is now deaf and has ringing in one ear. (For Miranda, marriage predominantly symbolises sacrificing her career as a lawyer for her husband and son.) In a rather sophisticated key, such an exchange seems actually to parody the expected female response to an engagement announcement and to recognise the limits of expression through screaming. Samantha's later shocked reaction to the news, in which she states she does not really believe in marriage and sees more value in Botox, also provides an alternative aural reaction to Carrie's news, thus further balancing Charlotte's high-pitched screaming, whilst confirming the different character types.

Other non-verbal communication that exists within the film is the sound of laughter. Astrid Henry notes that, when it appeared on TV, *Sex and the City* was unusual for its depiction of women's laughter. She recalls the work of feminist critic Nancy Reincke who has observed 'the threat to male dominance isn't women laughing at men; the threat is women laughing with women'.[31] Indeed, much of the female laughter depicted throughout the film is between the four main characters and often figures as an 'in joke' which can be threatening to anyone not in the group, particularly men who would never appropriate the group in a way that other women possibly could. Mikhail Bakhtin's discussion of laughter as part of the Renaissance carnival explores the ways in which laughter can function subversively, challenging traditional hierarchical societal roles. He also discusses the ways in which laughter is linked with renewal and regeneration, thus highlighting a seeming therapeutic aspect of laughter. In a comedic film such as *Sex and the City*, where our protagonist experiences heartbreak, there is an obvious, momentary lack of laughter in this section of the narrative. This is self-reflexively acknowledged by the characters themselves, projecting a sense that Carrie needs to re-acquire her ability to laugh in order to self-generate and renew herself.

After Carrie has been jilted by Big, her three friends accompany her to Mexico, where the newlyweds were due to embark on their honeymoon. Carrie initially hides herself away from her friends, and when she emerges from her bedroom one morning, much is made of her depressive mood and lack of laughter so at one point when her speech features her trademark wordplay: 'I need something to get me out of my Mexicoma', Samantha and Charlotte are delighted. Samantha gushes: 'Oh honey! You made a joke! Good for you!' while Charlotte beams with delight and nods in agreement since Carrie's jokey wordplay symbolises the beginning of a return to her 'normal self'. Later, during dinner, Carrie again acknowledges the lack of laughter in her life when the other characters are laughing. She questions, 'will I ever laugh again?' and is reassured by Miranda that she will, but only when something is '*really* funny'. That event turns out to be when Charlotte – the most 'proper' of all the women, and who eats only 'Poughkeepsie' chocolate puddings throughout their trip – loses control of her bowels and makes a true spectacle of herself by defecating in her trousers in front of her friends. This embarrassing moment is made comical through sound by the loud, extended noises of Charlotte's bowels rumbling while her contorted facial expressions denote her utter horror at her loss of bodily functions. This type of grotesque, bodily sounding is discussed in detail below in relation to the film *Bridesmaids*. For now, I use this episode to highlight the importance of female laughter here in restoring Carrie to her true 'self'. Bakhtin, when discussing the history of laughter and its literary influence on Rabelais, defines laughter as a universal philosophical principle that heals and regenerates; he notes that the characteristic trait of laughter was 'precisely the recognition of its positive, regenerating, creative meaning'.[32] In this scene, when the full realisation of what has happened to Charlotte hits the other women, the camera focuses on Carrie's face as she immediately erupts with laughter along with Miranda and Samantha. The scene is made more comical by Carrie's voice-over: 'and just like that, Charlotte Poughkeepsied in her pants' symbolising Carrie's ability to joke again. The sounds here of Samantha's high-pitched, squeaky laughter and Miranda's lower pitched guffaw fill the diegesis, along with Carrie's comparatively quiet laughter. Their combined laughter can be heard on screen for around twenty seconds and at some points, verges on screaming hysterics, signalling a kind of cathartic release for Carrie. This moment represents Carrie's departure from depression, restoring her ability to laugh and a return to the jokey, light-hearted character with whom we are familiar. In line with the wider topic of this chapter, this episode symbolises the strength and value in female friendship and camaraderie. This moment and others like it in the film also demonstrates the ways in which female characters can and do make spectacles of themselves for comic purposes.

Such subversive behaviour is also prevalent throughout the film *Bridesmaids*, which actually used the concept of female as comic spectacle to promote the film. In this way, the film is markedly different to many chick flicks that had come before it. This is evident in the way that *Bridesmaids* was marketed to film audiences in 2011: it was pitched as a female version of 'bromance' movie *The Hangover* (2009), largely due to its depiction of a group of women 'behaving badly' whilst engaging in the standard American pre-wedding experiences such as bachelorette parties and dress fittings. Roger Ebert has called the film a cross between a chick flick and a raunch comedy, saying 'it definitely proves that women are the equal of men in vulgarity, sexual frankness, lust, vulnerability, over-drinking, and insecurity'.[33] Indeed, much critical attention focused on the so-called masculine physical comedy which includes five of the six female characters suffering diarrhoea whilst trying on expensive gowns in a bridal shop, or the main character Annie (Kristen Wiig) getting drunk and arrested on a plane, and later erupting into a violent frenzy at the bridal shower. I focus my discussion on the naturalised vocal performances of the female characters in the film, with further discussion on the use of non-verbal, bodily or 'grotesque' sounding linked to the film's physical comedy and unruly female behaviour. In this way, the soundscape of *Bridesmaids* challenges traditional female friendship genre conventions, establishing an alternative representation of modern female characters in chick flicks.

The film focuses on Annie, whose best friend Lillian (Maya Rudolph) gets engaged at the start of the film and asks her to be her maid of honour at her wedding. The other members of the bridal party include Lillian's cousin and mother of three boys, Rita (Wendi McLendon–Covey), newly married Becca (Ellie Kemper), the groom's tomboy sister Megan (Melissa McCarthy) and rich, beautiful trophy wife Helen (Rose Byrne) to whom Annie takes an instant dislike. Rivalry ensues between Annie and Helen as they compete over Lillian's friendship. Eventually, after Annie has unintentionally ruined the dress fitting, the bachelorette party and the bridal shower, Lillian tells her not to come to the wedding and puts Helen in charge of the wedding planning. Annie's life goes from bad to worse as she loses her job, her apartment and her male love interest, police officer Rhodes (Chris O'Dowd). The film's culmination sees Helen and Annie obliged to join forces when Lillian goes missing the night before the wedding. Annie finds her and consoles her, they renew their friendship and end the movie singing along to the 1990s band Wilson Phillips at Lillian's wedding.

Bakhtin's carnival theory is easily applied to a film like *Bridesmaids*, which features diegetic laughter and provokes the audience's laughter by knowingly subverting comedy traditions and frequently displaying grotesque aspects of the female body in a comical manner. Kathleen Rowe explores these types of Bakhtinian subversions focused around women in her book *The Unruly Woman: Gender and the Genres of Laughter*. In this, she draws on the work of Natalie Zemon Davis, who extends Bakhtin's notion of the carnival as the space-time of the subversion of social class to focus on the subversion of gender in comparable circumstances. Rowe discusses unruly women or female characters in films and popular television series such as Mae West, Roseanne Arnold and Miss Piggy as females who knowingly make spectacles of themselves to provoke laughter. She explores the ways in which these females, who are often comical, overweight, loud and rebellious, use precisely these traits to provoke laughter. Such rebellion shapes the aural figuration of narrative in *Bridesmaids* too.

Rowe summarises that the unruly woman is a 'rule-breaker, joke-maker, and public, bodily spectacle'.[34] In line with some evocative descriptions of Rabelais's characters in Bakhtin's work on the carnival, much of Rowe's discussion is focused on large women. But taking away the point of physicality, which here only really applies to the character of Megan in *Bridesmaids*, and focusing merely on sound, we can see how voice performance and the sounds of bodily spectacle might provoke laughter. Therefore, I find more useful Rowe's parenthetical suggestion that on-screen female challenges to the traditional order are exacerbated by the female mouth 'and its dangerous emanations – laughter and speech'.[35] The sounds of female voices dominate the diegetic soundscape of Feig's film: in fact, there are very few male voices heard throughout *Bridesmaids*. The voices of Annie and Lillian establish the important bonds of female friendship from the outset, emphasising what is at stake when the two friends are temporarily separated. Furthermore, their voice performances are often the source of comedy throughout the film. Kathleen Rowe notes that historically, popular culture and high art have represented women as objects, not subjects of laughter. In *Bridesmaids*, female characters appropriate the conventions of comedy to *provoke* laughter, a circumstance that casts these characters as subversive and unruly women.

Like in *Sex and the City*, we hear the sounds of female laughter early on in the movie, but as the film progresses, and tension is created between the characters, the comedic situations are aimed at provoking audience laughter rather than shared amusement between the characters. In comparison with *Sex and the City*, the interaction between the women is more relaxed and convincing, contrasting with the comparatively polished dialogue and wordplay in *Sex and the City*. Speaking on the DVD commentary,[36] director Paul Feig notes the prevalence of free-flowing speech in key scenes in *Bridesmaids*, and attributes it largely to the naturalistic dialogue composed by scriptwriters Kristen Wiig and Annie Mumolo. Moreover, the film's actresses were given the freedom to improvise many scenes while filming and were encouraged to try out variations of different lines to see which dialogue came across best. This approach to speech is unusual in mainstream cinema, since, as noted by Todd Berliner, 'dialogue in Hollywood movies abides by conventions that do not pertain to regular conversation'[37] and as film audiences we are aware of the function of dialogue to provide information about narrative, character or setting. Therefore, we are used to hearing characters speak in a way that most of us would not in real life, as I have argued in regards to *Sex and They City* with its use of snappy wordplay. The improvised approach taken in *Bridesmaids* is key to producing speech that sounds more natural and realistic. Sarah Kozloff notes the development of improvised film dialogue in the late 1960s and early 1970s with experimental filmmakers such as John Cassavetes, which led to a more realistic representation of colloquial dialogue.[38] Returning to Berliner, he notes that Cassevetes strove to achieve 'the impression of improvisation'[39] in films such as *Shadows* (1959) and *A Woman Under the Influence* (1974) whereby the cast and crew would adapt or change lines from the film script in rehearsals and during recording. I argue that this same improvisational approach to female voice in *Bridesmaids* is to be credited for the impression that the female characters in this film are more realistic and fully-rounded than female incarnations in previous female friendship movies. Furthermore, this adds to the subversiveness of the bodily sounds discussed later in this chapter, since, if the speech and voice patterns performed by the characters are more 'realistic', then the sounds we later hear emitted by these characters must surely be linked with a more credible – and somehow more grotesque – representation of modern women.

Much like the female characters in *Sex and the City*, *Bridesmaids* features a group of strong, confident, individual characters who collectively represent an array of contemporary womanhood. Unlike *Sex and the City*, whose glamorous, wealthy, white, middle-class characters are likely to be far removed from the lives of most audience members who engage with the film, *Bridesmaids* portrays a range of women in terms of age, class, race and life experiences and furthermore unreservedly probes areas of dissatisfaction in their lives in a more realistic, but also a more comedic and subversive manner. In the analysis below, I discuss each character and her voice performance in *Bridesmaids*, uncovering the ways in which voice can be linked to the representation of a particular 'type' in American society and how this might contribute to political or gender based meanings about contemporary women. Furthermore, I link these voice performances to the comedic use of grotesque, bodily sounds to demonstrate the ways in which the characters are unruly women, subverting traditional gender norms and genre conventions and challenging patriarchy.

The film's protagonist, Annie Walker, can be described as a girl who tried and failed at the 'American Dream'. At the start of the film we discover that she owned a bakery but her business was unsuccessful, resulting in financial bankruptcy and the loss of her home and boyfriend. Her status as a single woman who is less financially affluent than the other women in the bridal party is the source of her discomfort throughout the movie. This is often reflected in her voice performance, which often sounds diffident and involves brief moments where she talks to herself in attempts at self-reassurance. In his article 'Neurotic in New York: the Woody Allen touches in *Sex and the City*', Tom Grochowski convincingly links *Sex and the City*'s Carrie Bradshaw with Woody Allen's neurotic, insecure, nervous comedy characters in films such as *Annie Hall* (1977). He highlights Carrie's status as an outsider often trying to fit in, her frequently neurotic behaviour, and the embarrassing situations in which she finds herself.[40] The character of Annie in *Bridesmaids* can be categorised in precisely the same way, which is highlighted aurally through her speech patterns, which are often nervy and fast-paced, especially when she attempts to integrate with the other girls in the bridal party. As a victim of global recession – unlike the other characters in the film – she is a character who requires constant support and friendship throughout the narrative and again this is represented through her high-pitched and sometimes childlike voice performance.

Lillian's voice performance likewise reflects her characterisation, and importantly, her racial background. Her voice is often deep and slow paced, reflecting her character as being laid back and affable, yet frequently acquires a scratchy, higher pitch to it when she is excited. In some of these excited moments, her vernacular frequently features stereotypical African American colloquialisms such as 'this is crazy good y'all' or in her description of her bridal party as 'a stone cold pack of weirdos'. Other than the presence of her father, who is black, at the engagement party and wedding, the only allusions to Lillian's black heritage are contained in moments of speech such as these. Through marrying Dougie, Lillian is clearly moving from being a working-class black woman (augmented by her father's frequent complaints about the cost of the wedding) to white, middle-class territory as signified by Dougie's membership at the Country Club, her ability to fly first class and her association with very affluent Helen Harris the Third – yet her black ethnic roots are still audible through aspects of her vocal performance.

Helen's voice performance, reflective of her characterisation, is wholly embellished and exaggerated. In the moment in which we meet her, we see her via a point-of-view shot from Annie's perspective. Before Lillian calls her name, she gasps and says 'there she is!' in an excited tone which builds the suspense to her introduction. The camera then focuses on Helen laughing and smiling with other guests before she spins around, her long hair flowing and with a dazzling smile, looks straight at the camera, and at Annie, who looks immediately intimidated. This parodic shot is filmed in slow motion and the camera draws back to reveal Helen in a full length, stunning ball gown as she floats towards Annie and Lillian, beaming with beauty. When she speaks, her voice is high-pitched, smooth and frequently has a patronising or insincere essence to it in what appears to be a very self-aware satire of the 'beauty queen' type so frequented in mainstream American films. As a rule, the 'beauty queen' appears intimidating to the ordinary girl-next-door type, like Annie. This is confirmed in the first, amusing words Annie blurts out when meeting Helen: 'you're so pretty!' which shocks Lillian and to which Helen responds with giggly, high-pitched laughter and a patronising 'aw, you're so cute!' that feigns embarrassment but really suggests her delight at such a compliment.

The comic tenor of *Bridesmaids* is reliant on the dialogue and its vocal performance, which is fully realised with the introduction of the other bridesmaids. Lillian's cousin, Rita, is the oldest member of the party (likely in her mid-forties) and the only one who is a mother. For her, motherhood represents a life of restriction and disrespect founded on the fact that her three children are boys who frequently swear at her. Her introduction in the film focuses on the sexual awakening of her sons where she shocks Annie and Lillian by announcing in a pleasant, high-pitched maternal voice: 'they're cute! But when they reach that age . . .,' her voice suddenly changes as she continues in a loud whisper, 'they're disgusting! They smell, they're sticky, they say things that are horrible and there is semen *all over everything*!' Here her tone changes to a feistier one and then gradually to a quieter, subtle tone as she describes her life as a full-time mother. Rita's voice is deeper and more gravelly than the other female characters and her speech is usually disparaging of her husband and sons – and of their sexual behaviour in particular. Her candid character adds a sense of women poking fun at men, which is often featured in chick flicks, and in this film, adds to the importance attached to female camaraderie. This also adds to the sense that Rita, as an older and more experienced member of the female group, is a 'woman of the world' and her slight New York accent and slangy spoken phrases suggest someone who, like her cousin Lillian, has risen from working-class status to a life of affluence. This is symbolised in her comments about being at home all day with her children (obviously not expected to work) as well as her clothing, jewellery and the images we see of her middle-class home. In great contrast, Lillian's work friend Becca, a newlywed, comes across as naive and romantic in her voice performance, gushing to Annie in a squeaky, high-pitched voice about her 'sweetheart' honeymoon trip to Disneyworld, conveying a childlike essence to their relationship. Yet she is an example of a married but unsatisfied woman as she later describes to Rita, in whispered tones, the lack of sexual gratification she experiences in her relationship, also revealing that she remained a virgin until she was married. Interestingly, Becca attempts to emphasise her verbal compatibility with her husband by saying that they finish each other's sentences, which they do not (a more accurate description would be that they answer one question at the same time). Becca's giggly attempts to paint a perfect picture of romance between her and her new husband seek to compensate for their lack of connection in other aspects of their relationship; we later learn that Helen and Rita are both also deeply dissatisfied in their respective marriages.

Megan, who is of a physically larger build than the other women, is presented as tomboyish and somewhat unrefined. This makes her one of the funnier characters in the group as she comes across as eccentric, yet as totally comfortable in her own skin. Her dialogue is often comical, featuring swearing and aggressive, direct objectifying phrases in reference to men she is attracted to, such as 'I'm gonna climb that like a tree'. Her voice is deep and masculine sounding and she is heard burping and breaking wind throughout the film. Megan's character speaks of the bullying she experienced at high school and the ways in which she rose above the mockery of her peers by becoming educated to secure a high-level security job working for the US government. In this way she appears as a refreshing alternative to the other types of women represented in this movie and others of its genre, which might also accompany such a transformation with a physical change. Megan is the moral voice at the end of the movie who, after comically physically attacking her, loudly convinces Annie to 'fight for your shitty life!', commanding that she stops blaming the world for her problems, thereby providing guidance where other characters, such as Annie's mother or best friend, do not.

From this analysis of their voice performances, Annie, Rita and Megan appear as 'unruly women' and, at the same time, the most comical and most subversive characters in the movie. Yet the introduction of the further three, more conventional, character types balances the group and reflects the social 'norms' against which the comedy characters rebel. Their combined interaction throughout the narrative ensures that female voices do not only dominate the soundscape, but when they do, they are frequently disparaging of men and heterosexual relationships. A brief analysis of the diegetic sounding in the opening scene confirms the prominence of this template.

In the opening scene, we hear Annie before we see her, or any other visual images, voiced over a black screen. This then fades up to reveal an establishing shot of the exterior of a large house. The first sounds we hear are Annie panting while having sex. Her first rushed words, said in a whispering, throaty, passionate voice are 'I'm so glad you called'. These words, accompanied by the sounds of her deep breathing immediately suggest that this is a casual relationship and is linked to the concept of female sexual liberation. The scene that follows is comical in that it is a montage of the couple in varied, awkward sexual positions, the first of which features Annie astride her partner Ted (John Hamm), not featuring him in the shot, ensuring the film's immediate focus is on her and representing her as attempting to sexually dominate him. As the scene continues, the sounds of pleasure coming from Ted seem to clash with the sounds coming from Annie, which are frequently uncomfortable, verging on 'ow' or observational, 'I think we're on different rhythms', symbolising their lack of physical-emotive connection. In her seminal discussion of the embodied female voice in mainstream cinema, Kaja Silverman argues that the female voice, being always encased 'within' the female body in the film's sound diegesis, is always denied any authority or subjectivity precisely because it is tied to the objectified body of the female. Silverman places this audio construct in contrast with the privileged, disembodied (usually male) theological voice-over in mainstream films or documentaries, which always represents, or speaks, the truth.[41] Silverman's theory of the female embodied voice points to the objectification of women through bodily sounds, adding to previous feminist discourse that focused on the visual objectification of women in mainstream movies.

In my discussion of this postfeminist, self-reflexive film I conversely argue that here such bodily sounds are used to parody previous representations of onscreen female heterosexuality and to subvert male superiority. Importantly for this discussion, in this scene, Annie's breathy, bodily voice takes prominence on the soundtrack and our focus is always on her as she attempts to experience some form of pleasure in this overall unsatisfying sexual encounter. As we see the couple in varied (perhaps unrealistic) sexual positions, the sounds of pleasure that we hear from her are highly performative: clichéd panting and groaning sounds that are an exaggerated version of what would often accompany a Hollywood sex scene, as if to make an aural mockery of this filmic tradition. The final sounds in this sex-montage are of laughter: loud, childish giggling from Ted and an obviously forced laugh from Annie before the scene cuts back to an establishing shot of the exterior of Ted's lavish home the following morning, accompanied by the sounds of birds singing. By ending this scene – which is a far cry from the tender, romantic scenes of love-making that pervade mainstream Hollywood – with the sound of laughter highlights the film's subversive and critical take on heterosexual relationships, which are represented throughout as unfulfilling, or in the case of Lillian and Doug's impending marriage, as actually temporarily destroying female friendship. From a sound perspective, this scene highlights the aural disharmony that exists between Annie and Ted, the lack of any diegetic or non-diegetic sound enhances this, much like the lovemaking scene between Bonnie and Clyde described in Chapter 3. Thus the opening scene posits female agency as a key theme both physically and acoustically and uses the sound of laughter to question heteronormative love-making as portrayed by Hollywood.

In contrast, the interaction that takes place between the women in the film is represented as harmonious and free-flowing, as discussed above. The juxtaposing scene featuring Annie and Lillian exercising in the park and eating breakfast demonstrates the verbal compatibility between them and is in marked contrast to the mismatched 'heterosexual sounding' in the previous scene. Furthermore, when the topics of conversation are the men in their lives, the women are disparaging, such as Lillian saying that Dougie unromantically calls her 'dude' a lot and Ted saying that Annie needs dental work. Thus the notion of unruly women laughing at men is continued from the opening scene, particularly when the topic falls on sex, at which point the women laugh and make fun of male appendages, which includes Annie doing an amusing impression of what she calls an 'aggressive' penis. The scene ends with further female laughter, confirming the notion of female camaraderie and also introducing the notion of women openly discussing intimate subjects in a comical manner. Such shared unruly female laughter, Rowe argues, 'hints at the collective power of women to shatter the symbolic authority of the patriarchy'.[42] But this behaviour also sets the comic tenor for the film, which looks frankly and humorously at intimate, physical experiences throughout, a fact that, as mentioned above, featured heavily in the promotion of the film.

Paul Julian Smith observed that in the eye-catching poster for *Bridesmaids*, 'six strong women stare down the spectator in a pink lineup: goodfellas in fuchsia'.[43] This comparison to the tight-knit, strong powerful male characters of the gangster genre, partakes in the view shared by many critics: that the characters in *Bridesmaids* display an overt masculinity. Indeed it is true that we see and hear female characters breaking wind, defecating, swearing and wrestling – activities that, parenthetically, need not be seen as an exclusive male prerogative. It is in some ways unfortunate that so much of the critical attention has fallen on this aspect of the film, and has fallen on it in a misplaced manner, because this movie, written by two women, is not about women behaving like men, and surely 'masculinity' does not merely reside in, nor is constructed by, the physicality of bodily functions. Yet this critical spotlight that repeatedly highlights a fascination with such subversive behaviour is worthy of discussion, especially in the way that sound is utilised to aurally construct such unruly female behaviour. The scene I have chosen for this analysis is perhaps the most talked about in the whole film since it shows five of the six main characters suddenly overcome by food poisoning, and then vomiting and defecating in a sophisticated and expensive bridal boutique. This scene epitomises Rowe's assertions 'that the unruly woman eats too much and speaks too much, [which] is no coincidence, [since] both involve failure to control the mouth'.[44] Here we see unruly women's inability to control their bowels, leading to carnivalesque, grotesque comedy. In Bakhtin's discussion of carnival, he explores the link between laughter and the lower regions of the body, or as he terms it the 'lower stratum'. He notes that, behind a 'culture of laughter' (he has the Medieval times in mind here) there is 'the drama of bodily life (copulation, birth, growth, eating, drinking, defecation)'.[45] In the 'defecating' scene in *Bridesmaids* we see these elements of the carnivalesque working on the level of sound, and serving as a disruption to accepted societal female behaviour which is represented through the disgusted reactions of Helen and the shop owner.

Before the food poisoning takes hold, the characters have all tried on different bridesmaid dresses and stand in a row, discussing which one they should purchase. In the tranquil ambience of the elegant bridal shop floor, the sounds of various stomachs rumbling are suddenly heard causing the women to look at one another in embarrassment. When the shop owner then compensates this awkward aural moment by presenting Lillian to the group, wearing a stunning, white, designer wedding gown, all six women excitedly gush at how beautiful she looks. Rita says, 'holy shit, you look amazing' and Megan adds, 'you look so pretty it makes my stomach hurt'. Both sentences, containing allusions to defecation, pre-empt what is about to take place. Shanti Elliot has observed that the grotesque 'expresses a pointed reversal of moral and logical expectations'[46] which, according to Bakhtin, is a main feature of the subversion of carnival and which now manifests itself in the grotesque scene that unfolds. Megan suddenly, and unexpectedly, gags loudly and lunges forward, creating the sense that she is on the verge of vomiting. She repeats this action and simultaneously breaks wind, much to the shock and disgust of the shop owner and Helen who is standing next to her. Here we see the introduction of grotesque sounding, which is loud and exaggerated and seemingly all the more grotesque in being emitted by women. Yet the character of Megan has been constructed from the outset as overtly boyish and less refined than the other women, so when Becca and Rita both start to gag and break wind, these bodily sounds emitted from their more sophisticated female forms seems all the more shocking. This is then exemplified by Rita's frank assertions that she needs to 'get off this white carpet' conjuring the potential image of faeces or vomit in the elegant décor of the bridal shop while the shop owner screeches in a very high-pitched voice for them to leave and use the bathroom across the street. Next we see the physical manifestation of Rita's words as she runs to the pristine bathroom while vomiting on herself, the expensive dress she is wearing and then over the toilet. As she continues being sick, she swears loudly and roars noisily and her already deep voice drops in pitch, sounding quite monstrous as the food poisoning takes hold. Until this moment, the scene has been grotesque and quite unpleasant to watch, but now shifts towards comedy when Megan enters the bathroom, shouting at Rita in a high-pitched, pained voice that she needs to use the toilet. Unable to use the toilet since Rita is being sick in it, she lifts her dress and seats herself over the sink while screaming loudly at Rita, 'look away! Look away!' emphasising that she is well aware of her subversive actions, but has no choice but to relieve herself in the sink. A juxtaposing overhead shot of the two women screaming while vomiting and defecating augments the comedy since this unusual, bird's eye perspective of a plush female bathroom is strange, grotesque, but also amusing bearing in mind the narrative situation. This shot is accompanied by further bodily sounds from the two women, adding to the subversive comedy.

These loud, raucous bathroom scenes are now contrasted with comparatively calm, hushed scenes featuring conversations between Annie and Helen on the shop floor. Helen is the only character unaffected by food poisoning. Bakhtin argues that the 'classical' or bourgeois body conceals such processes,[47] privileging the 'upper stratum'; thus the character of Helen embodies this classical, bourgeois body in her feminine behaviour and speech, represented initially in her refusal to eat the meat that causes the food poisoning. We see from Annie's behaviour in the scene that she is trying to emulate Helen's classical 'upper stratum' composure. This only adds to the comedy of the scene since Annie's face, hair and clothes are drenched with sweat as she strives to avoid the loud, embarrassing reactions of the other characters. As these subtle moments take place, they are juxtaposed with cuts back to the other characters. When Annie quietly stresses to Helen 'I don't have to throw up' the camera cuts to a shot of Becca vomiting over Rita's hair and back, and Megan loudly exclaiming 'it's coming out of me like lava!' as she continues to suffer with diarrhoea while sitting in the sink. At this point, the shop owner enters the bathroom, the sounds of stomachs rumbling, mouths gagging and vomiting and Megan defecating are exaggerated on the diegetic soundtrack to create a scene of grotesque carnivalesque comedy. The scene's climax comes when Lillian, still dressed in the pristine, designer white wedding gown begins to emit the loud sounds of her bowels rumbling. At which point she is forced to run from the shop in search of a bathroom. She nearly makes it across the road before beginning to squat down, quietly telling herself 'it's happening, it's happening' as she slowly sinks to the floor while defecating in the street. The horror of the shop owner, as she now almost breaks down in tears, emphasises this moment as a sort of grotesque finale to this bizarre scene. The camera then lingers on Lillian, a far cry from the glowing bride at the start of the scene, squatting in the road as cars drive by, loudly sounding their horns at her.

In scenes such as this, the construct of femininity as represented by mainstream Hollywood and the traditional realm of chick flicks appears to be subverted and challenged; this can be linked to Bakhtin's notion about the subversion of traditional hierarchies during carnival time. Yet previous scholarly discussion of Bakhtin's carnival urges us to also consider the short-lived element of the carnival in that once it is over, 'normality' and traditional hierarchies and structures are restored until the next carnival. However, in memorable and funny scenes such as these, that are so highly discussed in both scholarly and everyday circles, it seems that the subversive grotesque comedy lives on in the minds of audiences, precisely because they are fascinated by this frank display of women 'behaving badly'. The use of sound here, in terms of voice performance and exaggerated bodily sounds, is key in maintaining a sense of permanence about these scenes, allowing them to remain in the minds of audiences. Such sounding and displays of unruliness challenge the generic conventions of the chick flick as we see and hear elements of the 'gross-out' comedy merging with the well-known form of the female friendship movie. Importantly, in the context of mainstream cinema, the success of this film featuring grotesque and subversive female behaviour has predictably led to the incarnation of other films that also explore 'alternative' female behaviours.

One such film is *Bachelorette* (2012), written and directed by Leslye Headland. The film is based on a play, also written and directed by Headland in 2007, which became a huge success off Broadway in 2010, notably making it a predecessor to *Bridesmaids*. Like the other films discussed in this chapter, we see a narrative that focuses around an impending wedding, yet the subversive female behaviour takes on a whole new shape and level in this most recent rendering of the female friendship genre. The film focuses on Regan (Kirsten Dunst), Gena (Lizzy Caplan) and Katie (Isla Fisher) who have been best friends since they were at high school. When drunk and high on cocaine the night before their school friend Becky (Rebel Wilson) gets married to rich, handsome Dale (Hayes MacArthur), they accidentally rip her wedding dress. The narrative is driven by their desperate attempts to either replace or fix the dress whilst indulging the audience in stories from their troubled pasts, including Gena's abortion, Katie's drug and alcohol abuse and Regan's bulimia. In true, yet slightly quirky chick-flick style, the film ends with Becky getting married in a repaired (yet slightly blood-stained) dress, Gena reuniting with her old high school boyfriend Clyde (Adam Scott), and Katie achieving her desire of finding a boyfriend who has a job. Meanwhile Regan unconventionally ends the film with no significant coupling to speak of, and having re-ignited her eating disorder.

As mentioned above, the unruly female behaviour witnessed in this film is comparable to *Bridesmaids* in that we see women behaving in ways that are unexpected and unfeminine for this film genre. Such behaviour includes excessive drinking, snorting cocaine, sexual promiscuity and even more candid discussions of sex than heard in *Sex and the City*. Yet, unlike other films discussed here, or indeed most other chick flicks, there is a distinct presence of unlikeable female characters. From the film's outset, the women are portrayed as rude, selfish, narcissistic and bitchy, although this is often presented in a comical way within the realms of the diegesis. This idea is enhanced by the construction of the soundscape, which features delicate ambient noise, the foregrounding of female voicing and prominent non-diegetic music. This acoustic construction is established from the beginning of the film, which I discuss in detail below. In one scene, Regan is having lunch with Becky, where the use of medium and close up camera shots introduces the binary differences in their appearances and characterisation. Regan is very thin, with coifed blonde hair, wears classical style make-up and is smart and stylish in her dress. Becky is overweight and plump in the face, her hair is tied back and she wears little make-up. She is dressed in a plain cardigan and does not look chic or stylish in the way that Regan does. Throughout the film, the three main characters frequently express their disbelief that Becky, who is overweight and – by mainstream Hollywood chick flick standards – less conventionally attractive than the other three characters, is the first to get married out of their friendship group. Furthermore, her husband-to-be is rich and handsome, which further irritates and baffles her friends, leading them to comically conclude that she has a 'magic vagina' with which she has bewitched him. Yet the suggestion that Becky is a confident and happy young woman is established in the opening scene through her first words, where in comparison to Regan's bland food order of a cob salad with no chicken, bacon, cheese or avocado, Becky orders a burger and fries, and brownie cheesecake for dessert. When Regan refers to the 'stupid diet' that Becky used to be on, Becky agrees that it was making her a miserable person, which is an accurate comment on Regan's characterisation throughout the movie and is interestingly how she remains at the film's culmination. This short interchange in the film's opening establishes Regan as a narcissistic, neurotic character and Becky as a secure and confident young woman; these ideas are emphasised through their voice performances. Like Annie in *Bridesmaids*, Regan often speaks at a fast pace but also has a sharp and curt manner in her voice, constructing her as a frenzied, insecure and offensive character. In contrast, Becky's voice is soft and slow, sounding confident and relaxed, yet also with an essence of passivity to it, suggesting that Regan has always been the one 'in control' in their relationship.

The first words of the film come from Regan and, like in *Bridesmaids*, are spoken over a black screen, drawing our attention to the sounds of her clear, confident voice. Her words are prominent above the din of glasses and cutlery clinking as she proudly announces: 'Things have been going really well!' She talks about her work with terminally ill children and the camera now reveals Regan in a medium shot, remaining focused on her as she smiles and continues to talk about herself. This shot is revealed to be a point-of-view shot from Becky's perspective, as the camera turns around to reveal her. Once they have ordered their food, Becky tells Regan that she has some news. Since the film is about an impending wedding, we can probably guess what Becky is about to say, yet the film now works against the viewer's expectations and rather than revealing Becky's news, moves into a fast-paced, non-linear montage sequence.

From a formal perspective, the inclusion of a non-linear narrative is a now familiar postmodern technique that knowingly disrupts or plays with the film's chronology: at this moment in *Bachelorette*, it creates audience speculation about what Becky's news could be. This type of narrative play is a technique famously employed by Quentin Tarantino in *Pulp Fiction* (1994) where the entire film unfolds in a non-chronological, cyclical format. Tarantino's stylish aesthetics and his use of non-linear editing were quickly established as a pervading convention in postmodern cinema and have influenced many contemporary filmmakers at various sides of the mainstream or avant-garde spectrum.[48] *Bachelorette* is no exception, as the opening episode now jumps forwards and backwards in time, disquieting the viewer but also allowing for the introduction of the two other main characters, showing their reactions to Becky's news and establishing key aspects of their characterisation. Gena is introduced waking up in bed next to an unknown man, with a hangover and with no realisation that it is Monday and that she should be at work. She smokes a cigarette throughout this montage sequence and her voice is deep and gravelly, conveying the sense that she smokes and drinks a lot and suggesting a gritty, hard essence about her character. Conversely, Katie is shown working in Club Monaco, a high-end clothes store, doing all she can to avoid work.

Her voice is high-pitched and chirpy, conveying a childlike aura around her character and also constructing her as a dumb, bimbo type. The fast pace of the montage sequence also introduces us to the high-speed, frantic narrative situations that pervade the film. This establishes an aural format that features quick, often unconnected, snippets of dialogue from the female characters. These fragments of speech often serve comic purposes but also establish female banter as another sound trope that pervades the film and heralds the importance of female voice in this female friendship movie.

Returning to the scene under discussion, as mentioned above, this montage delays the revelation of Becky's news. The surprising nature of the news, however, is implicit aurally from the very beginning of the montage. When Becky says to Regan: 'I have some news', the scene instantly cuts to Gena violently bolting upright in bed while loudly gasping. The soundtrack emphasises her loud, long intake of breath and then hoarse coughing, before the ringing of her mobile phone can be dimly heard in the diegetic soundscape. The exaggerated sound of Gena's gasping creates a sense of the characters being brought back to reality or shaken up by this news, while furthermore developing the characterisation of Gena as she sleepily glances around in confusion at her current surroundings. The announcement of the news is now delayed further as Gena begins to talk about her 'weird little life' as Regan calls it, who, in turn, attempts to relay Becky's news. As she does so, the scene now cuts back to the restaurant, to emphasise that Regan is retelling Gena their conversation in its entirety. As Becky begins gently talking about Dale, attempting to announce her news, Regan's natural assumption is that the relationship is failing and she repeatedly interrupts Becky with sharp words of wisdom about 'guys like Dale'. Yet again we cut back to Gena as she now interrupts the story, saying she needs to call Katie, since Regan's story is so long that she will never remember it. She shouts loudly at Regan to 'hold on!', building the idea that these characters regularly yell at each other and that this is a standard way for them to interact. Regan's frustration at this delay echoes our own, as we are now becoming intent on knowing what this crucial piece of information could be. The scene cuts to Katie who, upon receiving a phone call, comically says 'I've gotta take this, it's work' despite the fact that she is already at work. The story continues by cutting back to the restaurant as Regan attempts to comfort her friend, who, she assumes, is about to announce that she has been dumped. After several attempts to interject, Becky finally manages to announce, quietly and awkwardly: 'Dale asked me to marry him.' Then, tearful with emotion, she reveals the diamond ring on her finger to Regan. What was previously a fast-paced montage featuring quick snippets of dialogue between the four characters now grinds to a halt, emphasising that this news has stopped Regan in her tracks. There is now total silence as Regan – for the only time in the film – is lost for words and merely stares at Becky with a shocked facial expression and then emits a quiet 'oohhh', expressing her apparent total disbelief and jealousy that anyone would want to marry Becky. This exhaling of breath aurally envelops the revelation of Becky's news, which began with a gasp from Gena, and is now ending with the releasing of Regan's breath as this news literally take the wind out of her sails. The next shot quickly cuts to Gena and Katie, shown in split screen, loudly screaming in unison, 'That's insane!' The montage now speeds up again, as Regan, stalking along a street in New York stormily rants that she was supposed to be the first one out of their group to get married.

Compared to the excited 'engagement scream' heard in other female friendship films, two of which have been discussed above, the wedding announcement reaction we are presented with in *Bachelorette* portrays an alternative aural response to the news of impending marriage. This new acoustic construction represents contemporary female friendship as competitive and malevolent and furthermore questions American attitudes about heterosexual compatibility – that is, only pretty women should marry handsome men – since much of this stunned reaction is based on the circumstances that Becky is overweight and was nicknamed 'pig face' in high school. The only enthusiasm about the wedding comes from Katie who excitedly gushes that they will all be able to dress up, 'look cool' and throw a bachelorette party. Thus when this sequence ends with the three girls all saying in high-pitched, smiley unison 'love you B's!', all of this excitement seems either a hollow sentiment, or is rather a postmodern, candid representation of modern female friendship. Significantly, this phrase introduces us to the postfeminist vernacular, as we soon discover that 'B's' stands for 'B Faces' or in its full form 'Bitch Faces', which is what the four girls called their friendship group in high school. Importantly, this opening montage sequence finishes by focusing not on the bride of this movie, but on the three bachelorettes who are all stunned and jealous about their friend's impending nuptials. Thus the labelling of these girls as 'Bitch Faces' is arguably an apt title, while also introducing a new, alternative representation of bitchy, unlikeable girls as a narrative focus within the female friendship, chick flick genre.

The modern appropriation of phrases like 'bitch' that many – for example, the second wave feminists – would consider offensive and derogatory to women, is manifest in the film's title sequence: another montage featuring old photos and yearbook pages showing the 'B Faces' in their younger days. The sequence is underscored by the angst-ridden, distorted punk track 'Infinity Guitars' by Sleighbells (2010) featuring strong female vocals and a powerful, sharp drumbeat, suggesting a hard, edgy, no-nonsense characterisation of the main characters. As the images flash up in quick succession, handwritten words are scrawled on the pictures of the girls in their school days, such as 'slut', 'twat' and 'bitch'. A closer inspection of many of these words reveals that the girls call each other these names, as seen on one page of a yearbook featuring messages between the girls. In these notes, they write sentiments such as 'love you slut' and 'hey scrotum sniffer, great year as usual, B-faces forever!' Laurel A. Sutton has commented on the appropriation of the word 'bitch' in particular, among young female friendship groups, suggesting its use is part of a search for an individual and group identity in a male-dominated world. Such could be the case in *Bachelorette*, where the male and female world is represented as distinctly segregated and where, although young women are arguably empowered, traditions such as waiting for men to propose, or in the case of Gena and Clyde, to apologise, or in the case of Katie and Joe (Kyle Bornheimer), to even strike up a conversation, demonstrates the ways in which modern women might feel that they live in a male-dominated world and must abide by the rules of patriarchy. Thus this 'bitchy' vernacular is accordingly used as a signal of female solidarity in that everyone in the group can address one another as 'bitch', but it would not be acceptable for an outsider to do so. Sutton notes that choosing language that deliberately runs counter to societal expectations of women's behaviour constructs 'an alternative model of the social world . . . a new societal identity that does not conform to traditional definitions of femininity'.[49] Thus the verbal propensity for words like 'bitch' or 'slut' exhibited by the three main characters throughout *Bachelorette* demonstrates the re-appropriation of derogatory words that have historically been used by men to insult women. Here we see that these words – whilst also capitalising on the historical relationship between the girls since the nicknames originated in high school – now come to signify modern female friendship and solidarity within their clique.

The strong aural presence of punk music that opens the film is closely linked to another key aural feature of *Bachelorette*: the ways in which music is incorporated within the soundscape. Along with the film's inclusion of non-linear editing, the function and placing of music in the film is comparable to Tarantino's postmodern approach to movie soundtracks. For Tarantino, the choice of music in his films is often decided before filming has even commenced.[50] Lisa Coulthard refers to him as an 'acoustic auteur', noting that the central role of music in his films is key to understanding his postmodern style and popular appeal. The foregrounding of pre-existing music within his films has become a stylistic trait, Coulthard argues, 'more than mere pastiche, musical reference in Tarantino indicates an affective, emotional attachment to, and investment in, the music being (re)played'.[51] The prevalence of edgy, nostalgic music throughout *Bachelorette* imbues key scenes with stylish affect, relaying information about the characters and their relationships. In Tarantino style, the music also playfully flits between being diegetic and non-diegetic, or is heard within the headspace of just one character. A case in point is the episode when Gena spots her ex-boyfriend Clyde from across the room at the rehearsal dinner. As soon as her eyes fall on him, the song 'Moving in Stereo' (1978) by The Cars plays loudly yet non-diegetically, seemingly in Gena's mind, as all other sound in the room fades down and she compulsively watches Clyde moving in slow motion. The loud electric guitar strumming and use of synthesised strings embody the style of popular 1980s music and invoke a sense of nostalgia linked to their past relationship. This sounding also signals Gena's contradictory feelings about Clyde, whom she seems to hate, yet for whom she still has feelings. Once Gena emerges from her daydream, the sounds of Katie's voice re-emerge in the diegesis, along with the delicate sounds of a string quartet playing in the background. Thus we see music being used solely to represent Gena's confusion and angst about seeing Clyde; yet this music is also markedly operative in the diegetic world as it spurs her on to go and speak to him, suggesting the power of nostalgic music that, in this case, forces Gena to confront her painful past experiences.

A further example of this nostalgic, and very Tarantino-like, use of music is the dress-ripping scene. Prior to this, Katie's stripper friend has ruined the bachelorette party by calling Becky 'pig face', a situation which leaves the bride dashing out in tears, and the three girls alone in the hotel room. Katie questions, 'what do you call a bachelorette party without a bride?' to which Gena replies, 'Friday?' as the scene immediately cuts to show the girls drinking champagne and snorting cocaine, suggesting that this is a normal activity for the girls on a Friday night. The Northern Soul song 'A Girl Like You' by Edwyn Collins (1995) plays and appears to be part of the diegesis, underscoring the scene with a musical genre that has its origins in the Northern England 1960s Mod youth movement.[52] This rebellious group was infamous for its drug use and thus the soundtrack here embroils this scene with a Tarantino sense that the girls are 'cool', rebellious and drug-users, comparable to *Pulp Fiction*'s Mia Wallace (Uma Thurman). Their hedonistic behaviour escalates when Katie appears wearing Becky's wedding dress, joking about how big it is: 'you guys, two people could fit in here!' As both Katie and Regan decide to fit into the dress while they ask Gena to take a picture (to tag on Facebook), their drunken swaying leads to Katie abruptly falling over, ripping the top section of the wedding dress in half. Throughout this scene, Edwyn Collins has continued to accompany their unruly behaviour and the sounds of their drunken shouting and laughter add to the rowdiness of this scene. However, at the point of the dress ripping, the track abruptly stops and the loud sound of the fabric ripping is accentuated in the diegesis, like a needle scratching across a record, followed by Regan's loud scream at the realisation of what they have done. Thus we now realise that this music was non-diegetic and used to inflect this scene with a rebellious milieu, not chosen by the girls themselves. However, later in the film we also witness the importance of characters selecting music to play in the diegesis; another key Tarantino acoustic trait.

Ken Garner has observed that in Tarantino's three major films (*Reservoir Dogs* (1992), *Pulp Fiction*, *Jackie Brown* (1997)) moments where characters take control of the score through the playing of diegetic music are 'explicitly celebrated'[53] by the characters themselves calling attention to it and are furthermore indicative of character or situation. One such moment in *Bachelorette* comes when Gena and Clyde are at his mother's house, getting the wedding dress repaired by his mother. In his old bedroom, while reminiscing about their high school days, Clyde finds an old cassette, inserts it in an old cassette player and the song 'I'm Gonna Be (500 Miles)' by The Proclaimers (1988) blasts loudly into the room. In fact, the song seems to be *too* loud, and so amplified that it could lead us to question the 'believability' of the diegetic source of the song. This unconvincing sounding introduces an element of self-reflexivity about the film itself and the film's formal strategies, which is linked to the believability of this narrative situation. Again this is arguably a very Tarantino-like approach to narrative and music. This nostalgic aural moment, with the playing of this popular track, is so heightened on the soundtrack that it forces the characters and audience to listen to the lyrics as Gena and Clyde sit on the bed, staring into the camera. The essence of the song, which is about a man's love and life commitment to his partner, is captured in the opening lines: 'when I wake up, I know I wanna be, I wanna be the man who wakes up next to you'. As Clyde and Gena stare at the camera, the song continues and the words about commitment seem to dawn on them, represented via their gradually saddening facial expressions which denote that Clyde was not prepared to stand by Gena when she underwent an abortion of their baby, causing the demise of their relationship. As they begin to talk, their voices are quietly whispered, but are heightened on the soundtrack and now heard above the playing of the music. Their close physical contact creates a scene of intimacy that now seems to be more in line with traditional, romantic sound tropes of Hollywood chick flicks than postmodern Tarantino. This is confirmed when they kiss, and the volume of the music increases, seemingly in celebration and then becomes a non-diegetic accompaniment to the following scene. This scene is set to display the power of musical nostalgia, a sound trope frequently used by Tarantino; but here it is used to unite the couple and to soften the character of Gena, who thus far has been a hard and sometimes unlikeable character. Coulthard has stressed the importance of repetition in the tracks Tarantino chooses for his films, both within the format of the songs themselves, and the repetition of tracks within the diegesis. She identifies such repetition as being a pleasurable experience for the audience since it reinforces a sense of recognition and familiarity.[54] In line with such use, the Proclaimers' track is later used again in *Bachelorette* to permanently reunite the couple in the film's culmination, and confirm the unison of affect with the audience. After delivering a speech about his love for Gena, Clyde then attempts to sing the song to her during the wedding breakfast to confirm his commitment to her. The repetition of this track also comes to symbolise the reunification of the 'B Faces' and their respective male partners, ending *Bachelorette* on a celebratory note where female friendship is concerned; and it draws the audience in through recognition and implication in musical nostalgia.

The emphasis on female solidarity and friendship at the end of this film, as in the others discussed in this chapter, highlights that the female friendship subgenre of the chick flick privileges female relationships over romance between men and women. This spectrum of meanings is enhanced through the vocal performances in each film, but specifically heightened through the fast-paced, energetic female dialogue heard in *Bachelorette*. This film, I argue, can be categorised as a postmodern screwball comedy. In this modern rendering of a classic genre, we see the three female characters experiencing a rift in their relationship, undergoing verbal battles and experiencing temporary separation, with the 'remarriage' narrative replaced by the renewing of female friendship in the film's resolution.

Unlike the voice performances discussed in Chapter 1, the banter that takes place in this film is between the female characters. Each of the women displays female wit, intelligence and the capacity to talk at speed but, unlike classical screwball comedy, they frequently display no real desire to enter into this type of interchange with male characters. The girls' use of words such as 'bitch' and 'slut' to address one another brings a further postmodern edge to the girls' banter, and is a coded way to prevent the male characters joining in, since such vernacular is reserved exclusively for the 'B Faces'. In contrast, the men are ill-equipped to engage in these high tempo, witty conversations and are in fact repeatedly silenced by the girls' fast quips, such as Regan's questioning if Dale, Joe, Trevor (James Marsden) and Clyde will get into a Gentlemen's Club – 'because I don't see any gentlemen here'. Indeed, the lack of verbal skills exhibited by the men is astounding. Joe can barely gather the courage to even say a word to Katie, and Clyde's stuttered, awkward public confession of his love for Gena is comically inadequate, whilst also emphasising that the film's verbal somersaults are reserved for the bachelorettes alone.

This discussion of female voice in contemporary chick flicks has highlighted that self-reflexive voice performance is a key aural aspect of this genre. Like the screwball comedy heroines examined in my opening chapter, the women discussed here are smart and quick-witted. Yet, on finding themselves in a postfeminist and postmodern American society, they are far more playful in their expression than their female predecessors. Furthermore, their sparring partners have changed: the soundscape of these films, enveloped as it is in female voices, suggests the importance of women engaging in discussion with other women, and of privileging their relationships with one another, over their relationships with male counterparts. For all the constraints of the genre, this sounding still might display a set of alternative sound tropes that does not centre on heteronormative, hegemonic perceptions of gender and gender performance.

NOTES

1. Suzanne Ferriss and Mallory Young (eds), *Chick Flicks: Contemporary Women at the Movies* (New York: Routledge, 2008), 2.
2. Diane Negra, *What a Girl Wants? Fantasizing the Reclamation of Self in Postfeminism* (New York: Routledge, 2009).
3. Angela McRobbie, *The Aftermath of Feminism: Gender, Culture and Social Change* (London: Sage Publications, 2009), 12.
4. Michele Schreiber, *American Postfeminist Cinema: Women, Romance and Contemporary Culture* (Edinburgh: Edinburgh University Press, 2014), 19.
5. Negra, 4.
6. Imelda Whelehan, *Helen Fielding's 'Bridget Jones's Diary': A Reader's Guide* (New York: Continuum International Publishing Group, 2002), 67.
7. See http://www.the-numbers.com/movies/2001/BJDIA.php (accessed 5 April 2012).
8. Helen Warner, '"A new feminist revolution in Hollywood comedy"? Postfeminist discourses and the critical reception of *Bridesmaids*', in Joel Gwynne and Nadine Muller (eds), *Postfeminism and Contemporary Hollywood Cinema* (Basingstoke: Palgrave Macmillan, 2013), 228.
9. Karen Hollinger, *In the Company of Women: Contemporary Female Friendship Films* (Minneapolis: University of Minnesota Press, 1998), 1.
10. Roberta Garrett, *Postmodern Chick Flicks: The Return of the Woman's Film* (New York: Palgrave Macmillan, 2007), 3.
11. Garrett, 4.
12. Val Hill, 'Postmodernism and cinema', in Stuart Sim (ed.), *The Routledge Companion to Postmodernism* (London and New York: Routledge, 2012), 146.
13. Michel Chion, *The Voice in Cinema* (New York: Columbia University Press, 1999), 164.
14. Arnt Maasø, 'The proxemics of the mediated voice', in Jay Beck and Tony Grajeda (eds), *Lowering the Boom: Critical Studies in Film Sound* (Urbana and Chicago: University of Illinois Press, 2008), 37.
15. Maasø, 39.
16. Chion, 166.
17. Maasø, 46.
18. Sarah Kozloff, *Overhearing Film Dialogue* (Berkeley, Los Angeles: University of California Press, 2000), 247.
19. Chion, 27.
20. Chion, 49.
21. The technical requirements to achieve this are, firstly, close miking to create a feeling of intimacy and, secondly, an absence of reverb so as not to inscribe the voice into a particular 'real' space.
22. Chion, 49.
23. Whelehan, 55.
24. Maasø, 38.
25. Seemingly, one of the pleasures of watching the show for some women is to determine

who they think they are most like, via 'what character are you?' style online quizzes; see Michael Ryan, *Cultural Studies: A Practical Introduction* (Chichester: Blackwell Publishing, 2010), 145.
26. Kim Akass and Janet McCabe, *Reading Sex and the City* (London: I. B. Tauris, 2004), 12.
27. Deborah Jermyn, *Sex and the City* (Detroit: Wayne State University Press, 2009), 10.
28. Akass and McCabe, 3.
29. Chion, 23.
30. Chion, 75.
31. Astrid Henry, 'Orgasms and empowerment: *Sex and the City* and the Third Wave Feminism', in Kim Akass and Janet McCabe (eds), *Reading Sex and the City* (New York: I. B. Tauris, 2004), 67.
32. Mikhail Bakhtin, *Rabelais and His World* (Bloomington: Indiana University Press, 1984), 71.
33. Roger Ebert, *Roger Ebert's Movie Yearbook 2012* (Kansas City: Andrews McMeel Publishing, 2011), 70.
34. Kathleen Rowe, *The Unruly Woman: Gender and the Genres of Laughter* (Austin: University of Texas Press, 1995), 11.
35. Rowe, 43.
36. Paul Feig, 'Feature commentary with filmmakers and cast', *Bridesmaids*, extended edition DVD, London: Universal Pictures, 2011.
37. Todd Berliner, 'Killing the writer: Movie dialogue conventions and John Cassavetes', in Jeff Jaeckle (ed.), *Film Dialogue* (New York: Wallflower Press, 2013), 104.
38. Kozloff, 23.
39. Berliner, 107.
40. Tom Grochowski, 'Neurotic in New York: the Woody Allen touches in *Sex and the City*', in Kim Akass and Janet McCabe (eds), *Reading Sex and the City* (London: I. B. Tauris, 2004), 153.
41. Kaja Silverman, *The Acoustic Mirror: The Female Voice in Psychoanalysis and Cinema* (Bloomington and Indianapolis: Indiana University Press, 1988), 49.
42. Rowe, 2.
43. Paul Julian Smith, 'Beneath the glamour', *Film Quarterly*, v. 65, no. 1 (Fall 2011): 8.
44. Rowe, 37.
45. Bakhtin, 88.
46. Shanti Elliot, 'Carnival and dialogue in Bakhtin's Poetics of Folklore', *Folklore Forum*, v. 30, no. 1(1999):130.
47. Bakhtin, 29.
48. Examples include *The Usual Suspects* (Singer, 1995); *Out of Sight* (Soderburgh, 1998); *Sliding Doors* (Howitt, 1998); *Memento* (Nolan, 2000).
49. Laurel A. Sutton, 'Bitches and Skankly Hobags, the place of women in contemporary slang', in Kira Hall and Mary Bucholtz (eds), *Gender Articulated: Language and the Socially Constructed Self* (New York and London: Routledge, 1995), 290.
50. Jeff Smith, 'Popular songs and comic allusion', in Pamela Robertson Wojcik and Arthur Knight (eds), *Soundtrack Available: Essays on Film and Popular Music* (Durham, NC: Duke University Press, 2001), 413.
51. Lisa Coulthard, 'The attractions of repetition: Tarantino's sonic style', in James Wierzbicki (ed.), *Music, Sound and Filmmakers: Sonic Style in Cinema* (New York: Routledge, 2012), 166.
52. For more on Northern Soul music, see Andy Wilson, *Northern Soul: Music, Drugs and Subcultural Identity* (Cullompton: Willan Publishing, 2007).

53. Ken Garner, '"Would you like to hear some music?" Music in-and-out-of-control in the films of Quentin Tarantino', in K. J. Donnelly (ed.), *Film Music: Critical Approaches* (Edinburgh: Edinburgh University Press, 2001), 189.
54. Coulthard, 170.

Conclusion

In *Adam's Rib*, Adam Bonner claims that he prefers 'two sexes'. Much of the film explores male anxieties about empowered women and the concept of equality between the sexes. Yet, as the voice performances of both Spencer Tracy and Katharine Hepburn in this film continuously intimate, the notion of biologically determined behaviours that are socially assigned to each sex seems an almost impossible – and outdated – view of gender. My exploration of these representations in this book has furthermore revealed that the blurring of boundaries between masculine and feminine behaviours – or, rather, performances thereof – is a liberating experience for men and women. Moreover, this sense of gender subversion offers a pleasurable and wide spectrum of meaning-generative audio, visual and narrative experiences for film audiences.

While working on this book, I have encountered diverse aural representations of masculinity and femininity. These were centred by and focalised through their production and distribution context: mainstream (mostly Hollywood) American genre films. In discussing sound in relation to genre, we can perhaps consider this selection of films in terms of their 'dominant soundscapes' and now begin to reflect on the ways in which film sound genre conventions might have changed or evolved in each case study. Since this study takes a socio-historic approach, these changes can be linked to developments taking place in American society and might furthermore indicate how or why they might have influenced the evolution of other genres.

The dominant soundscape of screwball comedy is constructed around vocal performance, mainly consisting of fast-paced speech, with limited music or sound effects, as witnessed throughout *It Happened One Night*. Yet in later incarnations of the genre, we see more fluctuations in female vocal performance, as witnessed from Hildy in *His Girl Friday*, musical performance from Susan and David in *Bringing Up Baby*, as well as a chorus of loud sound effects such as the dog barking and leopard growling. These examples demonstrate how changes in sound conventions intensify the fast-paced, madcap essence for which the genre is infamous. Later experiments with vocal performance in *Adam's Rib* demonstrate the ways in which changes to male vocal performance reflected post-war attitudes to gender and a more self-reflexive attitude to the genre by filmmakers themselves. This self-reflexivity and playfulness is then later encountered in contemporary chick flicks, such as *Bridesmaids* and *Bachelorette*, where snappy dialogue between female characters reflects postmodern, female relationships and challenges the genre conventions of the female friendship movie.

Melodrama is a genre that has famously made use of emotive music to represent female emotions in its dominant soundscape, and later versions of the genre discussed here have incorporated jazz, I argue, to signal 1950s female emancipation and often linked to female musical performance. This development in film sound conventions demonstrates a more complex approach in the representation of female subjectivity, and a more general link between jazz music and rebellion that reflects the emerging ideological concerns of the younger generation in the 1950s.

When discussing the New Hollywood era, my chosen texts are difficult to confine to one genre, yet the films feature a similar dominant soundscape through the prevalence of silent male characters. This sound convention is interesting to consider in the context of my later discussion of *Full Metal Jacket*, which is set in the 1970s (i.e. the New Hollywood era) and features a collective group of silent and silenced male characters. Stanley Kubrick fulfils war genre expectations during the training and fighting scenes, with sounds of the drill instructor and weaponry. Yet, his manipulation of military music, popular records and composed, synthesised tracks challenges audience expectations of the war film genre. These important aural interventions speak directly to the audience and enforce the inherent political message behind the film: to question and criticise America's involvement in the Vietnam conflict. As such, Kubrick uses genre conventions (both aurally and visually) to challenge his audience, demonstrating a way in which film genre can be used to establish a dialogic relationship with a film audience. When comparing this to *Aliens*, we encounter a loud, raucous group of masculine Marines, who appear to verbalise their every thought, and when the subject is of battling aliens, they 'talk the talk', but do not have the required skills and knowledge to substantiate their excessive boasting. Likewise, this demonstrates how sound conventions related to the science fiction/war genre can combine to speak directly to audiences as a comment on the US involvement in the Vietnam conflict.

The silent male, as part of the dominant soundscape of the films discussed in Chapter 3, is in stark contrast to the male characters discussed in *Aliens* and *The Deer Hunter* as well as the recent emergence of the 'bromance' genre film, which frequently features a plethora of heartfelt male dialogue, not unlike the chatty men encountered in *The Deer Hunter*. This demonstrates a contemporary shift in society, perhaps part of the 'new man' philosophy, where men should accordingly be more open with their feelings. This, however, also links back to my discussion of Jack Nicholson's performance as George in *Easy Rider*, where we likewise encounter a chatty, male character, who appears to be the sonic exception to the silent male rule in this particular body of films.

In the blockbuster era, the dominant soundscapes of the science fiction films discussed here are more complex, due to important developments in film sound technology. Thus we hear an intricate mix of dialogue, sound effects, music and silence. The dominant soundscape of *Aliens* merges the sounds of technology and 'otherness' to create a multifaceted aural dimension that one might expect from modern science fiction films, although such sounding is markedly different from previous incarnations of the genre, which tended to rely on manufactured sound libraries. As discussed in Chapter 5, *Aliens* uses visceral sounds to suggest the materiality and threat of the aliens and are set in aural opposition to the technological sounds linked with Ripley. Here we hear a facet of film sound linked to the changing status of women in the 1980s, whereby technological developments meant that females need not be excluded from labour-intensive work that could be achieved via machine and a push of a button – as represented by Ripley in the power loader.

As mentioned above, the dominant soundscape of the contemporary chick flicks discussed here tends to be the fast-paced female voice, demonstrating a postmodern take on screwball comedy sound conventions. The popularity of this genre, with its dominant sounds of 'girl talk' and paralinguistic sounds such as screaming and laughing suggests a societal shift in the importance contemporary women place on their female relationships. Furthermore, the carnivalesque display of female bodily sounds in *Sex and the City* and *Bridesmaids* demonstrates a film sound genre convention that audiences might expect to hear in male-centred, 'gross out' comedies rather than a female friendship movie. Such genre developments are illuminating and perhaps suggest changing social perceptions of masculinity and femininity as well as a subversion of the generic conventions of the chick flick.

The conclusions I have been able to draw about the representation of gender in the films discussed here have often been surprising, in that even in examples of early sound cinema, a sense of subversion and play has dominated the early sound portrayal of gender. So when examining the representation of gender through voice in screwball comedy, it became increasingly clear to me that as the genre developed, with repeat performances from key actors and actresses, the notions of masculinity and femininity as fixed, essentialist norms started to be challenged. In particular, voice performances from Cary Grant, Katharine Hepburn and Spencer Tracy can lead us to deduce that gender is a fluid and ever-changing concept, and that even as early as in the 1930s and 1940s, actors and actresses were freely (re)interpreting it in their individual performances. While much of my discussion focuses on the representation of women in this opening chapter, the surprisingly daring male performances remind us that the changing status of women in American society was a change that affected men as well as women, some of whom might have struggled with the notion of women being more active and liberated, but many of whom revelled in the idea of women as equals, or even in the idea of gender as a fundamentally unstable category.

The liberated female characters seen in screwball comedy are likewise present in the 1950s melodramas, yet during this post-war period we see a proliferation of narratives in which women are repeatedly re-inscribed back into the dominant, patriarchal ideology. The notion of liberated female characters is key to my discussion of women and jazz. The sound figuration of femininity in these films undoubtedly casts socially subversive women in a negative light, yet, I argue, it also fosters a sense of freedom and rebellion against the constraints of the 1950s patriarchal society. In my discussion of melodrama, I have considered the aural representation of older women – mothers in particular – which is currently a developing area of academic research, and one which might be worthy of further exploration from a film sound perspective. An important conclusion drawn from this chapter is the notion of an 'acoustic remainder' in the form of jazz music. I have argued that the use of jazz within the sound diegesis (which is linked to female liberation) can, when heard again in other situations, reignite this impulse of freedom and rebellion in the active film viewer, demonstrating how sound in film can be 'taken' away after a film viewing in ways that visual aesthetics cannot.

When looking at silent, alienated characters in my discussion of New Hollywood cinema, the filmic zeitgeist for incorporating popular pre-existing music into the film's soundscape provides a rich field for exploration of aural meanings associated with masculinity. This strategy leads us to question previously rigid representations of strong, stoic silent males as the music tracks in my selected films impart meanings about men both within dominant ideological modes, such as Ben's father in *The Graduate,* and those who were part of the counter-culture movement, such as Billy and Wyatt in *Easy Rider.* Such aural representations allow us to consider the portrayal of male characters outside of previously hegemonic models, and to further probe the category of masculinity as such. This repositioning places an emphasis on filmic modes that use sound to consider the inner essence of film characters instead of focusing on polished, idealised facades as previously represented by films of the studio era.

The soundscape of *Full Metal Jacket* re-posits traditional, military-inspired notions of masculinity as either unobtainable or irrelevant. Arguably, the light-hearted character of Joker, who easily qualifies as a Marine (and thus as a 'man' in his drill sergeant's eyes), struggles to cope with the realities of war in the narrative. Yet his aural coding presents him as a fully acceptable 'version' of masculinity, possibly alleviating male anxieties about what it means to be a 'man', but also, due to the clash between this aural figuration and the narrative line, rendering the category 'masculine' null and void.

The soundscapes of blockbuster movies of the 1980s again reveal surprisingly subversive representations of masculinity and femininity. This is partially because the 1980s blockbuster period is arguably perceived (both inside and outside of academia) as an era in which filmmaking became homogenous and formulaic. Thus notions of masculinity and femininity also seemed to fall into more traditional representations, with the action hero and 'damsel-in-distress' proliferating in popular narratives. Focusing on science fiction films, my discussion has revealed that the use of sound in *Star Wars* and *Aliens* can lead us to question the validity of labelling a person as 'masculine' or 'feminine' even in such an ostensibly hegemonic male genre. In these films, it is clear that the acoustic representation of empowered female characters reflects the strong legacy of second wave feminism. Yet these incarnations can also lead us to question the validity of categorising gender in narratives where men and women are fighting the same war, 'in it together' and where, in the diegetic world, the presence of strong women is largely unquestioned, even when they perform the traditionally 'male' role of hero. Unsurprising it is, then, that Donna Haraway refers to this 1980s period as a post-gender age: the sonic interrogation of gender in these films questions what it means to be a 'man' or a 'woman'.

The discussion of female voice in my final chapter uncovers the importance of the sounds of female interaction and the ways in which female friendship has been foregrounded in popular, contemporary chick flicks. The focus on all-female dialogue perpetuates the notion of female solidarity in a contemporary age. Furthermore, it is evident from a close examination of female voice in *Sex and the City* that postmodern chick flicks frequently use voice to stereotype or essentialise female characters, if playfully. Later incarnations of the genre, such as the films *Bridesmaids* and *Bachelorette*, then subvert these stereotypes and candidly foreground 'less pleasant' bodily sounds of female characters and modern vernacular in ways that challenge female stereotyping.

As is visible from this brief account of my findings, representations of gender have varied greatly during this sustained period of film. Furthermore, it seems that while stable, hegemonic – or stereotypical – notions of gender have arguably always been embedded in American mainstream cinema (including the idea of the strong, silent male and the chatty verbose female), these depictions have frequently been challenged and the audio element of the audiovisual cinematic experience has been key to these subversions. An important contributor to this operation of sound is the 'acoustic remainder', discussed in Chapter 2, a hermeneutic category arguably applicable to all films discussed here. The idea of quoting famous lines of film dialogue has become a particularly cherished meta-cinematic practice – a form of entertainment for film enthusiasts. Likewise, the film audience can 'take away' musical underscoring (who might repeat the song by playing a recording of the same song at home), thereby extending the sonic life of the film and its messages, potentially eternally. In this way, key sounds such as film dialogue and film music are able to 'remain' with audiences, and thus associative ideas about gender and sound are potentially able to do the same.

Bibliography

Adair, Gilbert, *Hollywood's Vietnam: From 'The Green Berets' to 'Full Metal Jacket'* (London: William Heinemann, 1989).
Akass, Kim and Janet McCabe (eds), *Reading Sex and the City* (London: I. B. Tauris, 2004).
Allen, Michael, *Contemporary US Cinema* (Harlow: Pearson Education, 2003).
Allen, Prudence, *The Concept of Woman: the Aristotelian Revolution, 750 BC–AD 1250* (Grand Rapids: W. B. Eerdmans Publishing, 1997).
Altman, Rick, *The American Film Musical* (Bloomington: Indiana University Press, 1987).
Altman, Rick, *Sound Theory, Sound Practice* (New York: Routledge, 1992).
Altman, Rick, *Film/Genre* (London: British Film Institute, 1999).
Altman, Rick, *Silent Film Sound* (New York: Columbia University Press, 2004).
Aristotle, *History of Animals* (Whitefish: Kessinger Publishing, 2004).
Ashworth, Jack, 'Banjo', in Dennis Hall and Susan G. Hall (eds), *American Icons: An Encyclopedia of the People, Places and Things that have Shaped our Culture* (Westport: Greenwood Publishing Group, 2006), 45–50.
Babington, Bruce and Peter William Evans, *Affairs to Remember: The Hollywood Comedy of the Sexes* (Manchester: Manchester University Press, 1989).
Baker, Brian, *Masculinity in Fiction and Film: Representing Men in Popular Genres 1945–2000* (London: Continuum International Publishing Group, 2007).
Bakhtin, Mikhail, *Rabelais and His World* (Bloomington: Indiana University Press, 1984).
Barthes, Roland, *Image-Music-Text* (London: Fontana, 1977).
Belton, John, '1950s magnetic sound: The frozen revolution', in Rick Altman (ed.), *Sound Theory, Sound Practice* (New York: Routledge, 1992), 154–70.
Belton, John, *American Cinema, American Culture* (New York: McGraw-Hill, 2005).
Benshoff, Harry M. and Sean Griffin, *America on Film: Representing Race, Class, Gender, and Sexuality at the Movies* (Malden: Wiley-Blackwell, 2004).
Berliner, Todd, 'Killing the writer: Movie dialogue conventions and John Cassavetes', in Jeff Jaeckle (ed.), *Film Dialogue* (New York: Wallflower Press, 2013), 103–15.
Beynon, John, *Masculinities and Culture* (Buckingham: Open University Press, 2002).
Biskind, Peter, *Easy Riders, Raging Bulls: How the Sex 'n' Drugs 'n' Rock 'n' Roll Generation saved Hollywood* (London: Bloomsbury, 1998).
Bloom, Gina, *Voice in Motion: Staging Gender, Shaping Sound in Early Modern England* (Philadelphia: University of Pennsylvania Press, 2007).

Brode, Douglas and Leah Deyneka (eds), *Sex, Politics and Religion in Star Wars: An Anthology* (Lanhan: Scarecrow Press, 2012).
Brown, Royal S., *Overtones and Undertones: Reading Film Music* (Berkeley: University of California Press, 1994).
Bruzzi, Stella, *Men's Cinema: Masculinity and Mise-en-scene in Hollywood* (Edinburgh: Edinburgh University Press, 2013).
Buhler, James, Caryl Flinn and David Neumeyer (eds), *Music and Cinema* (Hanover: Wesleyan University Press, 2000).
Buhler, James, David Neumeyer and Rob Deemer, *Hearing the Movies; Music and Sound in Film History* (Oxford: Oxford University Press, 2010).
Buscombe, Edward, *100 Westerns: BFI Screen Guides* (London: BFI, 2006).
Butler, David, *Jazz Noir: Listening to Music from The Phantom Lady to The Last Seduction* (Westport: Greenwood Publishing Group, 2002).
Butler, Judith, *Gender Trouble: Feminism and the Subversion of Identity* (New York: Routledge, 1990).
Byers, Jackie, *All That Hollywood Allows: Re-Reading Gender in 1950s Melodrama* (Chapel Hill: University of North Carolina Press, 1991).
Carson, Ann, 'The gender of sound', in Ann Carson, *Glass, Irony and God* (New York: New Directions Publishing Corporation, 1995).
Carson, Diane, 'To be seen but not heard: *The Awful Truth*', in Diane Carson, Linda Dittmar and Janice Welsch (eds), *Multiple Voices in Feminist Film Criticism* (Minneapolis: University of Minnesota Press, 1994), 213–25.
Cavell, Stanley, *Pursuits of Happiness: The Hollywood Comedy of Remarriage* (Cambridge, MA: Harvard University Press, 1981).
Chion, Michel, *Audio-Vision* (New York: Columbia University Press, 1994).
Chion, Michel, *The Voice in Cinema* (New York: Columbia University Press, 1999).
Chion, Michel, *Film, a Sound Art* (New York: Columbia University Press, 2009).
Clement, Catherine, *Opera, or, The Undoing of Women* (London: I. B. Tauris, 1997).
Cohen, Steven and Ina Rae Clark, *The Road Movie Book* (London: Routledge, 1997).
Comolli, Jean-Louis and Jean Narboni, 'Cinema/Ideology/Criticism', *Screen*, v. 12, no.1 (Spring 1971): 27–36.
Constable, Catherine, 'Becoming the monster's mother: Morphologies of identity in the *Alien* series', in Annette Kuhn (ed.), *Alien Zone II: The Spaces of Science Fiction in Cinema* (London: Verso, 1999), 173–202.
Cook, David A., *Lost Illusions: American Cinema in the Shadow of Watergate and Vietnam 1970–1979* (Berkeley: University of California Press, 2000).
Cook, Pam, 'Duplicity in *Mildred Pierce*', in Ann E. Kaplan (ed.), *Women in Film Noir* (London: BFI, 1978), 68–82.
Cook, Pam, *Screening the Past: Memory and Nostalgia in the Cinema* (London: Routledge, 2005).
Cooke, Mervyn, *A History of Film Music* (Cambridge: Cambridge University Press, 2008).
Coulthard, Lisa, 'The attractions of repetition: Tarantino's sonic style', in James Wierzbicki (ed.), *Music, Sound and Filmmakers: Sonic Style in Cinema* (New York: Routledge, 2012), 165–74.
Creed, Barbara, *The Monstrous-Feminine: Film, Feminism, Psychoanalysis* (London: Routledge, 1993).
De Beauvoir, Simone, *The Second Sex* (London: Vintage, 2000).
del Rio, Elena, *Deleuze and the Cinemas of Performance: Powers of Affection* (Edinburgh: Edinburgh University Press, 2008).

Denisoff, R. Serge and William D. Romanowski, *Risky Business: Rock in Film* (New Brunswick, NJ: Transaction Publishers, 1991).
DiBattista, Maria, *Fast Talking Dames* (New Haven: Yale University Press, 2001).
Dichos, Andrew, *Street with No Name: A History of the Classical American Film Noir* (Lexington: University Press of Kentucky, 2002).
Doherty, Thomas, Genre, gender, and the *Aliens* trilogy', in Barry Keith Grant (ed.), *The Dread of Difference: Gender and the Horror Film* (Austin: University of Texas Press, 1996), 181–99.
Dominguez, Diana, 'Feminism and the Force: Empowerment and disillusionment in a galaxy far, far, away', in Carl Silvio and Tony M. Vinci (eds), *Culture, Identities and Technology in the 'Star Wars' Films: Essays on the Trilogies* (Jefferson: McFarland & Co., 2007), 109–33.
Drachman, Virginia G., *Sisters in Law: Women Lawyers in Modern American History* (Boston, MA: Harvard University Press, 2001).
Dunn, Leslie C. and Nancy A. Jones (eds), *Embodied Voices: Representing Female Vocality in Western Culture* (Cambridge: Cambridge University Press, 1996).
Dyer, Richard, *Gays and Film* (New York: Zoetrope, 1984).
Dyer, Richard, 'Four films of Lana Turner', in Lucy Fischer (ed.), *Imitation of Life, Douglas Sirk, Director* (New Brunswick, NJ: Rutgers University Press, 1991), 186–206.
Ebert, Roger, *Roger Ebert's Movie Yearbook 2012* (Kansas City: Andrews McMeel Publishing, 2011).
Elliot, Shanti, 'Carnival and dialogue in Bakhtin's Poetics of Folklore', *Folklore Forum*, v. 30, no. 1 (1999): 129–39.
Elsaesser, Thomas, 'Tales of sound and fury: Observations on the family melodrama', in Christine Gledhill (ed.), *Home is Where the Heart is: Studies in Melodrama and the Woman's Film* (London: BFI, 2002), 43–69.
Elsaesser, Thomas, *Film Theory: An Introduction Through the Senses* (New York: Routledge, 2010).
Epstein, Cythia Fuchs, *Women in Law* (Champaign: University of Illinois Press, 1993).
Faludi, Susan, *Stiffed: The Betrayal of the Modern Man* (London: Chatto and Windus, 1999).
Ferriss, Suzanne and Mallory Young (eds), *Chick Flicks: Contemporary Women at the Movies* (New York: Routledge, 2008).
Flinn, Caryl, *Strains of Utopia: Gender, Nostalgia and Hollywood Film Music* (Princeton: Princeton University Press, 1992).
Friedan, Betty, *The Feminine Mystique* (New York: Norton, 2001).
Friedman, Lester D., *Arthur Penn's Bonnie and Clyde* (Cambridge: Cambridge University Press, 2000).
Gabbard, Krin and Shailja Sharma, 'Stanley Kubrick and the Art Cinema', in Stuart Y. McDougal (ed.), *Stanley Kubrick's 'A Clockwork Orange'* (Cambridge: Cambridge University Press, 2003), 85–108.
Garner, Ken, '"Would you like to hear some music?" Music in-and-out-of-control in the films of Quentin Tarantino', in K. J. Donnelly (ed.), *Film Music: Critical Approaches* (Edinburgh: Edinburgh University Press, 2001), 188–205.
Garrett, Roberta, *Postmodern Chick Flicks: The Return of the Woman's Film* (New York: Palgrave Macmillan, 2007).
Gauntlett, David, *Media, Gender and Identity: An Introduction* (London: Routledge, 2002).
Gledhill, Christine, 'Women reading men', in Pat Kirkham and Janet Thumin (eds), *Me Jane: Masculinity, Movies and Women* (London: Lawrence and Wishart, 1995), 73–93.
Gledhill, Christine (ed.), *Home is Where the Heart is: Studies in Melodrama and the Woman's Film* (London: BFI, 2002).

Gomery, Douglas, 'Writing the history of the American film industry: Warner Brothers and sound', in Bill Nichols (ed.), *Movies and Methods: An Anthology, Volume 2* (Berkeley: University of California Press, 1985), 108–20.
Gorbman, Claudia, *Unheard Melodies: Narrative Film Music* (London: BFI, 1987).
Grant, Barry Keith (ed.), *American Cinema of the 1960s: Themes and Variations* (New Brunswick, NJ: Rutgers University Press, 2008).
Grochowski, Tom, 'Neurotic in New York: the Woody Allen Touches in *Sex and the City*', in Kim Akass and Janet McCabe (eds), *Reading Sex and the City* (London: I. B. Tauris, 2004), 149–60.
Hagopian, Patrick, *The Vietnam War in American Memory: Veterans, Memorials, and the Politics of Healing* (Amherst: University of Massachusetts Press, 2011).
Hanson, Helen, *Hollywood Heroines: Women in Film Noir and the Gothic Film* (London: I. B. Tauris, 2007).
Hanson, Helen, 'Sound affects: Post-production sound, soundscapes and sound design in Hollywood's studio era', *Music, Sound and the Moving Image*, v. 1, no. 1 (2007): 27–49.
Hanson, Helen and Steve Neale, 'Commanding the sounds of the universe: Classical Hollywood sound in the 1930s and early 1940s', in Steve Neale (ed.), *The Classical Hollywood Reader* (New York: Routledge, 2012), 249–61.
Haraway, Donna, 'A cyborg manifesto: Science, technology, and socialist-feminism in the late twentieth century', in Amelia Jones (ed.), *The Feminism and Visual Culture Reader* (London: Routledge, 2010), 475–98.
Haskell, Molly, *From Reverence to Rape: The Treatment of Women in the Movies* (New York: Holt, Rinehart and Winston, 1975).
Henry, Astrid, 'Orgasms and empowerment: *Sex and the City* and the Third Wave Feminism', in Kim Akass and Janet McCabe (eds), *Reading Sex and the City* (New York: I. B. Tauris, 2004), 65–82.
Heung, Marina, '"What's the matter with Sarah Jane?": Daughters and mothers in Douglas Sirk's *Imitation of Life*', in Lucy Fischer (ed.), *Imitation of Life, Douglas Sirk, director* (New Brunswick, NJ: Rutgers University Press, 1991), 302–24.
Hill, Val, 'Postmodernism and cinema', in Stuart Sim (ed.), *The Routledge Companion to Postmodernism* (London: Routledge, 2012), 143–55.
Hollinger, Karen, *In the Company of Women: Contemporary Female Friendship Films* (Minneapolis: University of Minnesota Press, 1998).
Hollinger, Karen, *Feminist Film Studies* (London: Routledge, 2012).
hooks, bell, *Ain't I A Woman? Black Woman and Feminism* (Boston, MA: South End Press, 1981).
Horrocks, Roger, *Male Myths and Icons: Masculinity in Popular Culture* (Basingstoke: Macmillan, 1995).
Inglis, Ian, 'Music, masculinity and membership', in Steve Lannin and Matthew Caley (eds), *Pop Fiction: The Song in Cinema* (Bristol: Intellect Books, 2005).
Jeffords, Susan, *The Remasculinization of America: Gender and the Vietnam War* (Bloomington: Indiana University Press, 1989).
Jeffords, Susan, *Hard Bodies: Hollywood Masculinity in the Reagan Era* (New Brunswick, NJ: Rutgers University Press, 2004).
Jermyn, Deborah, *Sex and the City* (Detroit: Wayne State University Press, 2009).
Johnston, Claire, 'Women's cinema as counter-cinema', in E. Ann Kaplan (ed.), *Feminism and Film* (New York: Oxford University Press, 2000), 22–33.
Kalinak, Kathryn, *Settling the Score: Music and the Classical Hollywood Film* (Madison: University of Wisconsin Press, 1992).

Kalinak, Kathryn, *Film Music: A Very Short Introduction* (Oxford: Oxford University Press, 2010).
Kamir, Orit, *Framed: Women in Law and Film* (Durham, NC: Duke University Press, 2006).
Kaplan, E. Ann, 'A history of gender theory in cinema studies', in Krin Gabbard and William Luhr (eds), *Screening Genders* (New Brunswick, NJ: Rutgers University Press, 2008), 15–28.
Kassabian, Anahid, *Hearing Film: Tracking Identifications in Contemporary Hollywood Film Music* (New York: Routledge, 2001).
Kendall, Elizabeth, *The Runaway Bride: Hollywood Romantic Comedies of the 1930s* (New York: Cooper Square Press, 2002).
Kerins, Mark, *Beyond Dolby (Stereo): Cinema in the Digital Sound Age* (Bloomington: Indiana University Press, 2011).
King, Geoff, *New Hollywood Cinema: An Introduction* (London: I. B. Tauris, 2002).
Klein, Michael, 'Historical memory, film, and the Vietnam era', in Linda Dittmar and Gene Michaud (eds), *From Hanoi to Hollywood: The Vietnam War in American Film* (New Brunswick, NJ: Rutgers University Press, 2000), 19–40.
Klinger, Barbara, *Melodrama and Meaning: History, Culture and the Films of Douglas Sirk* (Bloomington: Indiana University Press, 1994).
Kolker, Robert, *A Cinema of Loneliness: Penn, Stone, Kubrick, Scorsese, Spielberg, Altman* (Oxford: Oxford University Press, 2000).
Kozloff, Sarah, *Overhearing Film Dialogue* (Berkeley: University of California Press, 2000).
Kramer, Lawrence, *Music and Meaning: Toward a Critical History, Volume 1* (Berkeley: University of California Press, 2002).
Kramer, Peter, *The New Hollywood: From* Bonnie and Clyde *to* Star Wars (London: Wallflower, 2005).
La Cruz, Anita, 'Is "Who wears the pants" an empty question? Comedy and marriage in *Adam's Rib*', *Bells: Barcelona English Language & Literature Studies*, v. 9, no. 2 (1998): 133–42.
Laing, Heather, *The Gendered Score: Music in 1940s Melodrama and the Woman's Film* (Aldershot: Ashgate, 2007).
Langford, Barry, *Post-Classical Hollywood: Film Industry, Style and Ideology since 1945* (Edinburgh: Edinburgh University Press, 2010).
Lastra, James, 'Film and the Wagnerian aspiration: Thoughts on sound design and the history of the senses', in Jay Beck and Tony Grajeda (eds), *Lowering the Boom: Critical Studies in Film Sound* (Chicago: University of Illinois Press, 2008), 123–38.
Lawrence, Amy, *Echo and Narcissus: Women's Voices in Classical Hollywood Cinema* (Berkeley: University of California Press, 1991).
Lee Gengaro, Christine, *Listening to Stanley Kubrick: The Music in His Films* (Lanham: Rowman and Littlefield, 2012).
Lent, Tina Olsin, 'Romantic love and friendship: The redefinition of gender relations in screwball comedy', in Kristine Brunovska Karnick and Henry Jenkins (eds), *Classical Hollywood Comedy* (London: Routledge, 1995), 314–31.
Link, Stan, 'Going gently: Contemplating silences and cinematic death', in Nicky Losseff and Jenny Doctor (eds), *Silence, Music, Silent Music* (Aldershot: Ashgate, 2007), 69–86.
LoBrutto, Vincent, *Sound-on-Film: Interviews with Creators of Film Sound* (Westport: Greenwood Publishing Group, 1994).
Lyotard, Jean François, *The Postmodern Condition: A Report on Knowledge* (Minneapolis: University of Minnesota Press, 1984).
Maasø, Arnt, 'The proxemics of the mediated voice', in Jay Beck and Tony Grajeda (eds),

Lowering the Boom: Critical Studies in Film Sound (Chicago: University of Illinois Press, 2008), 36–50.

Maltby, Richard, *Hollywood Cinema* (Malden: Wiley-Blackwell, 2003).

Mast, Gerald, *Bringing Up Baby* (New Brunswick, NJ: Rutgers University Press, 1988).

McDonagh, Maitland, 'The exploitation generation or: How marginal movies came in from the cold', in Alexanda Horwath, Thomas Elsaesser and Noel King (eds), *The Last Great American Picture Show: New Hollywood Cinema in the 1970s* (Amsterdam: Amsterdam University Press, 2004), 107–30.

McGee, Kristin A., *Some Liked It Hot: Jazz Women in Film and Television, 1928–1959* (Middletown: Wesleyan University Press, 2009).

McHugh, Kathleen Anne, *American Domesticity: From How-To Manual to Hollywood Melodrama* (Oxford: Oxford University Press, 1999).

McKay, Anne, 'Speaking up: Voice amplification and women's struggle for public expression', in Caroline Mitchell (ed.), *Women and Radio: Airing Differences* (London: Routledge, 2000), 15–28.

McRobbie, Angela, *The Aftermath of Feminism: Gender, Culture and Social Change* (London: Sage Publications, 2009).

Mead, Margaret, *Sex and Temperament in Three Primitive Societies* (New York: William Morrow, 1963).

Medovoi, Leerom, *Rebels: Youth and the Cold War Origins of Identity* (Durham, NC: Duke University Press, 2005).

Mercer, John and Martin Shingler, *Melodrama: Genre, Style, Sensibility* (London: Wallflower Press, 2004).

Mills, Sara, *Gender Matters: Feminist Linguistic Analysis* (Bristol: Equinox Publishing, 2012), 230.

Minh-ha, Trinh T., *Woman, Native, Other: Writing Postcoloniality and Feminism* (Bloomington: Indiana University Press, 1989).

Monaco, Paul, *History of the American Cinema, Volume 8, 1960–1969* (Berkeley: University of California Press, 2001).

Moriel, Liora, 'Erasure and taboo: A queer reading of *Bonnie and Clyde*', in Lester D. Friedman (ed.), *Arthur Penn's Bonnie and Clyde* (Cambridge: Cambridge University Press, 2000), 148–76.

Mulhall, Stephen, *Mulhall On Film* (London: Routledge, 2002).

Mulvey, Laura, *Fetishism and Curiosity* (London: BFI, 1996).

Mulvey, Laura, 'Visual pleasure and narrative cinema', in E. Ann Kaplan (ed.), *Feminism and Film* (New York: Oxford University Press, 2000), 34–47.

Mulvey, Laura, 'Notes on Sirk and melodrama', in Christine Gledhill (ed.), *Home is Where the Heart is: Studies in Melodrama and the Woman's Film* (London: BFI, 2002), 75–82.

Neale, Steve, *Genre* (London: British Film Institute, 1980).

Neale, Steve, 'Masculinity as spectacle: Reflections on men and mainstream cinema', *Screen*, v. 24, no. 6 (1983): 2–17.

Neale, Steve, *Genre and Hollywood* (London: Routledge, 2005).

Neale, Steve and Frank Krutnik, *Popular Film and Television Comedy* (London: Routledge, 1990).

Negra, Diane, *What a Girl Wants? Fantasizing the Reclamation of Self in Postfeminism* (New York: Routledge, 2009).

Nelson, Joyce, '*Mildred Pierce* reconsidered', in Bill Nichols (ed.), *Movies and Methods: An Anthology, Volume 1* (Berkeley: University of California Press, 1985), 450–8.

Newman, David, 'What's it really all about? Pictures at an execution', in Lester D. Friedman (ed.), *Arthur Penn's Bonnie and Clyde* (Cambridge: Cambridge University Press, 2000), 32–41.

Nowell-Smith, Geoffrey, 'Minnelli and melodrama', in Bill Nichols (ed.), *Movies and Methods: An Anthology, Volume 2* (Berkeley: University of California Press, 1985), 190–4.

Orr, Christopher, 'Closure and containment: Marylee Hadley in *Written on the Wind*', in Marcia Landy (ed.), *Imitations of Life: A Reader on Film and Television Melodrama* (Detroit: Wayne State University Press, 1991), 380–7.

Pardos, Manuela Ruiz, 'Addicted to fun: Courtship, play and romance in the screwball comedy', *Revista Alicantina de Estudios Ingleses*, 13 (2000): 153–60.

Pomerance, Murray, 'Movies and the specter of rebellion', in Barry Keith Grant (ed.), *American Cinema of the 1960s: Themes and Variations* (New Brunswick, NJ: Rutgers University Press, 2008), 172–92.

Prendergast, Roy M., *A Neglected Art: A Critical Study of Music in Films* (New York: New York University Press, 1977).

Prince, Stephen, 'Hollywood in the age of Reagan', in Linda Ruth Williams and Michael Hammond (eds), *Contemporary American Cinema* (London: Open University Press, 2006), 229–46.

Radner, Hilary, *Neo-Feminist Cinema: Girly Films, Chick Flicks and Consumer Culture* (New York: Routledge, 2011).

Rashussen, Randy, *Stanley Kubrick: Seven Films Analysed* (Jefferson: McFarland & Co., 2005).

Ray, Robert B., *A Certain Tendency of the Hollywood Cinema 1930–1980* (Princeton: Princeton University Press, 1985).

Reay, Pauline, *Music in Film: Soundtracks and Synergy* (London: Wallflower Press, 2004).

Rich, B. Ruby, *Chick Flicks: Theories and Memories of the Feminist Film Movement* (Durham, NC: Duke University Press, 1998).

Rodowick, David, 'The difficulty of difference', *Wide Angle*, v. 5, no. 1 (1982): 4–15.

Rosen, Marjorie, *Popcorn Venus: Women, Movies and the American Dream* (New York: Coward, McCann and Geoghegan, 1973).

Rosenburg, Neil, *Bluegrass: A History* (Champaign: University of Illinois Press, 2005).

Roth, Elaine, '"You just hate men!" Maternal sexuality and the nuclear family in *Gas, Food, Lodging*', in Heather Addison, Mary Kate Goodwin-Kelly and Elaine Roth (eds), *Motherhood Misconceived: Representing the Maternal in U.S Films* (New York: State University of New York Press, 2009), 111–23.

Rowe, Kathleen, *The Unruly Woman: Gender and the Genres of Laughter* (Austin: University of Texas Press, 1995).

Rubinstein, Eliot, 'The end of screwball comedy: *The Lady Eve* and *The Palm Beach Story*', *Post Script*, v. 1, no. 3 (1982): 33–47.

Ryan, Michael, *Cultural Studies: A Practical Introduction* (Chichester: Blackwell Publishing, 2010).

Ryan, Michael and Douglas Kellner, *Camera Politica: The Politics and Ideology of Contemporary Hollywood Film* (Bloomington: Indiana University Press, 1988).

Savran, David, *Taking It Like a Man: White Masculinity, Masochism and Contemporary American Culture* (Princeton: Princeton University Press, 1998).

Schatz, Thomas, *Hollywood Genres: Formulas, Filmmaking and the Studio System* (Boston, MA: McGraw-Hill, 1981).

Schreger, Charles, 'Altman, Dolby, and the second sound revolution', in Elizabeth Weis and John Belton (eds), *Film Sound: Theory and Practice* (New York: Columbia University Press, 1985), 348–55.

Schreiber, Michele, *American Postfeminist Cinema: Women, Romance and Contemporary Culture* (Edinburgh: Edinburgh University Press, 2014).
Sergi, Gianluca, *The Dolby Era: Film Sound in Contemporary Hollywood* (Manchester: Manchester University Press, 2004).
Shumway, David R., 'Screwball comedies: Constructing romance, mystifying marriage', *Cinema Journal*, v. 30, no. 4 (1991): 7–23.
Shumway, David, 'Rock 'n' roll sound tracks and the production of nostalgia', *Cinema Journal*, v. 38, no. 2 (1999): 36–51.
Sikov, Ed, 'Laughing hysterically: Sex, repression, and American film comedy', in Martin B. Duberman (ed.), *Queer Representations: Reading Lives, Reading Cultures* (New York: New York University Press, 1997), 85–104.
Silverman, Kaja, *The Acoustic Mirror: The Female Voice in Psychoanalysis and Cinema* (Bloomington: Indiana University Press, 1988).
Sirk, Douglas, *Sirk on Sirk: Conversations with Jon Halliday* (London: Faber and Faber, 1997).
Smith, Jeff, 'Popular songs and comic allusion', in Pamela Robertson Wojcik and Arthur Knight (eds), *Soundtrack Available: Essays on Film and Popular Music* (Durham, NC: Duke University Press, 2001), 407–30.
Smith, Paul Julian, 'Beneath the glamour', *Film Quarterly*, v. 65, no. 1 (2011): 8–9.
Stern, Michael, 'Imitation of life', in Lucy Fischer (ed.), *Imitation of Life, Douglas Sirk, Director* (New Brunswick, NJ: Rutgers University Press, 1991), 279–88.
Sutton, Laurel A., 'Bitches and Skankly Hobags, the place of women in contemporary slang', in Kira Hall and Mary Bucholtz (eds), *Gender Articulated: Language and the Socially Constructed Self* (New York: Routledge, 1995), 279–96.
Tasker, Yvonne, *Spectacular Bodies: Gender, Genre and the Action Cinema* (London: Routledge, 1993).
Taubin, Amy, 'The *Alien* trilogy: From feminism to Aids', in Pam Cook and Philip Dodd (eds), *Women and Film* (London: BFI, 1994), 93–100.
Théberge, Paul, 'The interplay of sound and silence in contemporary cinema and television', in Jay Beck and Tony Grajeda (eds), *Lowering the Boom: Critical Studies in Film Sound* (Champaign: University of Illinois Press, 2008), 51–67.
Treitler, Leo, 'Gender and other dualities of music history', in Ruth A. Solie (ed.), *Musicology and Difference: Gender and Sexuality in Music Scholarship* (Berkeley: University of California Press, 1995), 23–45.
Vanhala, Helena, *The Depiction of Terrorists in Blockbuster Hollywood Films 1980–2001: An Analytical Study* (Jefferson: McFarland & Co., 2011), 112.
Wajcman, Judy, *TechnoFeminism* (Cambridge: Polity Press, 2004).
Walker, Janet, 'Hollywood, Freud and the representation of women: Regulation and contradiction, 1945–early 1960s', in Christine Gledhill (ed.), *Home is Where the Heart is: Studies in Melodrama and the Woman's Film* (London: BFI, 2002), 197–216.
Walsh, Andrea, *Women's Film and Female Experience 1940–1950* (New York: Praeger Publishers, 1984).
Warner, Helen, '"A new feminist revolution in Hollywood comedy"? Postfeminist discourses and the critical reception of *Bridesmaids*', in Joel Gwynne and Nadine Muller (eds), *Postfeminism and Contemporary Hollywood Cinema* (Basingstoke: Palgrave Macmillan, 2013), 222–37.
Warshow, Robert, 'Movie chronicle: The Westerner', in Robert Warshow, *The Immediate Experience: Movies, Comics, Theatre & Other Aspects of Popular Culture* (Cambridge, MA: Harvard University Press, 2001), 105–24.

Whelehan, Imelda, *Helen Fielding's 'Bridget Jones's Diary': A Reader's Guide* (New York: Continuum International Publishing Group, 2002).

Whitehead, J. W., *Appraising The Graduate: The Mike Nichols classic and its impact on Hollywood* (Jefferson: McFarland & Co., 2011).

Whittington, William, *Sound Design and Science Fiction* (Austin: University of Texas Press, 2007).

Whittington, William, 'Sound design in New Hollywood cinema', in Graeme Harper, Ruth Doughty and Jochen Eisentraut (eds), *Sounds and Music in Film and Visual Media: An Overview* (New York: Continuum International Publishing Group, 2009), 555–68.

Wierzbicki, James, *Music, Sound and Filmmakers* (New York: Routledge, 2012).

Willemen, Paul, 'Distanciation and Douglas Sirk', *Screen*, v. 12, no. 2 (1971): 63–7.

Wilson, Andy, *Northern Soul: Music, Drugs and Subcultural Identity* (Cullompton: Willan Publishing, 2007).

Witchel, Harry, *You Are What You Hear: How Music and Territory Make Us Who We Are* (New York: Algora Publishing, 2010).

Wood, Robin, *Hollywood From Vietnam to Reagan and Beyond* (New York: Columbia University Press), 247.

Wright Wexman, Virginia, 'Masculinity in crisis: Method acting in Hollywood', in Pamela Robertson Wojcik (ed.), *Movie Acting: The Film Reader* (New York: Routledge, 2004), 127–44.

Filmography and Other Sources

FILMOGRAPHY

Adam's Rib, dir. George Cukor, feat. Spencer Tracy, Katharine Hepburn, Judy Holliday (Loew's Incorporated, 1949).
Alien, dir. Ridley Scott, feat. Sigourney Weaver, Tom Skerritt, John Hurt (Brandywine Productions, Twentieth Century Fox Productions, 1979).
Aliens, dir. James Cameron, feat. Sigourney Weaver, Michael Biehn, Carrie Henn (Twentieth Century Fox, Brandywine Productions, SLM Production Group, 1986).
Annie Hall, dir. Woody Allen, feat. Diane Keaton, Tony Roberts (Rollins-Joffe Productions, 1977).
Apocalypse Now, dir. Francis Ford Coppola, feat. Martin Sheen, Marlon Brando, Robert Duvall (Zoetrope Studios, 1979).
Awful Truth, The, dir. Leo McCarey, feat. Irene Dunn, Cary Grant, Ralph Bellamy (Columbia Pictures Corporation, 1937).
Bachelorette, dir. Leslye Headland, feat. Kirsten Dunst, Isla Fisher, Lizzy Caplan (Gary Sanchez Productions, BCDF Pictures, 2012).
Blue Velvet, dir. David Lynch, feat. Isabella Rossellini, Kyle MacLachlan, Dennis Hopper (De Laurentiis Entertainment Group, 1986).
Bonnie and Clyde, dir. Arthur Penn, feat. Warren Beatty, Faye Dunaway, Michael J. Pollard (Warner Brothers/Seven Arts, Tatira-Hiller Productions, 1967).
Bridesmaids, dir. Paul Feig, feat. Kristen Wiig, Maya Rudolph, Rose Byrne (Universal Pictures, Relativity Media, Apatow Productions, 2011).
Bride Wars, dir. Gary Winick, feat. Kate Hudson, Anne Hathaway, Candice Bergen (Fox 2000 Pictures, Regency Enterprises, New Regency Pictures, Firm Films, Sunrise Entertainment (ii) 2009).
Bridget Jones's Diary, dir. Sharon Maguire, feat. Renée Zellweger, Colin Firth, Hugh Grant (Miramax Films, Universal Pictures, Studio Canal, Working Title Films, Little Bird, 2001).
Bringing Up Baby, dir. Howard Hawks, feat. Katharine Hepburn, Cary Grant, Charles Ruggles (RKO Radio Pictures, 1938).
Clueless, dir. Amy Heckerling, feat Alicia Silverstone, Stacey Dash, Brittany Murphy (Paramount Pictures, 1995).
Commando, dir. Mark L. Lester, feat. Arnold Schwarzenegger, Rae Dawn Chong, Dan Hedaya

(SLM Production Group, Silver Pictures, Twentieth Century Fox Film Corporation, 1985).
Deer Hunter, The, dir. Michael Cimino, feat. Robert De Niro, Christopher Walken, John Cazale (EMI Films, Universal Pictures, 1978).
Deliverance, dir. John Boorman, feat. Jon Voight, Burt Reynolds, Ned Beatty (Warner Bros., Elmer Enterprises, 1972).
Desperately Seeking Susan, dir. Susan Seidelman, feat. Rosanna Arquette, Madonna, Aidan Quinn (Orion Pictures Corporation, 1985).
Devil Wears Prada, The, dir. David Frankel, feat. Anne Hathaway, Meryl Streep, Adrian Grenier (Fox 2000 Pictures, Dune Entertainment, Major Studio Partners, Peninsular Films, Twentieth Century Fox Film Corporation, 2006).
Dog Day Afternoon, dir. Sidney Lumet, feat. Al Pacino, John Cazale, Penelope Allen (Artists Entertainment Complex, 1975).
Don Juan, dir. Alan Crosland, feat. John Barrymore, Jane Winton, Mary Astor (Warner Bros. Pictures, 1926).
Easy Rider, dir. Dennis Hopper, feat. Peter Fonda, Dennis Hopper, Jack Nicholson (Columbia Pictures Corporation, Pando Company Inc., Raybert Productions, 1969).
E.T. The Extra-Terrestrial, dir. Steven Spielberg, feat. Henry Thomas, Drew Barrymore, Peter Coyote (Universal Pictures, Amblin Entertainment, 1982).
Exorcist, The, dir. William Friedkin, feat. Ellen Burstyn, Max von Sydow, Linda Blair (Warner Bros. Pictures, Hoya Productions, 1973).
First Blood (a.k.a. Rambo), dir. Ted Kotcheff, feat. Sylvester Stallone, Brian Dennehy, Richard Crenna (Anabasis N.V., Elcajo Productions, 1982).
French Connection, The, dir. William Friedkin, feat. Gene Hackman, Roy Scheider, Fernano Rey (D-Antoni Productions, Schine-Moore Productions, 1971).
Friends With Benefits, dir. Will Gluck, feat. Mila Kunis, Justin Timberlake, Patricia Clarkson (Screen Gems, Castle Rock Entertainment, Zucker Productions, Olive Bridge Entertainment, 2011).
Full Metal Jacket, dir. Stanley Kubrick, feat. Matthew Modine, R. Lee Ermey, Vincent D'Onofrio (Natant, Stanley Kubrick Productions, Warner Bros. Pictures, 1987).
Godfather, The, dir. Francis Ford Coppola, feat. Marlon Brando, Al Pacino, James Caan (Paramount Pictures, Alfran Productions, 1972).
Godfather, The, Part II, dir. Francis Ford Coppola, feat. Al Pacino, Robert De Niro, Robert Duvall (Paramount Pictures, The Coppola Company, 1974).
Graduate, The, dir. Mike Nichols, feat. Dustin Hoffman, Anne Bancroft, Katharine Ross (Lawrence Turman, Embassy Pictures Corporation, 1967).
Green Berets, The, dir. Ray Kellogg and John Wayne, feat. John Wayne, David Janssen, Jim Hutton (Batjac Productions, 1968).
Hangover, The, dir. Todd Phillips, feat. Zach Galifianakis, Bradley Cooper, Justin Bartha (Warner Bros., Pictures, Legendary Pictures, Green Hat Films, IFP Westcoast Erste, 2009).
His Girl Friday, dir. Howard Hawks, feat. Cary Grant, Rosalind Russell, Ralph Bellamy (Columbia Pictures Corporation, 1940).
Imitation of Life, dir. Douglas Sirk, feat. Lana Turner, John Gavin, Sandra Dee, Susan Kohner (Universal International Pictures, 1959).
It Happened One Night, dir. Frank Capra, feat. Clark Gable, Claudette Colbert, Walter Connolly (Columbia Pictures Corporation, 1934).
Jaws, dir. Steven Spielberg, feat. Roy Scheider, Robert Shaw, Richard Dreyfuss (Zanuck/Brown Productions, Universal Pictures, 1975).

Jazz Singer, The, dir. Alan Crosland, feat. Al Jolson, May McAvoy, Warner Oland (Warner Bros. Pictures, 1927).

Julia, dir. Fred Zinnemann, feat. Jane Fonda, Vanessa Redgrave, Jason Robards (Twentieth Century Fox Film Corporation, 1977).

Legally Blonde, dir. Robert Luketic, feat. Reece Witherspoon, Luke Wilson, Selma Blair (Metro-Goldwyn-Mayer, Marc Platt Productions, 2001).

Letter from an Unknown Woman, dir. Max Ophüls, feat. Joan Fontaine, Louise Jourdan, Mady Christians (Rampart Productions (I), 1948).

Mean Girls, dir. Mark Waters, feat. Lindsay Lohan, Jonathan Bennett, Rachel McAdams (Paramount Pictures, M. G. Films, Broadway Video, 2004).

Midnight Cowboy, dir. John Schlesinger, feat. Dustin Hoffman, John Voight, Sylvia Miles (Florin Productions, Jerome Hellman Productions, 1969).

Mildred Pierce, dir. Michael Curtiz, feat. Joan Crawford, Jack Carson, Zachary Scott, Ann Blyth (Warner Bros. Pictures, 1945).

Miss Congeniality, dir. Donald Petrie, feat. Sandra Bullock, Michael Caine, Benjamin Bratt (Castle Rock Entertainment, Village Roadshow Pictures, NPV Entertainment, Fortis Films, 2000).

Miss Congeniality 2: Armed and Fabulous, dir. John Pasquin, feat. Sandra Bullock, Regina King, William Shatner (Castle Rock Entertainment, Village Roadshow Pictures, Fortis Films, 2005).

Muriel's Wedding, dir. P. J. Hogan, feat. Toni Collette, Rachel Griffiths, Bill Hunter (CiBy 2000, Film Victoria, House & Moorhouse, 1994).

Nine to Five, dir. Colin Higgins, feat. Jane Fonda, Lilly Tomlin, Dolly Parton (IPC Films, Twentieth Century Fox Film Corporation, 1980).

Palm Beach Story, The, dir. Preston Sturges, feat. Claudette Colbert, Joel McCrea, Mary Astor (Paramount Pictures, 1942).

Pitch Perfect, dir. Jason Moore, feat. Anna Kendrick, Rebel Wilson, Brittany Snow (Brownstone Productions (III), Gold Circle Films, 2012).

Raiders of the Lost Ark, dir. Steven Spielberg, feat. Harrison Ford, Karen Allen, Paul Freeman (Paramount Pictures, Lucasfilm, 1981).

Sex and the City: The Movie, dir. Michael Patrick King, feat. Sarah Jessica Parker, Kim Cattrall, Cynthia Nixon, Kristin Davis (New Line Cinema, Home Box Office, Darren Star Productions, 2008).

Sex and the City 2, dir. Michael Patrick King, feat. Sarah Jessica Parker, Kim Cattrall, Cynthia Nixon, Kristin Davis (New Line Cinema, Home Box Office, HBO Films, Village Roadshow Pictures, 2010).

Shadows, dir. John Cassevetes, feat. Ben Carruthers, Lelia Goldoni, Hugh Hurd (Lion International, 1959).

Singing Fool, The, dir. Lloyd Bacon, feat. Al Jolson, Betty Bronson, Josephine Dunn (Warner Bros. Pictures, 1928).

Star is Born, A, dir. Frank Pierson, feat. Barbra Streisand, Kris Kristofferson, Gary Busey (Barwood Films, First Artists, Winters Hollywood Entertainment Holdings Corporation, 1976).

Star Wars: A New Hope, dir. George Lucas, feat. Mark Hamill, Harrison Ford, Carrie Fisher (Lucasfilm, Twentieth Century Fox Film Corporation, 1977).

Superbad, dir. Greg Mottola, feat. Jonah Hill, Michael Cera, Christopher Mintz-Plasse (Columbia Pictures, Apatow Company, 2007).

Taxi Driver, dir. Martin Scorsese, feat. Robert De Niro, Jodie Foster, Cybill Shepherd (Columbia pictures Corporation, Bill/Phillips, Italo/Judeo Producions, 1976).

Terminator, The, dir. James Cameron, feat. Arnold Schwarzenegger, Linda Hamilton, Michael Biehn (Hemdale Film, Pacific Western, Euro Film Funding, Cinema 84, 1984).

Thelma and Louise, dir. Ridley Scott, feat. Susan Sarandon, Geena Davis, Harvey Keitel (Pathé Entertainment, Percy Main, Star Partners III Ltd., Metro-Goldwyn-Mayer, 1991).

Tommy, dir. Ken Russell, feat. Roger Daltrey, Ann-Margret, Oliver Reed (Robert Stigwood Organization, Hemdale Film, 1975).

21 Jump Street, dir. Phil Lord, Christopher Miller, feat. Jonah Hill, Channing Tatum, Ice Cube (Columbia Pictures, Metro-Goldwyn-Mayer, Relativity Media, Original Film, SJC Studios, 2012).

Twin Peaks, dir. David Lynch, Mark Frost, feat. Kyle MacLachlan, Michael Ontkean, Mädchen Amick (Lynch/Frost Productions, Propaganda Films, Spelling Entertainment, Twin Peaks Productions, 1990–1).

Wild Bunch, The, dir. Sam Peckinpah, feat. William Holden, Ernest Borgnine, Robert Ryan (Warner Brothers/Seven Arts, 1969).

Woman Under the Influence, A, dir. John Cassevetes, feat. Gena Rowlands, Peter Falk, Fred Draper (Faces, 1974).

Women, The, dir. George Cukor, feat. Norma Shearer, Joan Crawford, Rosalind Russell (Metro-Goldwyn-Mayer, Loew's, 1939).

Women, The, dir. Diane English, feat. Meg Ryan, Annette Bening, Eva Mendes (Picturehouse Entertainment, Scion Films, Inferno Distribution, Jagged Films, New Line Cinema, Shukovsky English Entertainment, 2008).

Written on the Wind, dir. Douglas Sirk, feat. Rock Hudson, Lauren Bacall, Robert Stack, Dorothy Malone (Universal International Pictures, 1956).

DVDS

Feig, Paul, 'Feature commentary with filmmakers and cast', *Bridesmaids*, extended edition DVD, London: Universal Pictures, 2011.

WEBSITES

The Numbers Box Office Database, page for *Bridget Jones's Diary* http://www.the-numbers.com/movies/2001/BJDIA.php (accessed 5 April 2012).

MUSIC SOURCES

A Girl Like You, from *Gorgeous George*, written by Edwyn Collins. UK: AED Records Ltd, 1995.

Born To Be Wild, from *Easy Rider: The Soundtrack*, written by Mars Bonfire. USA: ABC Dunhill Records, 1969.

Can't Take My Eyes Off You, from *The Deer Hunter: The Soundtrack*, written by Bob Gaudio and Bob Crewe. USA: BMI Records, 1967.

Cavatina, from *The Deer Hunter: The Soundtrack*, music by Stanley Myers, performed on guitar by John Williams. USA: EMI Records, 1990.

Empty Arms, written by Arnold Hughes and Frederick Herbert.

Foggy Mountain Breakdown, written by Earl Scruggs. USA: Mercury Records, 1949.

God Bless America, music and lyrics by Irving Berlin, 1918.
Hello Vietnam, from *Full Metal Jacket: The Soundtrack*, written by Tom T. Hall. USA: Sony Classical Records, 1987.
I Can't Give You Anything But Love (Baby), lyrics by Dorothy Fields, music by Jimmy McHugh, 1928.
I'm Gonna Be (500 Miles), from *Sunshine on Leith*, written by Charles Reid and Craig Reid, UK: EMI Film and Television Music, 1988.
Infinity Guitars, from *Treats*, written by Derek Edward, Miller and Alexis Krauss. USA: Columbia Records, 2010.
Labels or Love, from *Sex and the City: Original Motion Picture Soundtrack*, written by Salaam Remi and Rico Love. USA: Decca Records, 2008.
Moving in Stereo, from *The Cars*, written by Ric Ocasek and Greg Hawkes. USA: Elektra Entertainment Group, 1984.
Mrs Robinson, from *The Graduate: The Soundtrack*, written by Paul Simon. USA: Columbia Records, 1968.
Oceana Roll, The, music by Lucien Denni, lyrics by Roger Lewis, 1911.
Pusher, The, from *Easy Rider: The Soundtrack*, music written by Hoyt Axton. USA: ABC Dunhill Records, 1969.
Sounds of Silence, The, from *The Graduate: The Soundtrack*, written by Paul Simon. USA: Columbia Records, 1968.
South American Way, music by Jimmy McHugh, lyrics by Al Dubin, 1939.
Temptation, music by Nacio Herb Brown, lyrics by Arthur Freed, 1933.
Waltz in E Flat Major (Grand Valse Brillante), music by Frédéric Chopin, 1834.
You Must Have Been a Beautiful Baby, music by Harry Warren, lyrics by Johnny Mercer, 1938.

Index

A Woman Under the Influence (1974), 166
acoustic remainder, the 5, 57, 72, 189, 190–1
Adam's Rib (1948), 33–41, 186, 187
Alien (1979), 135, 136
Aliens, (1986), 135–46, 187, 188, 190
Apocalypse Now (1979), 100, 129
Aristotle, voice and, 4, 13, 16, 31, 162

Bachelorette, 150, 174–82, 187, 190
Bakhtin, Mikhail, 163, 164, 165, 172, 173, 174
Barthes, Roland, 25
Beatty, Warren, 86, 88
blockbuster era, The, 100, 125, 126, 127, 128, 132, 188, 190
bluegrass music (in *Bonnie and Clyde*), 86, 87
Bonnie and Clyde (1967), 81, 85–91, 95, 171
Bridesmaids (2011), 6, 7, 149, 165–74, 175, 176, 187, 188, 190
Bridget Jones's Diary (2001), 150, 155–7
Bringing Up Baby (1938), 27–33, 34, 41, 68, 186
bromance genre, 151, 164, 187
Butler, Judith, 33, 34, 38, 39, 142, 143

Carson, Ann, 31
Cavell, Stanley, 19, 20, 24, 36, 39
Chion, Michel
   female scream, 162
   voice in cinema, 153, 154, 155, 158
Classical Hollywood, 10, 48, 58, 66, 125, 127, 128, 131
Colbert, Claudette, 15, 40
counter-culture, US, 77, 78, 81, 95

Deer Hunter, The (1978), 100, 112–22, 187

Deliverance (1972), 99
DiBattista, Maria, 3, 10, 21, 22, 29
diegetic music, 44–72, 114, 117, 181
Dolby Stereo, 128, 129, 130, 154
drag performance (Butler), 39
Dunn, Leslie C. and Nancy A. Jones, 25

Easy Rider (1969), 76–7, 82, 83–5, 86, 91, 95, 114, 188, 189

fast-talking dame, 11, 14, 19, 22, 29
female friendship genre, 151, 152, 154, 165, 174, 177, 178, 182, 187, 188, 190
female laughter, 161, 163, 164, 165, 166, 171, 172
film noir, 48, 51, 57
Friends With Benefits (2011), 1, 2, 7
Full Metal Jacket (1987), 100–12, 113, 119, 121, 122, 187, 189

Gable, Clark, 17, 40
gender performance (Butler), 11, 33–41, 145, 146, 183, 186, 187, 189
Graduate, The (1967), 80, 81, 84, 86, 91–6, 189
   Simon and Garfunkel, 91, 92
grain of the voice, the, 25
Grant, Cary, 22, 27, 33, 188
Green Berets, The (1968), 99

Haraway, Donna, cyborg manifesto, 137–8, 143, 145–6, 190
Hepburn, Katharine, 27, 30, 186, 188
His Girl Friday (1940), 22–7, 40, 41, 186
homosexuality in film, 33, 41, 47, 80, 84, 85, 151, 160

Imitation of Life (1934), 58
Imitation of Life (1959), 46, 50, 57–66, 68
It Happened One Night (1934), 9, 15–22, 23, 27, 40, 186

Jaws (1975), 127–8
jazz music in film, 48, 49, 51, 189
Jazz Singer, The (1927), 49
Jeffords, Susan, 101, 104, 126

Klinger, Barbara and melodrama, 47, 66
Kozloff, Sarah, 15, 17, 18, 20, 23, 24, 29

Laing, Heather, 45
Letter from an Unknown Woman (1948), 45, 154

marriage, 13, 14, 19, 20, 46, 59, 117, 169, 178
masculinity, 77, 80, 81, 88, 89, 90
 in *Aliens* 143–5
 silence and, 81–2, 87
 war and, 96, 100, 101, 112, 114, 190
melodrama, film genre, 44–75
method acting, 81
Mildred Pierce (1945), 45, 50–8, 68
Mills, Sara, 16, 25
'Movie Brats', 79
Mulvey, Laura and melodrama, 47

New Hollywood, 77, 78, 79
newspaper comedies, 18

postfeminism, 143, 144, 146, 149–50, 153, 158, 178, 182

postmodernism, 152, 153, 157, 158, 176, 178, 182, 187, 190
Production Code, The, 10, 13, 14, 21, 79
Pulp Fiction (1994), 176, 180, 181

Reagan, Ronald, 125–6

Schatz, Thomas, 23, 46
science fiction, sound in, 6, 125, 126, 130, 131, 135, 136, 187, 188, 190
screwball comedy, 9–43, 85, 144, 149, 152, 157, 182, 186, 188, 189
Sex and the City: The Movie (2008), 157–64, 166, 188
Shadows (1959), 166
silence in film, 77, 81, 84, 86, 87, 108
Silverman, Kaja, 170
Sirk, Douglas, 46, 57, 66
sound design, 6, 79, 100, 126, 129, 131, 132, 136
Star Wars: A New Hope (1977), 126, 130, 131–5, 146, 190

Taxi Driver (1976), 99
Tracy, Spencer, 33, 186, 188

Vietnam War, 99, 100, 101, 108, 110, 120, 121, 122, 143, 187

Wayne, John, 81, 82, 99
Whittington, William, 79, 130, 132, 136
Wild Bunch, The (1969), 99, 109–10
Women, The (1939) and (2008), 152
Written on the Wind (1956), 45, 50, 66–75

EU representative:
Easy Access System Europe
Mustamäe tee 50, 10621 Tallinn, Estonia
Gpsr.requests@easproject.com